Global Governance and Public Accountability

Global Governance and Public Accountability

Edited by
**David Held and
Mathais Koenig-Archibugi**

Blackwell
Publishing

First published as volume 39 issue 2 of *Government and Opposition*

BLACKWELL PUBLISHING
350 Main Street, Malden, MA 02148-5020, USA
108 Cowley Road, Oxford OX4 1JF, UK
550 Swanston Street, Carlton, Victoria 3053, Australia

First published 2005 by Blackwell Publishing Ltd

Library of Congress Cataloging-in-Publication Data has been applied for

ISBN 1-4051-2678-7

A catalogue record for this title is available from the British Library.

Set by SNP Best-set Typesetter Ltd., Hong Kong
Printed and bound in the United Kingdom
by MPG Books Ltd, Bodmin, Cornwall

For further informatin on
Blackwell Publishing, visit our website:
http://www.blackwellpublishing.com

CONTENTS

Notes on Contributors

Thorsten Benner *is Associate Director of the Global Public Policy Institute in Geneva and Berlin*

David Held *is Graham Wallas Professor of Political Science, London School of Economics*

Miles Kahler *is Rohr Professor of Pacific International Relations at the University of California*

Mathias Koenig-Archibugi *is Lecturer in Global Politics at the London School of Economics and Political Science*

Andrew Moravcsik *is Professor of Government and Director of the European Union Program at Harvard University*

Patrizia Nanz *is Junior Professor of International Relations and Political Theory in the Graduate School of Social Sciences at the University of Bremen*

Wolfgang H. Reinicke *is Director of the Global Public Policy Institute at Berlin and Geneva and a Non-Resident Senior Fellow of the Governance Studies Program at the Brookings Institution, Washington, DC*

Thomas Risse *is Chair in International Politics at the Otto Suhr Institute for Political Science, Freie Universität Berlin*

Jan Aart Scholte *is Professor in the Department of Politics and International Studies at the University of Warwick and Acting Director of the ESRC/Warwick Centre for the Study of Globalisation and Regionalisation*

Anne-Marie Slaughter *is Dean of the Woodrow Wilson School of Public and International Affairs at Princeton University*

Jens Steffek *is Assistant Professor at the Research Centre for Transformations of the State at the University of Bremen*

Jan Martin Witte *is Associate Director of the Global Public Policy Institute at Berlin and Geneva and a PhD candidate in European*

Studies at the Nitze School of Advanced International Studies, Johns Hopkins University

Michael Zürn *is Director at the Science Centre Berlin and Founding Dean of the Hertie School of Governance, Berlin*

1
Introduction

David Held and *Mathias Koenig-Archibugi*

TO WHAT EXTENT ARE THOSE WHO SHAPE GLOBAL PUBLIC POLICIES accountable to those affected by their decisions? Are the accountability deficits in global policy-making a serious obstacle to its effectiveness and legitimacy? And what can realistically be done to reduce these deficits?

This book explores questions such as these in order to examine the prospects of a viable and legitimate system of global governance.[1] In our democratic age, the exercise of authority requires the expressed consent of the governed and, more specifically, mechanisms through which policy-makers can be held accountable. While there is agreement among democrats that wherever power is exercised there should be mechanisms of accountability, what this means in relation to internationalized governance systems is contested.

Traditionally, it has been assumed that international institutions are legitimized indirectly by the consent of the participating governments and above all by their capacity to solve the problems that led to their creation. This view is increasingly questioned. The capacity to deliver effective policies is a basic requirement of the legitimacy of any political system, but usually it is not sufficient. This is because the conception of political legitimacy prevalent in most countries today is hostile to the idea of any form of power that is unaccountable to those over whom it is exercised and especially to those who are most affected by it. The legitimacy crisis of international

[1] This book stems from the Miliband Conference on Global Governance and Public Accountability held at the London School of Economics and Political Science, 17–18 May 2002. The chapters in this book are either revised versions of the conference papers or the elaboration of comments made during the discussion. The financial support of the LSE Miliband Programme is gratefully acknowledged. The Rockefeller Foundation provided further resources. In addition, we would like to thank the editors of *Government and Opposition* for their encouragement in publishing this collection as a special issue of their journal (volume 39 issue 2).

institutions such as the International Monetary Fund (IMF), the World Trade Organization (WTO) and the UN Security Council shows that the question of the public accountability of global governance is unavoidable and cannot be answered simply by pointing at the control exercised by national governments over them: in fact, collusion and disparities among governments are widely perceived as part of the problem. Ultimately, the debate about the foreign policy of the only remaining superpower is also about its lack of accountability to the billions affected by its decisions but excluded from its domestic democratic process.

The emerging consensus is that the legitimacy of global governance needs to be assessed from the point of view of both effectiveness and accountability.[2] By now there is a substantial amount of literature on the effectiveness of international regimes and other international governance mechanisms.[3] Scholars have devoted less attention to the exploration of accountability relationships and mechanisms at the international level. This relative neglect stands in stark contrast to the importance attributed to (the lack of) accountability by many political activists and commentators.[4] The articles in this special issue look at the conditions, the limits, and the potential for improvement of public accountability in global decision-making, and at how accountability interacts with other values such as policy effectiveness, participation and deliberation. While unilateral action by states often raises important questions of accountability, this issue leaves this particular bundle of questions aside and focuses instead on the sites of power where states and other organizations act collectively.

[2] Effectiveness and accountability roughly correspond to what Fritz Scharpf has called output-oriented legitimization and input-oriented legitimization. Fritz Scharpf, *Governing in Europe: Effective and Democratic?*, Oxford, Oxford University Press, 1999.

[3] Edward L. Miles, Arild Underdal, Steinar Andersen, Jorgen Wettestad, Jon Birger Skjaerseth and Elaine M. Carlin, *Environmental Regime Effectiveness: Confronting Theory with Evidence*, Cambridge, MA, MIT Press, 2001; P. J. Simmons and Chantal de Jounge Oudraat, *Managing Global Issues: Lessons Learned*, Washington, DC, Carnegie Endowment for International Peace, 2001; Oran R. Young (ed.), *The Effectiveness of International Environmental Regimes: Causal Connections and Behavioral Mechanisms*, Cambridge, MA, MIT Press, 1999.

[4] See for instance Lori Wallach and Michelle Sforza, *Whose Trade Organization?: Corporate Globalization and the Erosion of Democracy*, Washington, DC, Public Citizen, 1999.

Accountability refers to the fact that decision-makers do not enjoy unlimited autonomy but have to justify their actions vis-à-vis affected parties, that is, stakeholders. These stakeholders must be able to evaluate the actions of the decision-makers and to sanction them if their performance is poor, for instance by removing them from their positions of authority. Thus, effective accountability requires mechanisms for steady and reliable information and communication between decision-makers and stakeholders as well as mechanisms for imposing penalties.[5] In both national and international settings, these mechanisms include, amongst others, voting, appointment, withdrawal of political support, legal responsibility, shaming and physical sanctions. In most areas of global governance different forms of accountability co-exist and complement each other, even though some have come to be predominant. But there is no reason to assume that 'democratic' forms of accountability will necessarily prevail over 'non-democratic' ones.

The structure of this book reflects the conviction that (any systematic attempt to understand accountability relationships in global governance must be sensitive to the diversity of forms in which governance can be exercised.) While most scholars would still regard governments as pivotal actors in world politics, there is (an increasing awareness that governance functions are exercised through a variety of institutional forms, and that in certain contexts governments are not necessarily the most important actors.[6] Various developments have stimulated interest in the diversity of governance mechanisms in world affairs. First, many believe that the demand for global governance is increasing because of processes of growing interdependence and globalization in the economic, military, cultural and environmental domains.[7] There is a growing appreciation that the failure to address global issues such as the stability of financial markets, the spread of communicable diseases, or mass migrations induced by poverty and war, has adverse and disruptive

[5] James G. March and Johan P. Olsen, *Democratic Governance*, New York, Free Press, 1995. Robert O. Keohane, 'Global Governance and Democratic Accountability', in David Held and Mathias Koenig-Archibugi (eds), *Taming Globalization: Frontiers of Governance*, Cambridge, Polity Press, 2002.

[6] David Held and Anthony McGrew (eds), *Governing Globalization: Power, Authority, and Global Governance*, Cambridge, Polity Press, 2002.

[7] David Held, Anthony McGrew, David Goldblatt and Jonathan Perraton, *Global Transformations: Politics, Economics and Culture*, Cambridge, Polity Press, 1999.

consequences on the security and well-being of many communities around the world, and not just in those most immediately affected.

Second, the classic solution to international interdependence – cooperation among sovereign states – is far from being a homogeneous phenomenon. (Comparative research on traditional intergovernmental arrangements shows that they are highly diverse with respect to their level of formality and legalization, their instruments and resources, their responsiveness to the preferences of powerful and weaker members, and several other important dimensions.[8] This diversity is evident by comparing two prominent intergovernmental organizations: the WTO and the IMF. Even in intergovernmental structures there is substantial institutional variation and scope for design. More specifically, the staff of certain international organizations have a substantial degree of discretion in formulating and implementing policies, and thus should be regarded as distinct actors in global governance.[9] Supranational bureaucracies, such as the IMF staff, take decisions of great importance and this inevitably raises questions about their public accountability.

Third, an increasing number of public agencies other than national executives, such as central bankers and securities regulators, establish links with their counterparts in other countries and thus form transgovernmental networks that take decisions on issues of common concern.[10] Informal networks of this sort are sometimes welcomed as a way to improve the effectiveness of global policies, but they also represent sites of power that may elude traditional forms of democratic oversight.

Fourth, business actors have created a number of transnational governance mechanisms in the domains of technical standardization,

[8] Judith L. Goldstein, Miles Kahler, Robert O. Keohane and Anne-Marie Slaughter (eds), *Legalization and World Politics*, Cambridge, MA, MIT Press, 2001; Oran R. Young, *Governance in World Affairs*, Ithaca, NY, Cornell University Press, 1999.

[9] Kenneth W. Abbott and Duncan Snidal, 'Why States Act Through Formal International Organizations', *Journal of Conflict Resolution*, 42 (1998), pp. 3–32; Bob Reinalda and Bertjan Verbeek (eds), *Autonomous Policymaking by International Organizations*, London, Routledge, 1998.

[10] Anne-Marie Slaughter, 'Governing the Global Economy Through Government Networks', in Michael Byers (ed.), *The Role of Law in International Politics*, Oxford, Oxford University Press, 2000.

safety regulation, dispute resolution and other regulatory areas.[11] These forms of corporate self-regulation might add a useful element of flexibility to global governance, but private rule-setting is particularly prone to exclude important stakeholders from the decisions. Often, as in the case of the Code on Pharmaceutical Marketing Practices launched by the International Federation of Pharmaceutical Manufacturers Association, companies choose a strategy of 'preventive self-regulation' in order to avoid the adoption of stricter regulation by public bodies, i.e., bodies that at least in principle are responsive to a broader range of interests and values.

Fifth, global civil society – that is, nongovernmental organizations and transnational advocacy networks – is increasingly important in processes of global governance: it contributes to problem identification and definition, influences the formulation of the options and the making of binding decisions, collaborates with public agencies in implementing those decisions and sometimes provides services directly to people when governments are unable to do so.[12] The success of the International Campaign to Ban Landmines testifies that advocacy coalitions can have a substantial effect even in areas that traditionally are the preserve of states, such as arms control.

Sixth, civil society organizations, companies, national public agencies and intergovernmental organizations are forming policy networks that enhance the prospects of finding consensual solutions to social problems.[13] Examples of 'multistakeholder' networks include the World Commission on Dams, the Roll Back Malaria Initiative, the Global Alliance for Vaccines and Immunization, the Apparel

[11] Virginia Haufler, *A Public Role for the Private Sector: Industry Self-Regulation in a Global Economy*, Washington, DC, Carnegie Endowment for International Peace, 2001; John Braithwaite and Peter Drahos, *Global Business Regulation*, Cambridge, Cambridge University Press, 2000; Karsten Ronit and Volker Schneider (eds), *Private Organisations in Global Politics*, London, Routledge, 2000.

[12] *Global Civil Society Yearbook*, Oxford, Oxford University Press, 2001, 2002, 2003; Margaret E. Keck and Kathryn Sikkink, *Activists Beyond Borders: Advocacy Networks in International Politics*, Ithaca and London, Cornell University Press, 1998; Robert O'Brien, Anne-Marie Goetz, Jan Aart Scholte and Marc Williams, *Contesting Global Governance: Multilateral Economic Institutions and Global Social Movements*, Cambridge, Cambridge University Press, 2000.

[13] Wolfgang H. Reinicke et al., *Critical Choices: The United Nations, Networks, and the Future of Global Governance*, Ottawa, International Development Research Centre, 2000; John G. Ruggie, 'Taking Embedded Liberalism Global: the Corporate Connection', in Held and Koenig-Archibugi, *Taming Globalization*, op. cit.

Industry Partnership, and Kofi Annan's Global Compact. These mostly informal partnerships between diverse actors have been hailed by some as the most promising way to tackle global problems and promote responsiveness to a plurality of interests and views.

\\In sum, global governance is a highly complex phenomenon in terms of participating actors, modes of operation and institutional forms.)The following chapters explore the conditions of legitimacy of global governance by taking this complexity into account. A first set of chapters examines how accountability is practised in the main types of governance systems that operate in the global arena. Miles Kahler examines the major multilateral organizations in the economic domain, the World Bank, the IMF and the WTO. Anne-Marie Slaughter assesses transgovernmental networks of relatively independent public officials, such as central bankers, security regulators and judges. Thorsten Benner, Wolfgang Reinicke and Jan Martin Witte explore accountability relationships in partnerships among public agencies, companies and nongovernmental organizations for the resolution of problems such as landmines, corruption, debt relief, child soldiers, the construction of large dams, and malaria. Jan Aart Scholte considers the role of civil society organizations in promoting accountability in global governance, and the circumstances that have affected and limited the extent of their success. Mathias Koenig-Archibugi examines how the global reach of transnational corporations creates or exacerbates gaps in public accountability, and evaluates the ability of intergovernmental and private arrangements to reduce these gaps.

A second set of chapters examines global governance as a whole. Michael Zürn discusses the transition from traditional intergovernmental cooperation to new international institutions that are more intrusive into national society and thus require stronger legitimization. Thomas Risse looks at the role of argument and communicative action in global governance and explores its multifaceted relationship to legitimacy and public accountability. Patrizia Nanz and Jens Steffek argue that the legitimacy of global governance can be enhanced by creating sites of public deliberation open to transnational civil society.

The two concluding chapters assess whether the current level of public accountability in global governance justifies the diagnosis of a 'democratic deficit' and consider the implications for the debate on the reform of global governance institutions. Andrew Moravcsik denies that existing international organizations suffer necessarily from a democratic deficit: the current practices of managerial governance and intergovernmental bargaining may be efficient and legitimate, and his article develops a general framework for assessing transnational democratic legitimacy. On the other hand, David Held argues from a cosmopolitan perspective that contemporary global governance is plagued by a serious deficit of democracy and that this requires the thorough reform of existing institutions as well as the creation of new ones.

The chapters in this book provide an analysis of major arenas of global decision-making from the perspective of accountability and an evaluation of the democratic quality of the current efforts to manage global issues. They reflect a variety of analytical and normative perspectives, but they share the view that the current state of accountability in supranational, intergovernmental and transnational governance arrangements is an important topic of political research, and that the question of the development of democratic practices in these domains deserves intense consideration.

2
Defining Accountability Up:
the Global Economic Multilaterals

Miles Kahler[1]

IN THE SWIRL OF ANTI-GLOBALIZATION RHETORIC AND MOBILIZATION
that has besieged the streets of Seattle, Genoa and Washington in
recent years, the key global economic institutions – the International
Monetary Fund (IMF), the World Bank and the World Trade Organization (WTO) – have been principal targets. Their identification
with the liberal economic principles partly explains their rapid
transformation from organizations understood only by a small international policy network to regular subjects of the evening news.
Another criticism of these organizations has resonated outside the
anti-globalization ranks: their lack of democratic accountability.
Critics of the global economic multilaterals (GEMs) often paint the
paradox in stark terms. The most influential members of the organizations, whether measured in voting shares or informal influence,
were liberal democratic polities. In their own governance, however,
these central international institutions have, in the eyes of their
critics, violated democratic precepts.

This simple juxtaposition of national governments that are democratically accountable with global institutions that are not obscures
several important distinctions. First, should emphasis be placed
on *democratic* or on *accountability*? Many member governments of
the GEMs are not democratic. Even among formally democratic
governments, longstanding political institutions may not ensure
accountability. For example, elections – a key index of democracy –
are no guarantee of the accountability of politicians to their

[1] The author wishes to thank the participants in the Miliband Conference on
Global Governance and Accountability at the London School of Economics and
Political Science, an anonymous referee for Cambridge University Press, and Professor Stephan Haggard for comments on an earlier version of this chapter. He also
thanks Kelly Wurtz for research assistance.

electorates.[2] Equally important, electoral institutions are only one part of the institutional panoply of a modern democracy. Contemporary democracies have assigned a large and growing role to non-majoritarian institutions (NMIs), such as the judiciary (whose accountability to electorates and governments varies widely) and central banks, whose independence from direct political control has increased over the past decade.[3] The accountability of international institutions, particularly global ones, may compare favourably to these domestic analogues. Finally, democratic accountability must also be weighed against other criteria for evaluating the performance of polities. Although majoritarian democracies win high scores for accountability to their electorates, consensus democracies outperform them on other criteria of good governance.[4] The rigorous standards of democratic accountability applied by critics of the GEMs may not only be rare in national governments, they may provide the wrong benchmarks for international institutions.

WARRING ANALOGIES: GLOBAL POLITY OR DELEGATED AUTHORITY?

Two distinct measures of democratic accountability have been applied to the GEMs and other global institutions. Although the association is not perfect, these views coincide with European and North American perspectives on supranational governance. For many European observers, arguments applied to the European Union (EU) are readily transposed to the GEMs. The GEMs are, in this view, at the core of an emerging system of global governance, a protopolity, one traceable to the consequences of globalization.[5] As

[2] Bernard Manin, Adam Przeworski and Susan C. Stokes, 'Elections and Representation', in Adam Przeworski, Susan C. Stokes and Bernard Manin (eds), *Democracy, Accountability, and Representation*, Cambridge, Cambridge University Press, 1999, p. 50.

[3] Mark A. Pollack, 'Learning from the Americanists (Again): Theory and Method in the Study of Delegation', *West European Politics*, 25: 1 (2002), pp. 200–19.

[4] Arend Lijphart, *Patterns of Democracy: Government Forms and Performance in Thirty-Six Countries*, New Haven, Yale University Press, 1999; Arend Lijphart, 'The Pros and Cons – But Mainly Pros – of Consensus Democracy', *Acta Politica* (2001–2), pp. 129–39.

[5] David Held, 'The Transformation of Political Community: Rethinking Democracy in the Context of Globalization', in Ian Shapiro and Casiano Hacker-Cordón (eds), *Democracy's Edges*, Cambridge, Cambridge University Press, 1999, p. 103.

globalization diminishes the capabilities of national states, the 'shaky foundations' of international institutions in democratic theory become more apparent.[6] The preferred replacement for existing international governance is less clear in these accounts. Using 'western democracy' as the 'appropriate benchmark', points to 'democratic public law' and 'a community' of all democratic communities for some; constitutionalization for others.[7] These proponents of the democratization of global institutions do not regard the absence of a global political community or demos as an absolute barrier to deploying domestically originated terms, such as 'democracy' or 'constitution', in a global political context. The criteria or benchmarks employed in national regimes are appropriate for the GEMs and other international institutions, even though their institutional expression may be different.

For some sceptics, promotion of a global polity organized along democratic lines is a simple pipe dream. Although they endorse the desirability of democracy at the global level, they contend that it is probably impossible to realize. The scale of global governance may enhance collective abilities to deal with transnational issues, but that advance will only occur at the expense of effective self-government by the citizens of nation-states.[8] Polyglot and culturally diverse national communities will not be able to engage in the type of political discourse that is essential to democratic governance.[9]

[6] Michael Zürn, 'Democratic Governance beyond the Nation-State', in Michael T. Greven and Louis W. Pauly (eds), *Democracy Beyond the State? The European Dilemma and the Emerging Global Order*, Lanham, MD, Rowman & Littlefield, 2000, p. 91.

[7] Michael T. Greven, 'Can the European Union Finally Become a Democracy?', in Greven and Pauly, *Democracy Beyond the State?*, op. cit., pp. 36, 55–6. On democratic public law, see Held, 'The Transformation of Political Community', op. cit., p. 105; on constitutionalism, see Neil Walker, 'The EU and the WTO: Constitutionalism in a New Key', in Gráinne de Búrca and Joanne Scott (eds), *The EU and the WTO: Legal and Constitutional Issues*, Oxford, Hart Publishing, 2001, pp. 31–57 and Ernst-Ulrich Petersmann, 'European and International Constitutional Law: Time for Promoting "Cosmopolitan Democracy" in the WTO', in Búrca and Scott, *The EU and the WTO*, op. cit., pp. 81–110.

[8] Robert A. Dahl, 'Can International Organizations Be Democratic? A Skeptic's View', in Ian Shapiro and Casiano Hacker-Cordón (eds), *Democracy's Edges*, Cambridge, Cambridge University Press, 1999, pp. 19–36.

[9] Will Kymlicka, 'Citizenship in an Era of Globalization: Commentary on Held', in Shapiro and Hacker-Cordón, *Democracy's Edges*, op. cit., pp. 112–26.

A second group of sceptics – to which the author belongs – also believes that certain forms of democratic accountability may be restricted to national political communities. That barrier is of less concern, however, since this group does not view the GEMs as a proto-polity or a fully-fledged system of global governance. The appropriate analogy for these observers is the array of NMIs to which democratic polities delegate important functions. Sol Picciotto, for example, diagnoses the barrier to accountability as systems of 'multi-layered governance' in which specialized organizations at different levels circumvent national governments and build networks that coordinate diverse regulatory activities.[10] Robert O. Keohane and Joseph Nye describe different forms of accountability within democratic polities. For them, the core issue is determining the kinds of accountability that should apply to international institutions.[11]

For members of this group, globalization has not produced a global polity-in-the-making. As Fiona McGillivray remarks bluntly, 'The WTO is not about global governance, it's about the right to trade; as such it's simply a set of rules about multinational negotiations and dispute settlement.'[12] The appropriate benchmark for these institutions is not democratic governance writ large, but a particular slice of democratic governance that has grown in importance in recent decades: specialized regulatory agencies that exercise considerable delegated authority without direct democratic control. Central banks and regulatory agencies present the same challenge to democratic governance as the GEMs. The prescriptive corollary is not rebuilding at the global level a 'version of an already outdated national model of representative democracy'.[13] Rather reformers should aim at mechanisms of accountability for these organizations that are compatible with democratic norms. As principals of the GEMs, democratic governments and their electorates face a central dilemma: how to delegate sufficient authority to render global

[10] Sol Picciotto, 'Democratizing Globalism', in Daniel Drache (ed.), *The Market or the Public Domain?: Global Governance and the Asymmetry of Power*, London, Routledge, 2001, pp. 335–59.

[11] Robert O. Keohane and Joseph Nye, 'Redefining Accountability for Global Governance', in Miles Kahler and David A. Lake (eds), *Governance in a Global Economy: Political Authority in Transition*, Princeton, Princeton University Press, 2003.

[12] Fiona McGillivray, *Democratizing the World Trade Organization*, Stanford, Hoover Institution on War, Revolution, and Peace, Stanford University, 2000, p. 2.

[13] Picciotto, 'Democratizing Globalism', op. cit., p. 339.

institutions effective without having that authority deployed for unintended purposes.

The divide between proponents of an emerging global polity and those who see delegation of authority from national governments to their institutional agents coincides with two other distinctions: input-oriented legitimacy versus output-oriented legitimacy and stakeholders versus shareholders.[14] For those who see the GEMs as centrepieces in an emerging global polity, the principles and processes by which they are governed are of central importance. The direct involvement of stakeholders – those who are directly affected by the GEMs – in their governance becomes an important proxy for democratic governance. The lens of delegation, on the other hand, implies a concentration on the effectiveness of these organizations in advancing the interests of their shareholders, the national governments that 'own' them by authority of treaty.

In this debate over the character of global governance and the appropriate measure and meaning of accountability, one element of democratic governance is seldom awarded the place that it deserves: equality among national governments and citizens, who are the principals of these organizations. Weighted voting at the IMF and the World Bank explicitly awards greater influence to the industrialized countries through their larger quotas. Although the WTO is governed by consensus, in which countries are accorded the same formal weight, it awards the largest share of influence to the major trading powers. Demands by the developing countries for decision-making closer to a 'one country, one vote' model at the international financial institutions (IFIs) – the IMF and the World Bank – would not overcome completely the influence that the major economic powers enjoy. If global institutions fail to serve their purposes, those more influential members can exercise a credible threat to exit and form their own clubs, such as the Group of Seven, the Group of Ten and the Organization for Economic Cooperation and Development (OECD). In any case, one country, one vote is hardly a democratic principle, since it over-weights the citizens of the smaller countries. Equality of representation among principals – whether defined as national governments or individual citizens – is important to both the legitimacy of these organizations, particularly among the

---

[14] On the distinction between these forms of legitimacy, see Fritz W. Scharpf, *Governing in Europe: Effective and Democratic?*, Oxford, Oxford University Press, 1999.

developing countries. Their claims for more equality of representation may conflict, however, with the claims of nongovernmental organizations (NGOs) for a larger role in GEM governance.

Proposals for rendering the GEMs more accountable to member governments and their electorates, proposals that may undermine accountability in the interests of a particular definition of democracy, lie at the centre of the following discussion. The controversies surrounding accountability and legitimacy are critical to the political future of the GEMs. Suspicion of supranational governance and embrace of market alternatives on the right have been matched by left-wing hostility towards globalization and its promotion by the GEMs. The domestic base of support for these institutions has eroded. Addressing the issue of accountability is essential for rebuilding that support.

MYTHOLOGIES OF GLOBAL GOVERNANCE: NATIONAL GOVERNMENTS AND THE GEMS

If GEMs are instruments of national governments rather than reflections of a global polity, an expansion in the scope of these organizations and their influence over national policies will reflect a calculated response to the demands of globalization rather than aggrandizement by the multilaterals themselves or the emergence of a global polity. The mythology that surrounds the GEMs in anti-globalization rhetoric claims that faceless international bureaucrats exercise increasing sway over a widening range of national policies. Inflated rhetoric reflects an element of political reality: opening national borders to economic and cultural exchange has increased both the number of national policies of concern to other societies and pressure to scrutinize those policies in the interests of economic openness.

For the WTO, this has meant growing attention to 'trade-related' measures that are argued to impede market access. Inclusion of such issues – from intellectual property rights to environmental and consumer protection regulations – on the WTO agenda is controversial. The expansion of the WTO's scope can be exaggerated, however. Although anti-WTO activists allege that there is a campaign to undermine national regulatory regimes, the WTO has not defined the scope of 'trade-related' regulation very broadly. Only a few General

Agreement on Tariffs and Trade (GATT) or WTO panel proceedings have concerned environmental, labour or consumer protection regulations. With regard to exchange rate policy and the industrialized countries, the scope of IMF intervention has actually declined since 1970. The IMF, which once monitored an exchange rate regime of fixed parities and provided large-scale external financing to industrialized countries, no longer does so. The IMF and World Bank participation in financial crisis management has important implications for the economic well-being of the industrialized economies but role has also declined in significance when compared to the 1980s. The scope of IFI policy interventions in developing economies has undoubtedly increased. This 'mission creep', however, influences primarily those governments that seek IFI financing. The central conflict over IMF and World Bank intervention lies less with any overall expansion of their scope than with their use of conditional finance to obtain policy change from a concentrated group of clients in the developing world.

Just as expansion in the scope of the GEMs has been uneven, the instruments of their influence over national policies have changed little over time and have remained uncertain in effect. Although the WTO incorporates streamlined dispute settlement procedures (only a consensus of members can block its forward momentum), the dispute settlement process relies entirely on actions taken by member governments. As Martin Wolf emphasizes, the WTO has no power of enforcement of its own; despite popular misconceptions, it cannot change domestic laws, change tariff rates or impose sanctions on member governments.[15] In the absence of financial assistance to a member government, the influence of the IMF and the World Bank is limited to surveillance of national macroeconomic policies, technical assistance and policy advice. The effectiveness of conditionality – the exchange of financial support for policy change – is hard to evaluate. The appropriate measure of IFI influence is a difficult counterfactual: whether policy changed from its likely trajectory in the absence of conditionality. When the IMF intervenes in a particular economy, the government is typically in difficult straits, and policy change of some kind is often inevitable. To pretend that the

---

[15] Martin Wolf, 'What the World Needs from the Multilateral Trading System', in Gary P. Sampson (ed.), *The Role of the World Trade Organization in Global Governance*, Tokyo, United Nations University Press, 2001, p. 196.

IFIs produced the crisis or that the policies implemented were entirely imposed is often a convenient fiction for governments. The evidence rarely supports those assertions, however.[16]

A second argument regarding institutional influence – that liberalization, promoted by the GEMs, will produce a regulatory 'race to the bottom' on the part of national governments – is equally overstated. For a competition in regulatory laxity to occur, certain restrictive conditions must apply. In other instances, economic openness may add to pressure for *greater* regulatory stringency. The race to the bottom has proven to be a powerful and superficially appealing political argument; the evidence for such a race (or even crawl) at the global level is far more limited.[17]

Although the GEMs may not display the issue scope or influence over national policies that would merit the label global governance, their accountability to the governments of member states might still be questioned. Critics of both the left and the right often portray the GEMs as rogue or runaway agencies, pursuing their own ideological or bureaucratic goals rather than the legitimate ends of their member societies. This argument of bureaucratic autonomy and lack of accountability is often muddled with a different argument, particularly on the left: these organizations are accountable, but they are accountable to corporate elites, not to democratic governments.[18] This is an argument for capture rather than bureaucratic drift. Both claims, however, imply that global organizations are not accountable to the national governments that originally delegated authority to them.

Accountability to national governments (or any principal) could be undermined by two important properties of these institutions.

---

[16] For a review of conditionality and the conditions under which it is likely to be effective, see Miles Kahler, 'External Actors, Conditionality, and the Politics of Adjustment', in Stephan Haggard and Robert Kaufman (eds), *The Politics of Economic Adjustment: International Constraints, Distributive Conflicts, and the State*, Princeton, Princeton University Press, 1992, pp. 89–136.

[17] Miles Kahler, 'Modeling Races to the Bottom', paper presented at the Annual Conference of the American Political Science Association, Washington, DC, September 1998, pp. 3–6; David Vogel, *Trading Up: Consumer and Environmental Regulation in a Global Economy*, Cambridge, MA, Harvard University Press, 1995.

[18] Belén Balanyá, Ann Doherty, Olivier Hoedeman, Adam Ma'anit and Erik Wesselius, *Europe Inc.: Regional and Global Restructuring and the Rise of Corporate Power*, London, Pluto Press, 2000.

The first is their proprietary control of information that is not accessible to their national masters. Technical expertise or confidential information has often been a threat to democratic control of specialized agencies. A second route to unwanted autonomy lies in the presence of multiple principals who may have divergent preferences over the institution's policies, not an unrealistic assumption for a global organization. The organization's managers can exploit these divisions in order to enhance their autonomy.[19]

Although these concerns about information asymmetries, agency slack and loss of control by principals are not implausible, national governments have been able to set the outlines of GEM policy and to exercise adequate oversight of the organizations. Expertise and proprietary information – particularly unbiased information – are reasons for delegating authority to these organizations, but the GEMs monopolize neither expertise nor information. The major member governments can claim equivalent or superior sources of information; even confidential or politically sensitive information may be shared as readily with other member governments as with the staff of the IMF or the World Bank. The expertise embedded in these organizations is not without parallel in universities, research institutions, or member governments. A shared professional outlook across government bureaucracies and international organizations that limits any divergence in policy preferences between governments and GEMs.

Divisions among member governments are also real, but their effect on member government influence is diminished by the preponderant weight in the GEMs of the major industrialized countries – the United States, Japan and the European Union. In the IFIs, this influence is formalized in a system of weighted voting. In the WTO, consensus rules protect the position of the major economic powers; the scale of their domestic markets also awards them considerable informal sway. Although the developing countries as a group exercise less influence over GEM policies, their leverage can also be significant, amplified by a strong norm of consensus decision-making.[20]

---

[19] For an excellent examination of agency autonomy in the IMF, see Lisa Martin, 'Agency and Delegation in IMF Conditionality', unpublished paper, Department of Government, Harvard University, 2002.

[20] On decision rules and practices, see Miles Kahler, *Leadership Selection in the Major Multilaterals*, Washington, DC, Institute for International Economics, 2001, pp. 20–4, 53–5.

The influence of national governments over the GEMs is further enhanced by the presence of outside organizational options: clubs of the industrialized countries in the case of the IFIs (the Bank for International Settlements or the Group of Seven (G7), for example), regional trading arrangements in the case of the WTO. These options set up a competition among the GEMs and their rivals that makes deviation from the wishes of their member governments unlikely.[21] Finally, the ability of national governments to delegate authority without creating runaway bureaucracies is increased by the small scale of these organizations. Anti-globalization mythology paints the GEMs as vast bureaucracies. In fact, the WTO staff numbers in the hundreds and is less than one-tenth the size of the World Bank Group (5,700), which itself has a staff less than 25 per cent the size of the European Commission. A more accurate measure of government influence over GEMs is the ratio of GEM staff to national government staff overseeing their work. The WTO ranks the lowest of the three, given large national delegations in Geneva; the World Bank ranks the highest.[22]

The logic traced thus far – the GEMs are instruments of national governments that have been delegated their authority by those governments; national governments are able to ensure accountability to their interests by the GEMs – leads to the following conclusion: to the degree that these organizations display 'accountability deficits', those deficiencies are more likely the result of choices by the most influential national governments than a symptom of the dysfunctions of international bureaucracies. Remedies for an alleged lack of accountability fail to take into account the key source of resistance to reform: national governments. Governments have used delegation to international organizations to skew policy outcomes away from those that are likely in the national political arena. Mechanisms of accountability are shifted to bias policy over time. Particular interests

---

[21] On the importance of outside options in principal–agent relationships, see John Ferejohn, 'Accountability and Authority: Toward a Theory of Political Accountability', in Przeworski, Stokes and Manin, *Democracy, Accountability, and Representation*, op. cit., pp. 131–53.

[22] Figures from the mid-1990s in David Henderson, 'International Agencies and Cross-Border Liberalization: The WTO in Context', in Anne O. Krueger (ed.), *The WTO as an International Organization*, Chicago, University of Chicago Press, Table 3.1 and pp. 102–6.

are disenfranchised by design – just as they are by national NMIs. Fiona McGillivray, for example, argues that the over-representation of protectionist interests in domestic politics (in part the result of their ease of organization) is countered by the WTO, which produces outcomes that are closer to the interests of the median voter.[23] Paradoxically, 'opening' the WTO to a wider array of interests in the name of accountability might make negotiation outcomes *less* representative of the interests of the electorate as a whole.[24]

The use of delegation to skew policy outcomes over time is a familiar tactic in domestic politics that is imitated in international institutions. These commitment mechanisms may be defended on the basis of outcomes that represent the electorate's wishes more faithfully than processes that are subject to capture by special interests. On the other hand, the wishes of the electorate may be unclear or may change over time, raising the question of whether large and long-lasting policy biases in the GEMs violate democratic legitimacy. This use of GEMs, other international institutions and NMIs poses the knottiest normative issue regarding delegation and accountability in international institutions.

ACCOUNTABILITY AND ITS COSTS: REFORMING THE GEMS

Three techniques for enhancing accountability of the GEMs are illustrated in the following cases: transparency (more information for those outside the institution), competition (imitation of democratic accountability) and changes in rules of representation (accountability to stakeholders rather than shareholders). These accounts emphasize the preferences and actions of key national governments, in line with the argument that those governments ultimately design the mechanisms of accountability in the GEMs. They also emphasize the costs of accountability and particular mechanisms for improving or changing accountability. Too often accountability has been treated as an absolute value in discussions of international institutions. Here, central dilemmas are outlined, dilemmas that emerge from actual or proposed changes in the GEMs. More accountability may ultimately

[23] McGillivray, *Democratizing the World Trade Organization*, op. cit.
[24] On the relationship of representation, responsiveness, and accountability, see Manin, Przeworski and Stokes, 'Election and Representation', op. cit.

contribute to both the effectiveness and legitimacy of the GEMs, but that hope must be demonstrated, not assumed.

Transparency and the Audiences for Information

Although the IMF became an apostle of transparency in the wake of financial crises during the 1990s, it was also a convenient target for those who criticized its opaque decision-making and the tight controls that it exercised over member-related information. Initially its transparency agenda was directed to information provision by financial institutions and national governments, enforced by peer pressure and international standard-setting. The IMF promoted reduction in information asymmetries as a central part of the new international financial architecture and a contribution to global financial stability. Although widely applauded, some cautioned that the new world of greater transparency would not prevent an occurrence of international financial crises.[25]

Outside critics argued that similar standards of transparency and accountability should be applied to the Fund itself. The justification was often a pragmatic one. Echoing students of principal–agent relations, internal transparency – 'greater agent observability' – was required to win the confidence of principals and cause them to invest more in the IMF. The wider role advocated for the IMF in preventing and managing financial crises therefore implied more openness to outside scrutiny.[26] The flaw in this argument was its assumption that national governments (or the Executive Board that represented them) demanded greater transparency in exchange for commitment to an expanded Fund role. In fact, a major obstacle to enhanced transparency at the GEMs has been the resistance of national governments. Greater transparency conflicted with national cultures of secrecy, often built on fears of domestic accountability exercised by

[25] Barry Eichengreen, *Toward a New International Financial Architecture*, Washington, DC, Institute for International Economics, 1999; Miles Kahler, 'The New International Financial Architecture and Its Limits', in Gregory W. Noble and John Ravenhill (eds), *The Asian Financial Crisis and the Structure of Global Finance*, Cambridge, Cambridge University Press, 2000, pp. 235–60.

[26] Ferejohn, 'Accountability and Authority', op. cit., pp. 148–9; Eichengreen, *Toward a New International Financial Architecture*, op. cit., p. 114.

political opponents. Blame-shifting to the GEMs also becomes more difficult with greater transparency. National bureaucracies (finance ministries and central banks) that are deeply involved in oversight of the IFIs are unlikely to advocate greater public transparency that would reduce their leverage vis-à-vis bureaucratic and political rivals.

Recommendations for greater internal transparency at the IMF demonstrated the confusion that may result from a simple transfer of domestic mechanisms of accountability to the GEMs. Some reformers pressed for greater accountability through *closer* government oversight of the Fund through a formalization of the Interim Committee, a reform that was eventually implemented. Others, promoting the analogy of a central bank or national regulatory agency, proposed *reducing* direct oversight by national governments. At the same time, they recommended an increase in internal transparency by replacing consensus decision-making with recorded votes and by publishing minutes of Executive Board discussions.[27]

The diagnosis underlying these contradictory prescriptions was often questionable. Although meddling in Fund policies by self-interested national governments was easily documented (most recently in Russia), few observers of the IFIs would place its elimination at the top of a list of desirable Fund reforms. The IMF's foreign policy usefulness is a major incentive for engagement on the part of major powers. Fund governance that is completely independent of such behaviour would lose support in national capitals. The analogy to central bank independence – itself often questioned as an encroachment on democratic accountability – is also dubious. The IMF is not a world central bank. Whether greater transparency at the IMF would serve a stabilizing function in a crisis-prone international financial system is open to doubt. In any case, central banks have not acted in a transparent fashion during financial crises; witness the behaviour of the New York Federal Reserve during the failure of Long Term Capital Management in 1998.

Some reformers hope to enhance accountability by transferring majoritarian democratic principles to the IMF, an attack on consensus decision-making. One of the great strengths of the IMF and its

[27] José De Gregorio, Barry Eichengreen, Takatoshi Ito and Charles Wyplosz, *An Independent and Accountable IMF*, Geneva, International Centre for Monetary and Banking Studies, 1999; Ngaire Woods, 'The Challenge of Good Governance for the IMF and the World Bank Themselves', *World Development*, 28: 5 (2000), pp. 823–41.

Executive Board is their ability to act effectively and (by the standards of intergovernmental organizations) expeditiously. Recorded votes and majoritarian decision-making could seriously erode those positive qualities of the organization, producing clear winners and embittered losers over time. A peculiar vision of accountability in this case is allowed to trump other valuable ends.

The agenda of national transparency and code construction that has been adopted by the IMF and its major shareholders represented voluntary measures taken by national governments and did not involve the Fund in additional direct data-gathering and publication. Instead, in its new special data dissemination standard (SDDS) and general data dissemination standard (GDDS) the IMF sought to create standards understood and accepted by both governments (the suppliers) and private financial markets (the principal consumers). The IMF encouraged the release of Public Information Notices (PINs) and Article IV staff reports and established a presumption that documentation for Fund country programmes would be released (although the member in question could still refuse that release).[28]

Peer and market pressures were mobilized in favour of these voluntary measures by governments, but one dimension of increased Fund transparency, its relations with member governments, was left relatively untouched by pressures for reform. The IMF could increase the accountability of national governments to financial markets and to their own electorates by judicious deployment of its private information against wayward clients. However, advocates of the Fund as a financial 'traffic cop' – flashing green, amber and red signals to international investors – encountered resistance from national elites, who would risk political embarrassment, and from crisis managers, who predicted financial crises created by misguided attempts to prevent them. The IMF's value as a gatherer of credible financial information could be undermined in the longer run, as governments doctored information or avoided supplying it to the organization.[29] In response to these fears, the Fund made clear in the wake of the Asian

[28] Current IMF transparency policy is described in International Monetary Fund, 'The Fund's Transparency Policy – Review of the Experience and Next Steps', Washington, DC, 24 May 2002.

[29] Eichengreen, *Toward a New International Financial Architecture*, op. cit., p. 114; Kahler, 'The New International Financial Architecture', op. cit.

financial crisis that any public disclosure of differences with a member government would be very rare. The risks of rupture with an offended government and the prospect of exacerbating financial instability overrode any extension of IMF–member government transparency beyond its existing and largely voluntary boundaries.

Calls for greater transparency and accountability at the IMF produced limited change because the Fund's principals, national governments, were relatively satisfied with their own supply of information from the Fund. Key external audiences, particularly the private financial markets, did not clamour for radical changes in information provision or governance at the IMF. NGOs exerted less influence at the IMF than at other global institutions. One change illustrated the definition of accountability that members of the IMF found most useful. In 2001 the Fund created an Independent Evaluation Office (IEO), designed to operate 'at arm's length' from the Executive Board'.[30] This independent entity, committed to transparency in its own operations, was directed to promote organizational learning by the Fund and to build external credibility. The IEO will seek feedback from 'external stakeholders' on its work programme and on published evaluation reports. The IEO's work programmes have emphasized analysis of recent, controversial cases of IMF intervention, such as Argentina, as well as broader issues (poverty reduction, prolonged use of Fund resources). Its work embodies a key prerequisite to any discussion of accountability: determining whether and how the IMF has influenced government policies and international economic outcomes. Rendering the IMF accountable requires a clear understanding of its policy interventions and their effects in particular circumstances, or, as the first Director of the IEO declared, a quantification of the counterfactual.[31] Only with that understanding can steps be taken to correct past mistakes and reset future policies.

The World Bank has initiated a similar experiment in responsiveness and accountability in keeping with its concentration on project lending. NGOs and citizen groups have accused the Bank and borrowing governments of ignoring the protests and legitimate interests

[30] Information on the IEO can be found at http://www.imf.org/external/np/ieo/index.htm.

[31] 'Independent Evaluations Should Put IMF on a Faster Learning Track', *IMF Survey*, 31: 1 (14 January 2002), p. 3.

of those who are affected by World Bank lending. Environmental groups in particular have aligned themselves with indigenous peoples and local groups in the developing countries to oppose large infrastructure projects financed by the Bank in collaboration with national agencies. The World Bank established its Inspection Panel in 1993 'to provide an independent forum to private citizens who believe that they or their interests have been or could be directly harmed by a project financed by the World Bank.'[32] The Inspection Panel provides direct access to a type of appeals process, one that is situated in the Bank but is not part of the World Bank hierarchy. The Inspection Panel has received 27 formal requests since it began operations in 1994. Like the IMF Independent Evaluation Office, member governments have awarded the Inspection Panel substantial delegated authority and allowed it to distance itself from the Bank's management. Although its role is that of an ombudsman, addressing complaints from those affected by Bank activities, its analysis is directed to the same issue as the IEO: ascertaining the effects of Bank programmes, in this case on particular communities and individuals.

Transparency for whom has been a more pressing issue at the WTO. Developing country governments define internal transparency as ensuring that all members are kept abreast of inter-governmental negotiations and granted access to those negotiations if their interests are at stake. NGOs, on the other hand, see transparency as an avenue of influence in the organization. Their demands have produced a rapid increase in the volume of derestricted documents and a website that provides considerable detail on the progress of negotiations and the findings of dispute settlement panels and the Appellate Body. NGO participation in or observation of formal WTO meetings produces 'widespread anxiety' among most member governments, however, who view such access as a threat to the success of intergovernmental negotiations.[33] Equally sensitive are the dispute settlement proceedings, which have received disproportionate attention from NGOs. The proceedings are quasi-judicial in form, which encourages comparison to international courts that are open to the public, such as the International Court

[32] http://wbln0018.worldbank.org/lpn/ipnweb.nsf/WOverview/overview?operdocument#1 (29 April 2001).

[33] Frank Loy, 'Public Participation in the World Trade Organization', in Sampson, *The World Trade Organization in Global Governance*, op. cit., pp. 126–7.

of Justice and the European Court of Justice. Dispute settlement is also quasi-diplomatic, however. Panel findings are only one part of the process of settling commercial disputes between member governments. The diplomatic dimension of dispute settlement might be less successful in full view of the public and interested NGOs.

Competition and Leadership Selection

Reformers have often overlooked one mechanism for reinforcing accountability at the GEMs: selection of the top leadership in the organizations. In a democratic context, the ability to sanction leaders who diverge from the electorate's preferences is a central avenue of accountability; replacement of incompetent CEOs at private corporations serves the same purpose. In successive episodes of selection during the 1990s, the IMF and the WTO were embroiled in contentious battles over the choice of managing director or director-general.[34] One striking feature of these conflicts, however, has been the low priority assigned to leadership accountability as a criterion for selecting top management. Selecting leaders who are aligned with member government policy preferences might be expected to dominate the behaviour of government representatives. Instead, most governments have supported candidates on the basis of national or regional loyalties. Although indices of identity might be taken as a proxy for future behaviour, little evidence exists that such markers are good predictors of future management actions.

Dominance of the nationality principle – maximizing fellow nationals in top positions – in selection contests points to other ways in which the selection process has failed to enhance accountability. Procedures for selecting leaders in these organizations were unusually opaque to those outside the organizations and to many national representatives within. The criteria guiding the selection were seldom specified clearly. Accountability mechanisms that are widely employed in other organizations, public and private, have not been implemented in the GEMs. For example, reappointment of a managing director, president, or director-general has never required a formal performance review of top management.

---

[34] This account is based on Kahler, *Leadership Selection*, op. cit.

The WTO's selection of a director-general in 1998–99 was a partial exception to the past practice of closed selections driven by the nationality principle. The contest also demonstrated the dangers of open competition for the organization. The most powerful players at the WTO, the United States and the EU, equivocated in their choice of a candidate. In the absence of strong leadership from the United States or the EU, the field included candidates from two developing countries (Morocco and Thailand) and two OECD members (New Zealand and Canada). Support for the candidates, apart from consistent Asian support for Supachai Panitchpakdi of Thailand, did not cohere consistently along national or regional lines. Supachai, however, was clearly viewed as the candidate of most large developing economies, whose governments were discontented with implementation of the Uruguay Round agreements.

Selection of the WTO director-general in 1998–99 came closer to an open and competitive selection process than ever before. Although the 'electors' remained national governments, candidates campaigned among politicians and interest groups in key capitals. For example, Mike Moore captured the Clinton administration's support in part because of the positive impression he made on US labour. In best democratic fashion, candidates were accused of promising patronage positions within the WTO to their supporting governments. Unfortunately, openness and competition – a selection free-for-all – did not produce agreement on a candidate who was more representative of and accountable to the WTO membership. Instead, in the final stages of the leadership contest, the deeply polarized supporters of finalists Moore and Supachai produced a lengthy deadlock. Many member governments rejected resort to a vote, even though such recourse was stipulated under WTO rules.

The unsatisfactory device of term-sharing finally broke the impasse: Moore and Supachai would each serve three years as director-general without reappointment or extension of their terms. Since the shortened terms cover no more than a fraction of a new trade round, accountability of the director-general for negotiation results was undermined. Competitive deadlock also created persistent bitterness between the two camps that would spill over into other settings. The stalemate delayed selection of a new director-general and impeded preparations for the Seattle ministerial meeting. An absence of active leadership during 1998 and much of 1999 contributed to the WTO debacle in Seattle in December 1999.

The WTO breakdown underlined the shortcomings of a majoritarian model of decision-making in the GEMs. Openness and competition in the selection process – characteristics endorsed by the proponents of accountability – created division and deadlock. Simple transfer of a majoritarian model of democratic accountability neglects other values in governance that are equally important. Transparency and heightened competition may contribute to the legitimacy of these organizations in the longer term, but they may also discourage talented candidates for top leadership positions. Consensus decision-making, on the other hand, may sacrifice some transparency and accountability, in favour of avoiding conflict that damages other arenas of foreign relations. Polarized coalitions may win clear-cut victories at the cost of undermining organizational efficiency and legitimacy by creating clear losing coalitions. These competing values deserve equal attention when contemplating changes that are purported to enhance transparency and accountability. Selection procedures can be made more transparent through means less polarizing and public.

GEMs, NGOs and Government Gatekeepers

A final dilemma of accountability is perhaps the most difficult politically for the GEMs: incorporating nongovernmental actors into their decision-making. Robert O. Keohane has noted that the politics of accountability often involve 'struggles over who should be accepted as principal'.[35] It reflects directly on the issues of equality of representation among national governments, which pits rich countries against poor and large countries against small. Few would deny that the citizens of member states are principals of these organizations; they are simply not the proximate principals. By delegating authority to the GEMs, national governments have established a different arena of policy-making that is at least one step removed from the national political arena. As already described, that arena may be skewed to favour certain types of expertise or interest in order to promote the purposes of the organization. Nongovernmental organizations, noting the

---

[35] Robert O. Keohane, 'Global Governance and Democratic Accountability', in David Held and Mathias Koenig-Archibugi (eds), *Taming Globalization: Frontiers of Governance*, Cambridge, Polity Press, 2003, p. 140.

expanded scope of these organizations (particularly the WTO), have argued that this bias in policy-making is no longer legitimate and have attempted to circumvent their own government gatekeepers. At the centre of the controversy is this self-initiated reduction in the chain of delegation by NGOs (over the opposition of interests that have benefited from the existing policy bias), based on claims by NGOs to represent their national societies and an emerging international civil society. More fundamentally, conflict centres on the jealously guarded role of national governments as gatekeepers between their own societies and the GEMs.

NGO engagement with the GEMs has deepened on so many fronts that the new international policy-making process has been labelled 'complex multilateralism' or 'contested issue networks'.[36] Although NGO engagement has affected all of the GEMs, NGOs have devoted most attention to the WTO, given its expanded scope and its perceived impact on a range of domestic regulatory issues. Ironically, post-war plans for an International Trade Organization (ITO), designed as the companion to the Bretton Woods IFIs, had envisaged that nongovernmental interests would maintain 'regular contact' with its secretariat.[37] After the failure of the ITO, its successor, the GATT, became a negotiating forum dominated by the trade ministries of the major industrialized economies. The club model of organization that emerged at the GATT offered little space for active participation by either the developing countries or 'non-trade-related' political organizations in the industrialized countries. Since most developing countries avoided trade liberalization and deeper engagement with the international economy, however, their 'special and differential' participation was seldom a point of conflict. Labour, environmental, and consumer protection groups also viewed the GATT as peripheral to their interests during these decades.

As the club model of organization weakened in the 1990s, demands for changes in governance of the new WTO came from two

[36] Robert O'Brien, Anne Marie Goetz, Jan Aart Scholte and Marc Williams, *Contesting Global Governance: Multilateral Economic Institutions and Global Social Movements*, Cambridge, Cambridge University Press, 2000, p. 207; Keohane and Nye, 'Redefining Accountability for Global Governance', op. cit. O'Brien et al. provides an excellent series of case studies of NGO involvement with the GEMs.

[37] Loy, 'Public Participation in the World Trade Organization', op. cit., p. 116. The designers of the ITO may have had in mind the quasi-corporatist model of the International Labour Organization (ILO), founded immediately after the First World War.

different but equally persistent sets of actors. Although the WTO incorporated a strengthened Dispute Settlement Understanding (DSU), its internal governance had not been reformed to deal with either increased participation from a large number of new member governments (developing and transitional economies) or involvement by NGOs that were often deeply suspicious of WTO operations and hostile to its core agenda.

Conflict over openness and accountability at the WTO revealed a new underlying fault line in the politics surrounding the GEMs. Since the WTO had only a small secretariat and a member-driven agenda, bureaucratic opposition within the organization was not a plausible explanation for resistance to NGO demands. The major points of resistance were two: established trade bureaucracies in the major industrialized states, who resisted NGO attempts to broaden the WTO agenda (but not *all* attempts to broaden the agenda) and, most significantly and vehemently, developing country governments, now deeply engaged with the global trade regime and the new organization that governed it.

Reformers who argued for opening the WTO to greater participation by NGOs advanced a clear governing principle: 'those who believe that they have an interest in the outcome of decisions should have an opportunity to be part of the decision-making process.'[38] The WTO had ventured into issue-areas that impinged on domestic regulatory regimes. The NGOs who supported those regulatory goals claimed a right to be heard at the WTO, balancing the pro-liberalization bias of commercial interests – governmental and non-governmental – that had traditionally been represented in Geneva.

For trade experts and trade ministries in the industrialized countries, the new issues raised by the NGOs were peripheral to the core concerns of the WTO – reducing barriers to economic exchange in the interests of their national economies and global economic welfare. In their view, the criterion for participation should be expertise: if a dispute settlement panel dealt with environmental or scientific issues, the WTO should consult with available experts, whether based in NGOs or elsewhere. If NGOs were to be heard in WTO negotiations or dispute settlement proceedings 'as of right', then other groups could not be excluded, further slowing the WTO's cumbersome decision-making. Funding for dispute settlement

---

[38] Ibid., p. 128.

proceedings would require a substantial increase to deal with the prospective increase in participants.[39] Specialists in trade policy also questioned the legitimacy of NGOs on democratic grounds. The question 'accountable to whom?' that the NGOs had applied to the GEMs was used to question the NGOs' right of representation.[40]

Developing country governments were even more resistant to NGO inclusion in WTO decision-making. For both rich and poor countries, NGO demands often ran counter to national economic interests as defined by trade bureaucracies and their business allies. The developing countries, however, viewed any expansion of the WTO agenda with particular suspicion. In their view, the 'old' agenda – removing trade barriers to the exports in the industrialized countries – had not been completed. Labour rights and environmental protection, they feared, would become new impositions on their over-taxed political institutions, requirements backed by a threat of trade sanctions. Like supporters of liberalized trade in the north, they saw protectionists behind many NGO critics of the WTO, interests that were happy to use the vocabulary of democracy and accountability to obstruct the removal of trade barriers.

Skewed representation among the most prominent and influential NGOs also heightened developing country resistance. The centre of support for NGOs backing environmental, labour and consumer protection lay overwhelmingly in the industrialized countries. Successful NGOs in the developing countries often relied on a 'boomerang effect' that used influential NGO allies in the north to exert leverage on their own national governments.[41] The budgets and resources of the major NGOs 'far exceed those that many – if not most – of the member states of the WTO can bring to bear on either policymaking or litigation'.[42] For the developing countries, then, incorporating the NGOs into WTO decision-making would represent an additional tilt in organizational power towards the industrialized countries.[43] By circumventing the chain of delegation from

[39] Wolf, 'What the World Needs', op. cit., p. 199.

[40] Ibid., pp. 197–8; O'Brien et al., *Contesting Global Governance*, op. cit., pp. 200–1.

[41] Margaret E. Keck and Kathryn Sikkink, *Activists Beyond Border: Advocacy Networks in International Politics*, Ithaca, Cornell University Press, 1998.

[42] Claude E. Barfield, *Free Trade, Sovereignty, Democracy: The Future of the World Trade Organization*, Washington, DC, AEI Press, 2001, p. 88.

[43] Loy, 'Public Participation in the World Trade Organization', op. cit., p. 124.

national politics, the NGOs would permit the industrialized world a form of double counting in its representation at the WTO. Far more important than NGO participation for developing country spokesmen is the 'blatant under-representation' of the poorest developing countries at the WTO, governments that lack the resources to participate fully and to benefit from the global trading system.[44] Demands for greater influence from one group of aspirant principals, the NGOs, have collided with claims by the developing countries for more equitable representation and participation.

On one issue, the WTO's Appellate Body has advanced towards the position of the NGOs. In overturning the panel finding in an important environmental proceeding, the Appellate Body found that interested nongovernmental parties could file *amicus curiae* briefs, which panels could accept or reject. In the event that a panel does not accept such briefs, however, it is likely that a friendly government (an 'interested party') could incorporate NGO positions in their own filings with a panel. At the same time, the Appellate Body reaffirmed that the WTO Charter permitted only member governments to initiate or participate in a dispute settlement proceeding.[45]

CONCLUSIONS: DILEMMAS OF ACCOUNTABILITY IN THE GEMs

Debates over accountability in the GEMs are important for reasons international and domestic. The institutional supports for international cooperation are typically undersupplied. A perceived lack of accountability on the part of global institutions may discourage additional, necessary delegations of authority to international institutions. Echoing Philippe Schmitter, we should also ask that these institutions not contribute to the malaise of national democratic governance by operating in a 'remote, secretive, unintelligible, and

[44] McGillivray, *Democratizing the World Trade Organization*, op. cit., p. 3; Rubens Ricupero, 'Rebuilding Confidence in the Multilateral Trading System: Closing the "Legitimacy Gap"', in Sampson, *The World Trade Organization in Global Governance*, op. cit., pp. 47–9.

[45] WTO, 'United States – Prohibition of Certain Shrimp and Shrimp Products: Report of the Appellate Body', AB-1998-4, 12 October 1998.

unaccountable fashion'.[46] Spillovers of this kind from the global to the national level are corrosive of democratic rule.

In considering the issues of transparency at the IMF, competition in leadership selection at the WTO, and engagement with NGOs at the WTO (an experience that could be replicated with some variation at the other GEMs), the central role of government gatekeepers becomes apparent. The ability of governments to engage and co-opt nongovernmental actors has been documented in the context of international environmental negotiations and in other global settings. The pattern of delegation, accountability and participation in the GEMs is not primarily the result of inadvertence or agency deviation; it is the result of design by member governments. Changes will also require government acquiescence or action. Conflict over these issues of governance typically involves bureaucratic insiders in the member governments on the one hand and nongovernmental outsiders (often based in the same societies) on the other, even though the conflict is played out in a global setting.

Neither of the 'warring analogies' described earlier fully captures the new pattern of policy-making at the GEMs. These remain institutions created of, by, and for national governments. They are technical, specialized instruments of those governments. As their authority expands, however, nongovernmental actors seek to influence their activities directly, avoiding the intermediation of their own national representatives. That pattern, so disturbing to veterans of these organizations, is not likely to disappear. How those interested parties – whether interest groups or, occasionally, the wider public – are incorporated into the practices of these organizations will be a central issue in evaluating their accountability, even if national governments are largely successful in ensuring GEM accountability to themselves. The different mechanisms through which the GEMs are or may become accountable to others remain 'under construction'.

Each of the issues and cases has illustrated key dilemmas of accountability that are often overlooked by reformers. Transparency – rendering information more readily accessible – has been the easiest agenda for governments to advance. Nevertheless, information that might embarrass a government at the hands of its

[46] Philippe Schmitter, *How to Democratize the European Union . . . and Why Bother?*, Lanham, MD, Rowman & Littlefield Publishers, 2000, p. 116.

domestic opponents has remained carefully guarded at the IMF; the
WTO has resisted moves that would allow public oversight of negotiating sessions or dispute settlement proceedings for the same
reason. By and large, the GEMs have been able to increase available
information in order to enhance their public accountability and at
the same time to avoid excessive transparency that would impair their
core negotiating missions. Although 'opaque' decision-making at the
GEMs has been criticized, these are not large and impenetrable
bureaucracies, for their larger members at least.

The most recent leadership selection at the WTO revealed the
risks of increased competition as a means to greater accountability.
The contest between Supachai and Moore had many of the hallmarks
of a domestic electoral contest, with an audience that extended
beyond government agencies. Competition, which increased the
transparency of the process and elicited additional information on
the candidates, also imposed significant costs on the WTO. Institutional reformers have often argued for accountability practices at
the GEMs that borrow from majoritarian democracies. The critical,
perhaps essential, quality of consensus – also the hallmark of successful democracies – is too often slighted. In its last leadership selection, the WTO did ignore the value of consensus, and it paid a heavy
price.

The most difficult accountability issues are raised by claims to
direct participation in the work of the GEMs by nongovernmental
actors. Few clear guidelines exist at the global level for enfranchis-
ing those who are not member governments. Issues of representation and internal accountability are profound and divisive among
governments and nongovernmental organizations. Should groups
that have democratic access to their national governments be allowed
a second chance to influence policy through direct access to these
organizations? Should governments that do not allow democratic
access to their policy-making be subject to different requirements of
transparency and accountability within the organization (a distinction that has never been made by the GEMs)? Allowing access to
GEM decision-making without considering such criteria for participation could result in a more open, but less legitimate decision-
making process, one in which powerful governments weigh even
more heavily and the marginalized become the disenfranchised.

The issue of accountability to whom, which is most often framed
by the NGOs, conflicts with another agenda of representation

promoted by the developing countries. The weighting of influence within these organizations toward the industrialized countries has been challenged as a violation of democratic accountability, if all citizens of the world are taken as equal. More often, however, governments of the developing world have framed their representation demands in terms of equality of governments, a return to the old model of consensus decision-making that has plagued the WTO. One country, one vote is no more a principle of democratic accountability than weighted voting. Whether any system of revised representation can overcome the de facto influence of the largest economies within these organizations is unlikely. Internal transparency, however, would reduce the sense of exclusion and powerlessness felt by many smaller developing countries. Any measures to increase participation by NGOs based in the industrialized countries should be paired with additional steps to ensure that their participation does not further tilt these organizations against poor countries with inadequate capabilities or representation.

Each of these dilemmas can be resolved hypothetically in a manner that increases accountability without a steep trade-off against other important values – decision-making efficiency, consensus and effectiveness in achieving organizational goals – that also contribute to organizational legitimacy. Informational asymmetries can be reduced by 'accountability agencies', staffed by those who are removed from the influence of an organization's management. The IMF's IEO and the World Bank Inspection Panel represent first initiatives of this kind. Competitive analysis from outside experts – which could be institutionalized – also enhances accountability. Reformed leadership selection practices could incorporate both openness to nongovernmental judgements on candidates and restrained competition that elicits more information on a broader slate of candidates. Nongovernmental participation could be subjected to stringent standards of accountability – 'accountability all the way down' – requiring greater transparency and representational evidence from those who request access to the GEMs. Internal transparency should be defined in ways that empower the smaller and poorer members of the GEMs, and NGO involvement should be calibrated to prevent reinforcement of the preponderant influence of the rich countries.

Delegation and accountability in modern democracy remain larger issues that are reflected in the global economic institutions.

The GEMs are part of a proliferation of NMIs that have become an important feature of contemporary democratic governance. Paradoxically, as democratic governance has spread across the globe, democracies have turned to institutions that limit or violate democratic practices by design. As commitment devices, these institutions purposely bias policy and establish barriers to change for future governments and electorates. The GEMs do the same: under the GATT and the WTO, tariffs are bound by international agreement to prevent backsliding by future governments; governments assume similar commitments to liberalizing current account transactions under Article IV of the IMF. The World Bank is unlikely to fund projects or programmes that undermine economic openness or set back economic development. To the degree that the bias chosen decades ago is now the subject of political controversy, the instruments of that bias – whether domestic or international – will also remain at the centre of those controversies.

3
Disaggregated Sovereignty: Towards the Public Accountability of Global Government Networks

Anne-Marie Slaughter

Only governments bear the political imprimatur that is bestowed by political accountability. Neither multinational corporations nor international bureaucracies are a substitute. Addressing the most complex challenges posed by globalization requires the direct accountability carried by the representatives of sovereign nations. (Paul Martin, former Canadian Finance Minister and Chair of the G-20[1])

TERRORISTS, ARMS DEALERS, MONEY LAUNDERERS, DRUG DEALERS, traffickers in women and children, and the modern pirates of intellectual property all operate through global networks.[2] So, increasingly, do governments. Networks of government officials – police investigators, financial regulators, even judges and legislators – increasingly exchange information and coordinate activity to combat global crime and address common problems on a global scale. These government networks are a key feature of world order in the twenty-first century. But they are under-appreciated, under-supported and under-used to address the central problems of global governance.

Consider the examples simply in the wake of 11 September. The Bush administration immediately set about assembling an 'ad hoc coalition' of states to aid in the war on terrorism. Public attention focused on military cooperation, but the networks of financial regulators working to identify and freeze terrorist assets, of law enforcement officials sharing vital information on terrorist suspects, and of intelligence operatives working to pre-empt the next attack have been equally important. Indeed, the leading expert in the 'new

---

[1] Paul Martin, 'Notes for an Address by the Honourable Paul Martin to the Royal Institute of International Affairs', London, 24 January 2001, on Department of Finance Canada homepage (accessed 22 June 2003); available from http://www.fin.gc.ca/news01/01-009e.html.

[2] Moises Naim, 'Five Wars of Globalization', *Foreign Policy* (January/February 2003), pp. 28–37.

security' of borders and container bombs insists that the domestic agencies responsible for customs, food safety and regulation of all kinds must extend their reach abroad, through reorganization and much closer cooperation with their foreign counterparts.[3] And after the US concluded that it did not have authority under international law to interdict a shipment of missiles from North Korea to Yemen, it turned to national law enforcement authorities to coordinate the extraterritorial enforcement of their national criminal laws.[4] Networked threats require a networked response.

Turning to the global economy, networks of finance ministers and central bankers have been critical players in responding to national and regional financial crises. The G8 is as much a network of finance ministers as of heads of state; it is the finance ministers who take key decisions on how to respond to calls for debt relief for the most highly indebted countries. The finance ministers and central bankers hold separate news conferences to announce policy responses to crises such as the East Asian financial crisis in 1997 and the Russian crisis in 1998.[5] The G20, a network specifically created to help prevent future crises, is led by the Indian finance minister and is composed of the finance ministers of 20 developed and developing countries. More broadly, the International Organization of Securities Commissioners (IOSCO) emerged in 1984. It was followed in the 1990s by the creation of the International Association of Insurance Supervisors and a network of all three of these organizations and other national and international officials responsible for financial stability around the world called the Financial Stability Forum.[6]

[3] Stephen Flynn, 'America the Vulnerable', *Foreign Affairs*, 81 (2002), pp. 60–74.

[4] David E. Sanger, 'The World: When Laws Don't Apply; Cracking Down on the Terror-Arms Trade', *New York Times*, 15 June 2003, section 4, p. 4.

[5] Robert Chote, 'A World in the Woods', *Financial Times*, 2 November 1998, p. 20.

[6] The Financial Stability Forum was initiated by the Finance Ministers and Central Bank Governors of the Group of Seven industrial countries in February 1999, following a report on international cooperation and coordination in the area of financial market supervision and surveillance by the President of the Deutsche Bundesbank. In additions to representatives from the Basle Committee, IOSCO and IAIS, its members include senior representative from national authorities responsible for financial stability in significant international financial centres; international financial institutions such as the BIS, the IMF, the OECD and the World Bank; and committees of central bank experts. See 'A Guide to Fund Committees, Groups, and Clubs:

Beyond national security and the global economy, networks of national officials are working to improve environmental policy across borders. Within NAFTA, US, Mexican and Canadian environmental agencies have created an environmental enforcement network, which has enhanced the effectiveness of environmental regulation in all three states, particularly in Mexico. Globally, the EPA and its Dutch equivalent have founded the International Network for Environmental Compliance and Enforcement, which offers technical assistance to environmental agencies around the world, holds global conferences for environmental regulators to learn and exchange information, and sponsors a website with training videos and other information.

Nor are regulators the only ones networking. National judges are exchanging decisions with one another through conferences, judicial organizations, and the internet. Constitutional judges increasingly cite one another's decisions on issues from free speech to privacy rights. Bankruptcy judges in different countries negotiate mini-treaties to resolve complicated international cases; judges in transnational commercial disputes have begun to see themselves as part of a global judicial system. National judges are also interacting directly with their supranational counterparts on trade and human rights issues.

Finally, even legislators, the most naturally parochial government officials due to their direct ties to territorially rooted constituents, are reaching across borders. International parliamentary organizations have been traditionally well meaning but ineffective. But today national parliamentarians are meeting to adopt and publicize common positions on the death penalty, human rights and environmental issues. They support one another in legislative initiatives and offer training programmes and technical assistance.[7]

Financial Stability Forum', on International Monetary Fund homepage (accessed 20 December 2002); available from http://www.imf.org/external/np/exr/facts/groups. htm#FSF.

[7] American readers may be sceptical of these reports due to the widespread and completely false statistic about how few members of Congress have a passport. In fact, 93% of all members hold passports and average two trips abroad a year. Indeed, 20% claim to speak a foreign language. Eric Schmitt and Elizabeth Becker, 'Insular Congress Appears to be Myth', *New York Times*, 4 November 2000, section A, p. 9. What is true is that some members fear that their constituents will identify trips to meet their counterparts abroad with 'junkets', but that is a matter of public education.

Each of these networks has specific aims and activities, depending on its subject area, membership and history. But taken together, they also perform certain common functions. They expand regulatory reach, allowing national government officials to keep up with corporations, civic organizations and criminals. They build trust and establish relationships among their participants that then create incentives to establish a good reputation and avoid a bad one. These are the conditions essential for long-term cooperation. They exchange regular information about their own activities and develop databases of best practices, or, in the judicial case, different approaches to common legal issues. They offer technical assistance and professional socialization to members from less developed nations – whether regulators, judges, or legislators.

In a world of global markets, global travel and global information networks, of weapons of mass destruction and looming environmental disasters of global magnitude, governments must have global reach. In a world in which their ability to use their hard power is often limited, governments must be able to exploit the uses of soft power – the power of persuasion and information.[8] Similarly, in a world in which a major set of obstacles to effective global regulation is a simple inability on the part of many developing countries to translate paper rules into changes in actual behaviour, governments must be able not only to negotiate treaties but also to create the capacity to comply with them.

Understood as a form of global governance, government networks meet these needs. As commercial and civic organizations have already discovered, their networked form is ideal for providing the speed and flexibility necessary to function effectively in an information age. But unlike amorphous 'global policy networks', in which it is never clear who is exercising power on behalf of whom, these are networks comprised of national government officials – appointed by elected officials or directly elected themselves. Best of all, they can perform many of the functions of a world government – legislation, administration and adjudication – without the form.

No form of government is perfect, least of all at the global level. And even if, as with Winston Churchill's view of democracy, global governance through government networks is the 'least worst' alter-

---

[8] Joseph S. Nye, Jr, *The Paradox of American Power: Why the World's Only Superpower Can't Go It Alone*, New York, Oxford University Press, 2002, p. 9.

native, it still poses many problems that must ultimately be addressed. And indeed, observers of existing government networks, as well as critics of what they could become, have pointed out plenty of problems, as reviewed in the first part of the article below.

To respond to these various charges, and more importantly to ensure that a global governance system of government networks – what I have called a networked world order – is not only effective but also as accountable and just as possible, the members of government networks will need to be responsive to an entire complex of rules, principles and norms. First, they must be accountable to their domestic constituents for their transgovernmental activities to the same extent that they are accountable for their domestic activities. Second, as participants in structures of global governance, they must have a basic operating code that takes account of the rights and interests of all peoples. Third, they should ultimately be directly subject to the international legal obligations that currently apply to their nations as unitary states.

The next part sets forth a menu of possibilities for increasing the accountability of members of government networks to their domestic constituencies, including: 1) developing a concept of dual function for all government officials; 2) increasing the visibility and accessibility of government networks; 3) developing more legislative networks; 4) using government networks to mobilize a wide range of nongovernmental actors; and 5) a customized set of solutions developed by domestic polities themselves. The third section of this paper turns to potential global norms governing members of government networks in their relations with one another. I suggest five such norms: some to operate primarily in horizontal relations between national government officials and others to operate more generally in vertical relations between national government officials and their supranational counterparts. They include global deliberative equality, legitimate difference, positive comity, checks and balances and subsidiarity.

The final part reaches further afield, exploring the concept of disaggregated sovereignty. If unitary states can disaggregate into their component government institutions and those government officials can interact quasi-autonomously with their foreign counterparts, then they should also be able to exercise a measure of sovereignty. Disaggregated sovereignty, however, would be defined as positive sovereignty, as the capacity to enter into international regulatory regimes of various types, rather than as the negative right to be left alone. The right to exercise this type of sovereignty, however, would also carry with it an obligation to be independently bound by the existing corpus of international law.

PROBLEMS WITH GOVERNMENT NETWORKS

At the moment, government networks are like the proverbial elephant – different observers see different phenomena and hence discern different types of problems. Those who primarily observe regulatory and judicial networks worry about the triumph of technocracy over democracy and the distortion of domestic political processes and judicial decision-making. A typical response to this criticism, at least in the regulatory context, is to open up the decision-making process of government networks to the many different types of pressure groups that participate in a democratic domestic political process. Yet this solution alarms another set of critics who insist that government authority be clearly exercised by government officials rather than be diffused among a vast array of public, semi-public and private actors in a global policy network. A final, unavoidable problem is the way in which power is exercised in government networks by strong countries against weak countries, both through exclusion from certain networks or from powerful groups within them, and through inclusion in networks that serve as conduits for soft power.

1 A Global Technocracy

Perhaps the most frequent charge against government networks is that they are networks of technocrats – unelected regulators and judges who share a common functional outlook on the world but who do not respond to the social, economic and political concerns of ordinary citizens. Antonio Perez, for instance, accuses government networks of adopting 'Platonic Guardianship as a mode of transnational governance', an open 'move toward technocratic elitism'.[9]

---

[9] Antonio F. Perez, 'Who Killed Sovereignty? Or: Changing Norms Concerning Sovereignty In International Law', *Wisconsin International Law Journal*, 14 (1996), pp. 463, 476.

The affinity and even solidarity felt among central bankers, securities regulators, antitrust officials, environmental regulators and judges, in this view, socializes them to believe that deeply political trade-offs are value-neutral choices based on 'objective' expertise. To allow these officials to come together offshore, free from the usual mandated intrusions of public representatives and private interest groups in their decision-making process, is to allow them to escape politics.

A related concern is a lack of transparency, generally. According to Philip Alston, the rise of government networks 'suggests a move away from arenas of relative transparency into the back rooms and the bypassing of the national political arenas to which the United States and other proponents of the importance of healthy democratic institutions attach so much importance'.[10] Sol Picciotto agrees: 'A chronic lack of legitimacy plagues direct international contacts at the sub-state level among national officials and administrators.[11] He attributes this lack of legitimacy to the informality and confidentiality of such contacts, precisely the attributes that make them so attractive to the participants.[12]

The standard response to concerns about technocracy is to increase transparency. Yet transparency can make the network even more accessible to sectoral interest pressures, leading to 'over-politicization' in the form of distorted representation of specific domestic or international preferences. At the same time, government networks can pose the problem of not knowing enough about who is making decisions and when they are being made to have meaningful input into them. As Joseph Weiler observes with regard to charges of a democracy deficit within the EU: 'Transparency and access to documents are often invoked as a possible remedy to this issue. But if you do not know what is going on, which documents will you ask to see?'[13]

---

[10] Philip Alston, 'The Myopia of the Handmaidens: International Lawyers and Globalization', *European Journal of International Law*, 8 (1997), pp. 435, 441.

[11] See Sol Picciotto, 'Networks in International Economic Integration: Fragmented States and the Dilemmas of Neo-liberalism', *Northwestern Journal of International Law and Business*, 17 (1997), pp. 1014, 1047.

[12] Ibid., p. 1049.

[13] Joseph H. H. Weiler, 'To Be a European Citizen: Eros and Civilization', in Joseph H. H. Weiler, *The Constitution of Europe*, Cambridge, Cambridge University Press, 1999, p. 349.

2 *Distortion of National Political Processes*

Click on the website of the US public interest organization Public Citizen.[14] The left side lists buttons identifying the issue areas that are of specific concern to the organization. They include 'Fast Track, WTO, NAFTA, China', and 'Harmonization'. Click on harmonization and read on. Here is the definition of what harmonization is and why the American public should be concerned about it: 'Harmonization is the name given to the effort by industry to replace the variety of product standards and other regulatory policies adopted by nations in favor of uniform global standards'.[15]

Public Citizen blames international trade regimes such as NAFTA and the WTO for a major boost in harmonization efforts, arguing that they 'require or encourage' national governments either to harmonize standards or recognize foreign government standards as equivalent to their own.[16] This substantive commitment is implemented through the establishment of 'an ever-increasing number of committees and working groups to implement the harmonization mandate'.[17] The problem with all these efforts, from Public Citizen's perspective, is that

most of these working groups are industry-dominated, do not provide an opportunity for input by interested individuals or potentially-affected communities, and generally conduct their operations behind closed doors. Yet, under current trade rules, these standard-setting processes can directly affect our national, state and local policies.[18]

At first glance, concern over harmonization arises primarily from the goal of harmonizing regulations, with the resulting danger of 'levelling down' the protections for public health, the environment, consumer safety, and other areas but it is also the process. The idea of regulators meeting behind closed doors, without input from a wide variety of interested public groups at a time when they can still have

[14] On Public Citizen homepage (accessed 1 July 2003); available from http://www.citizen.org.

[15] 'Harmonization', on Public Citizen homepage (accessed 1 July 2003): available from http://www.citizen.org/trade/harmonization.

[16] 'What Is Harmonization?', on Public Citizen homepage (accessed 1 July 2003); available from http://www.citizen.org/trade/harmonization/articles.cfm?ID=4390.

[17] Ibid.

[18] Ibid.

impact on the discussion and the outcome, is deeply worrying in itself. Knowing that they are just exchanging information about common problems or providing technical assistance to one another will trigger less immediate alarm than knowing that they are actively engaged in harmonizing national regulations. Yet to the extent that the deeper concern is that regulators in a particular issue area are operating on a technocratic, professional set of assumptions that do not take into account other perspectives, interests and politics, trans-governmental regulatory interaction of any kind is likely to prompt demands for more public participation, or at least sufficient transparency to allow interested groups to decide for themselves whether they want to have input.

3 Unrepresentative Input into National Judicial Decision-Making

How troubling is it that judges draw on the decisions of foreign and international courts as part of their deliberations on how to decide a domestic case? US Supreme Court justices differ over this question, quite heatedly. Should we leave it to them to resolve? Should Congress take a hand? Should the solicitor-general, as the president's top advocate, take a position in arguments before the Court?

According to a former justice of the Supreme Judicial Court of Massachusetts, Charles Fried, drawing on foreign decisions could change the course of American law. Fried writes thoughtfully on the difference between scholarship and adjudication, noting that rejection of comparative analysis on the part of scholars 'would seem philistine indeed', but is not necessarily so on the part of judges.[19] Judges must hand down answers, constrained by a confined set of sources. By way of example, Fried points to the significance of allowing judges to cite sources other than pure case law, such as scientific reports, policy analyses, and other nonlegal materials. Expanding a judge's universe of information will expand the range of considerations she thinks is relevant to a decision. Expanding the range of considerations, in turn, makes it possible to make a wider range of arguments for or against a particular decision.

[19] Charles Fried, 'Scholars and Judges: Reason and Power', *Harvard Journal of Law and Public Policy*, 23 (2000), pp. 807–32, 818.

Thus, for instance, when Justice Ruth Bader Ginsburg faces a decision under US law on the constitutionality of affirmative action, she finds it valuable to look to the Indian experience as well as the US experience.[20] Knowing the Indian experience gives her a different perspective on the problems that US institutions may encounter with affirmative action programmes; it also gives her a wider sense of the available options. Yet is the Indian experience really relevant to the United States? The enormous differences between the two countries raise the possibility – indeed the likelihood – that the same policy initiatives will have completely different results. More fundamentally, though, does democracy imply the right to make our own mistakes?

Similar concerns have been expressed outside the United States. Christopher McCrudden documents debates about the appropriateness of drawing on foreign judicial decisions in Israel, Singapore, South Africa, Australia and Hong Kong.[21] A principal concern in these debates is arbitrariness in choosing when to pay attention to foreign law and when to ignore it, as well as in deciding which foreign courts to pay attention to. Yash Ghai reports from Hong Kong that 'the approach to the use of foreign cases is not very consistent; they are invoked when they support the position preferred by the court, otherwise they are dismissed as irrelevant'.[22]

4 Unrepresentative Input into Global Political Processes

Another group of critics is less worried about existing government networks as described here, but rather about the larger phenomenon of 'global policy networks' or 'global issue networks' – networks of all individuals, groups and organizations, governmental and nongovernmental, interested in a particular set of issues. The UN Secretary-General, a vice-president of the World Bank and numerous scholars have championed these networks as optimal mechanisms of

[20] Ruth Bader Ginsburg and Deborah Jones Merritt, 'Affirmative Action: an International Human Rights Dialogue', *Cardozo Law Review*, 21 (1999), pp. 253, 273.

[21] Christopher McCrudden, 'A Common Law of Human Rights?: Transnational Judicial Conversations on Constitutional Rights', *Oxford Journal of Legal Studies*, 20 (2000), pp. 499–532, 507–8.

[22] Yash Ghai, 'Sentinels of Liberty or Sheep in Wolf's Clothing? Judicial Politics and the Hong Kong Bill of Rights', *Modern Law Review*, 60 (1997), pp. 459, 479, quoted in ibid., p. 507.

global governance.[23] And, as just noted, these wider networks are often invoked as the solution to the problem of technocracy with pure government networks. Still, the problem that immediately arises is how to separate out the structures of government from the much more amorphous webs of governance.

According to Martin Shapiro, the shift from government to governance marks 'a significant erosion of the boundaries separating what lies inside a government and its administration and what lies outside them.'[24] The result is to advantage 'experts and enthusiasts', the two groups outside government that have the greatest incentive and desire to participate in governance processes but who are not representative of the larger polity.[25] From this perspective, relatively neutral government officials who are aware of the larger social trade-offs surrounding decision-making on a particular issue will produce more democratic outcomes than decisions shaped primarily by deeply interested private citizens – even those acting with substantial knowledge of the issue and the best of intentions. The merging and blurring of lines of authority are ultimately likely to blur the distinction between public legitimacy and private power.

5 The Ineradicability of Power

A final problem is the way in which government networks either replicate or even magnify asymmetries of power in the existing international system. Some government networks represent exclusive preserves of officials from the most economically developed, and hence powerful nations. The Basel Committee – with its membership of Belgium, Canada, France, Germany, Great Britain, Italy, Japan, Luxembourg, the Netherlands, Sweden and the United States – is again a prime example. Similarly, the Technical Committee of IOSCO, where most of the important work is done, is comprised of

[23] Kofi A. Annan, *We the Peoples: The Role of the United Nations in the 21st Century*, New York, United Nations, Department of Public Information, 2000, p. 70; Jean-François Rischard, 'A Novel Approach to Problem-Solving', *Global Agenda 2003, World Economic Forum*, 1 (2003), pp. 30, 31; Wolfgang H. Reinicke, 'The Other World Wide Web: Global Public Policy Networks', *Foreign Policy* (Winter 1999/2000), p. 44.

[24] Martin Shapiro, 'Administrative Law Unbounded: Reflections on Government and Governance', *Indiana Journal of Global Legal Studies*, 8 (2001), pp. 369–78, 369.

[25] Ibid., p. 376.

a fairly predictable group of nations with well-developed securities markets.[26] If such networks are to form the infrastructure for a networked world order, they must be given incentives to expand their membership in meaningful ways, inviting in government officials from poorer, less powerful, and often marginalized countries as genuine participants rather than as largely passive observers.

Supporters of government networks as mechanisms of global governance are well aware of this problem. Lord Howell celebrates the Commonwealth over institutions such as the OECD for its greater inclusiveness. The OECD, he writes, 'lacks an obvious and centrally valuable feature of the Commonwealth – namely, its scope for bringing together and giving a common voice to both richer and poorer, developed and developing societies'.[27] Greater inclusiveness also drives former Canadian Finance Minister Paul Martin's insistence on using the G20 instead of the G7. The 'breadth of [the G20's] membership is crucial', he writes, 'for we have learned a fundamental truth about policies to promote development: they will work only if the developing countries and emerging markets help shape them, because inclusiveness lies at the heart of legitimacy and effectiveness'. And the G20 *is* inclusive. Nations at all phases of development are at the G20 table – and no one side of it is dictating to another.[28]

If 'global government networks' are in fact only partial government networks, they will ultimately fail. They cannot address the world's problems, or even what appear to be only regional problems, as members of an exclusive club. This point is problematic for the members of some current networks, at least to the extent that one of the major intuitive advantages of networking over more formal international institutions is the ability to engage selectively with other like-minded governments in pondering hard problems rather than enduring the tedious procedural formalities of global deliberation. If all government networks were to become mini-UNs in different substantive areas, little would be gained. Yet as the example of the Commonwealth and Asia Pacific Economic Cooperation (APEC)

[26] Members of the Technical Committee include: Australia, Canada, France, Germany, Hong Kong, Italy, Japan, the Netherlands, Switzerland, the UK and the USA. On OICU–IOSCO homepage (accessed 1 July 2003); available from http://www.iosco.org/lists/display_committees.cfm?cmtid=3.

[27] David Howell, 'The Place of the Commonwealth in the International Order', *Round Table*, 345 (1998), p. 30.

[28] Martin, 'Notes for an Address', op. cit., n. 1.

demonstrate, it is possible to have much more inclusive government networks without formalizing procedures.

From the perspective of weaker countries, however, being included does not solve the problem of power. On the contrary, officials – regulators, judges, legislators – are simply subject to the soft power of the strongest members of the network. Even training, information and assistance that they seek out is likely to push them steadily toward convergence with both the substance and style of more developed countries in any particular subject area, from constitutional rights to utilities regulation. Having a voice in collective discussions is better than being silenced by exclusion, but it does not guarantee that you will be heard.

IMPROVING THE ACCOUNTABILITY OF GOVERNMENT NETWORKS TO DOMESTIC CONSTITUENCIES

The critics of government networks are themselves a diverse lot, criticizing a diverse phenomenon for a variety of different faults. If one group sees government without politics, another worries that the 'politics' sought to be introduced are likely to be selective and distorted. Still others, largely approving of government networks as a form of governance, charge them with too much selectivity in choosing their members. And all these perceived problems take on a different cast when the vantage point is a particular national polity versus a hypothetical global community.

Ultimately, policy-makers who wish to respond seriously to these various problems will have to formulate a solution on a case-by-case basis, after conducting more systematic research to verify the substance and the scope of each problem across different government networks. Yet even at this level of generality, it is possible to put forward some broader proposals.

First is to develop a concept of dual function for all national officials – an assumption that their responsibilities will include both a national and a transgovernmental component. They must thus be accountable to their national constituents for both categories of activity. Fully-fledged international agreements would still have to be struck by chief executives and ratified by the full legislature as specified under domestic law, but the legislators themselves would be much more involved in the process *with their foreign counterparts*.

Regulators of all kinds, from health to education to the environment, would conduct their own foreign relations, subject to some kind of domestic inter-agency process that accepted this phenomenon but nevertheless attempted to aggregate interests. Prosecutors, judges and law enforcement agents of all kinds would work actively with their foreign counterparts on problems requiring multiple coordinated initiatives across borders.

This concept of dual function would make it far easier for organizations like Public Citizen to mobilize ordinary Americans to understand that their government officials may well be playing on a larger global or regional playing field and to monitor their activities. These officials may have two faces, internal and external, but they still have only one audience. It would also make it more realistic for critics like Martin Shapiro to insist that government officials be held separately accountable for their activities in larger 'policy networks'.

A second step toward holding government networks as accountable as possible to domestic constituents is to make their activity as visible as possible to legislators, interest groups and ordinary citizens by ensuring that they operate in a real or virtual public space. The space must be the equivalent of a physical site, for symbolic and practical reasons. We must replace the image of shadowy networks making 'offshore' decisions with an actual vision of regularized governance processes in accessible places.

One solution is to create virtual space. It is possible to centralize information on a website that is the global equivalent of the massive carved buildings that host national departments of justice, treasury, defence and social services. At the same time, this website would be linked to as many different national websites in the particular issue area as possible. On the European Union website, for instance, citizens of member states and other interested individuals can review the EU's official journal; treaties; legislation (both acts that are in force and those in preparation), case law; parliamentary questions and documents of public interest.[29] Clicking on 'legislation in preparation' produces a page entitled 'pre-lex', which allows a viewer to see a host of commission proposals, records of parliamentary activity and council documents. It also offers a specific guide to 'monitoring the decision-making process between institutions'.

---

[29] On EUR-Lex, European Union Law homepage (accessed 1 July 2003); available from http://www.europa.eu.int/eur-lex/.

Third is to ensure that government networks link legislators across borders as much as they do regulators and judges, to ensure that all three branches of government, with their relative strengths and weaknesses, are represented. In some areas, such as human rights and the environment, national legislators are increasingly recognizing that they have common interests. Global Legislators for a Balanced Environment (GLOBE) was founded in 1989 and is essentially an environmental nongovernmental organization (NGO) composed of parliamentarians.[30] Governments in the EU must increasingly submit their European policies to special parliamentary committees, who are themselves networking.

Legislative networks are also emerging to monitor the activities of traditional international organizations such as the World Bank and the WTO. The Parliamentary Network on the World Bank held its first conference in May 2000 and its second in January 2001 in London, where it was hosted by a select committee of the House of Commons.[31] The network has no official connection to the World Bank; it is an independent initiative by parliamentarians who want to play a more active role in global governance. Similar efforts to organize parliamentarians to oversee the activities of the WTO are ongoing, spurred by a meeting of parliamentarians at the WTO Ministerial Conference in Doha, Qatar, in November 2001, which was organized by the Inter-Parliamentary Union.[32] In his speech to the assembled parliamentarians at Doha, WTO Director-General Michael Moore urged the assembled parliamentarians at Doha to 'assemble more often' and to assist and scrutinize 'all the multilateral institutions that you have created, that you own'.[33]

Fourth is to use government networks as the spines of larger policy networks, helping to mobilize transnational society but at the same time remaining identifiably distinct from nongovernmental actors.

[30] See Globe International homepage (accessed 1 July 2003); available from http://www.globeinternational.org.

[31] Steve Charnovitz, 'Trans-Parliamentary Associations in Global Functional Agencies', *Transnational Associations*, 31: 2 (2002), pp. 88–91, 88.

[32] Ibid., p. 89.

[33] Mike Moore, 'Promoting Openness, Fairness and Predictability in International Trade for the Benefit of Humanity', Speech to the Inter-Parliamentary Union meeting on international trade, 8 June 2001, on World Trade Organization homepage (accessed 1 July 2003); available from http://www.wto.org/french/news_f/spmm_f/spmm64_f.htm.

Kofi Annan has encouraged the formation and use of such networks from his UN bully pulpit, calling for the 'creation of global policy networks' to 'bring together international institutions, civil society and private sector organizations, and national governments in pursuit of common goals'.[34] More generally, Wolfgang Reinicke and Francis Deng have developed both the concept and practice of the global public interest, promoted and pursued through networks.[35] Reinicke describes global public policy networks as 'loose alliances of government agencies, international organizations, corporations, and elements of civil society such as nongovernmental organizations, professional associations, or religious groups that join together to achieve what none can accomplish on its own'.[36]

A final set of measures to address perceived or actual problems with the activities of existing government networks should come from domestic polities. The citizens of different countries, and their government officials, are likely to have different degrees of concern about these activities. The US debate over citing foreign judicial decisions has been replicated in some other countries, but by no means all, and it has a different resonance depending on the length and nature of a particular country's legal tradition. Similarly, the citizens of some countries might be content with the role of their regulators in global or regional regulatory networks, whereas the citizens of other countries might seek more monitoring of, or direct input into, those networks.

GLOBAL NORMS REGULATING GOVERNMENT NETWORKS

Even if participants in government networks around the world were satisfactorily accountable to their domestic constituents, what duty do they owe to other nations? It may seem an odd question, but if these networks were in fact primary structures of global governance, together with more formal international and supranational organizations, then they would have to be subject to global as well as

---

[34] Annan, *We the Peoples*, op. cit., p. 70, n. 23.

[35] Wolfgang H. Reinicke and Francis Deng, *Critical Choices: The United Nations, Networks, and the Future of Global Governance*, Ottawa, International Development Research Centre, 2000.

[36] Reinicke, 'The Other World Wide Web', op. cit., n. 23.

national norms. They would be responsible for collectively formulating and implementing policies in the global public interest. Equally important, the participants in these networks would have to develop and implement norms governing their relations with one another. Such norms may seem unnecessary when the principal activity in which these participants engage is information exchange; however, harmonization and enforcement activity requires the development of global ground rules. Finally, these networks should operate on a presumption of inclusivity rather than exclusivity.

What are the potential sources of these norms? First, it is natural to project domestic constitutional principles, developed by visionaries and thinkers from Madison to Monnet. Political philosophers are also relevant, providing first principles that can be adapted to this particular global context. Finally, norms are emerging from contemporary practice that can be generalized, adding an inductive dimension to the project.

It is particularly important to note the informal character of these norms, like that of the government networks they regulate. Proposals for global constitutions are already on the table, most notably from scholars such as Ernst-Ulrich Petersmann, but an actual global constitution suggests a formal global government, even if in fragmentary form.[37] I seek to develop an informal alternative – a set of principles and norms that can operate independently of formal codification, even as the actors and activities they would regulate form and reform in shifting patterns of governance. Both visions seek to underpin world order, but they diverge with respect to world government.

1 Global Deliberative Equality

The foundational norm of global governance should be global deliberative equality. Michael Ignatieff derives this concept from the basic moral precept that 'our species is one, and each of the individuals

---

[37] Ernst-Ulrich Petersmann, 'Constitutionalism and International Organizations', *Northwestern Journal of International Law and Business*, 17 (1997), p. 398; Ernst-Ulrich Petersmann, 'Constitutionalism and International Adjudication: How to Constitutionalize the U.N. Dispute Settlement System?', *New York University Journal of International Law and Politics*, 31 (1999), p. 753.

who compose it is entitled to equal moral consideration.'[38] His account of the progress of the human rights movement since 1945 builds from this precept, which lies at the heart of human rights, to the recognition that 'we live in a plural world of cultures that have a right to equal consideration in the argument about what we can and cannot, should and should not, do to human beings.'[39]

This idea, that 'all human beings belong at the table, in the essential conversation about how we should treat each other', does not posit utopian harmony. On the contrary, it assumes a world 'of conflict, deliberation, argument, and contention', but to the extent that the process of global governance is, at bottom, a conversation, a collective deliberation about common problems and towards common global objectives, then all affected individuals, or their representatives, are entitled to participate.[40]

This presumption of inclusion lies at the heart of the 'Montreal Consensus' that former Canadian Finance Minister Paul Martin has put forward to counter the 'Washington Consensus' concerning economic development. The heart of the Montreal Consensus is a 'more balanced vision of how developing countries and poor countries can share in the benefits of the global economy'.[41] It arises from the perception that developing countries are not threatened by globalization per se as much as by being left out and left behind. The solution is not to reverse globalization itself, but rather to find ways to share the wealth and integration it brings. That, for Martin and the G20, is the essence of global accountability.

A principle or even a presumption of inclusion does not mean that government institutions from all countries will become members of all government networks. Many networks will address problems common only to a group of countries, or a region. And even where the problems themselves are global, government networks such as the G20 reflect a philosophy of representation rather than direct participation.

[38] Michael Ignatieff, *Human Rights as Politics and Idolatry*, Princeton, Princeton University Press, 2001, p. 4.

[39] Ibid., p. 94.

[40] Ibid., pp. 94–5.

[41] 'Notes for an address by the Honourable Paul Martin, to the Royal Institute of International Affairs', Ottawa, 24 January 2001, On G20 homepage (accessed 1 July 2003); available from http://www.fin.gc.ca/news01/01-008e.html.

What such a principle should mean, however, is that all government networks adopt clear criteria for participation that will be fairly applied. These criteria can require a particular degree of economic or political development or a level of performance in terms of compliance with agreed principles. It is also certainly permissible for some nations to move faster or deeper than others in making particular commitments – just as the EU has multispeed integration in which some nations adopt a common currency and others do not. The World Intellectual Property Organization has incorporated a network of some advanced industrial countries alongside its traditional global decision-making processes. Yet countries that want to join such networks and that meet the stated criteria must be allowed in, in some form or other. At the same time, deliberative equality, as an ideal, means that those countries that have decided to join a network receive an equal opportunity to participate in agenda-setting, to advance their position, and to challenge the proposals or positions of others.[42]

More generally, government networks should be explicitly designed to engage, enmesh, and assist specific government institutions. One of the great values of this form of governance is the ability to bolster the court or regulatory agency or legislature of any country – to offer directly targeted technical assistance, political support where necessary, and an all-important sense of professionalism and belonging in a wider global community. That in itself is a form of global deliberative equality.

2 Legitimate Difference

The second principle of transnational governance should be the principle of legitimate difference. As Justice Benjamin Cardozo put it while sitting on the Second Circuit:

We are not so provincial as to say that every solution of a problem is wrong because we deal with it otherwise at home. The courts are not free to enforce a foreign right at the pleasure of the judges, to suit the individual notion of expediency or fairness. They do not close their doors unless help would

---

[42] Joshua Cohen, 'Deliberation and Democratic Legitimacy', in Alan Hamlin and Philip Pettit (eds), *The Good Polity: Normative Analysis of the State*, New York, Blackwell, 1989, p. 74.

violate some fundamental principle of justice, some prevalent conception of good morals, some deep-rooted tradition of the common weal.[43]

In conflicts of law, the principle of legitimate difference is limited by the public policy exception, whereby a court will not apply a foreign law that would be applicable if it violates a fundamental principle of domestic public policy. The principle of legitimate difference assumes that the public policy exception would be applied only rarely, in cases involving the violation of truly fundamental values. In the US context, fundamental equates with constitutional, in the sense that state courts cannot invoke the public policy exception to bar enforcement of another state's act unless that act arguably violates the Constitution itself.[44]

Transposed from the judicial to the regulatory context and from the US to the global context, the principle of legitimate difference should be adopted as a foundational premise of transgovernmental cooperation. All regulators participating in cooperative ventures of various kinds with their foreign counterparts should begin from the premise that 'difference' per se reflects a desirable diversity of ideas about how to order an economy or society. That 'we deal with it otherwise at home' is not a reason for rejecting a foreign law or regulation or regulatory practice unless it can be shown to violate the rejecting country's constitutional rules and values.

The principle of legitimate difference applies most precisely to foreign laws and regulations, but a corollary of the principle is a presumption that foreign government officials should be accorded the same respect due to national officials unless a specific reason exists to suspect that they will chauvinistically privilege their own citizens. An example from the judicial context illustrates the point. In a highly publicized antitrust litigation brought by Sir Freddie Laker against both US and British airlines for trying to drive his low-cost airline out of business, US federal district judge Harold Green decided not to restrain the British parties from petitioning the British government for help.[45] Judge Green was presuming the same good faith on the

---

[43] *Loucks v. Standard Oil Co.*, 120 N.E. 198, 201 (NY 1918).

[44] The full faith and credit clause of the constitution requires each state to recognize the acts of another. US Const., art. 4, §1, cl. 1. It is a basic instrument of federalism, knitting the states into one larger polity.

[45] *Laker Airways Ltd. v. Sabena, Belgian World Airlines* 731 F. 2d 909 (DC Cir. 1984).

part of the British executive as he would on the part of the US executive in a parallel circumstance and assuming that the British executive would not automatically ally with its own citizens in a case involving a foreign citizen in a foreign court.

In sum, legitimate difference is a principle that preserves diversity within a framework of a specified degree of convergence. It enshrines pluralism as a basis for, rather than a bar to, regulatory cooperation, leaving open the possibility of further convergence between legal systems in the form of mutual recognition or even harmonization, but not requiring it. At the same time, however, it does not try to stitch together or cover over differences concerning fundamental values, whether those involving basic human rights and liberties or the organizing principles for a social, political, or economic system. At a more practical level, the principle of legitimate difference would encourage the development of model codes or compilations of best practices in particular regulatory issue areas, letting the regulators in different countries figure out for themselves how best to adapt them to local circumstance.

It is also important, however, to be clear as to what a principle of legitimate difference will *not* do. It does not help individuals or government institutions figure out which nation should be the primary regulator in a particular issue area or with regard to a set of entities or transactions subject to regulation. Thus it cannot answer the question of which nation should be in the position of deciding whether to recognize which other nation's laws, regulations, or decisions based on legitimate difference. Nevertheless, it can serve as a *Grundnorm* of global governance for regulators exploring a wide variety of relationships with their transnational counterparts. If regulators are not prepared to go even this far, then they are unlikely to be able to push beyond paper cooperation.

3 Positive Comity

Comity is a long-standing principle of relations between nations. The classic definition for American lawyers is the formulation in *Hilton v. Guyot*: 'neither a matter of obligation on the one hand, nor of mere courtesy and good will on the other . . . comity is the recognition which one nation allows within its territory to the legislative, executive, or judicial acts of another nation.'[46] 'Recognition' is essentially a passive affair, signalling deference to another nation's action.

Positive comity, on the other hand, mandates a move from deference to dialogue. It is a principle of affirmative cooperation between government agencies of different nations. As a principle of governance for transnational regulatory cooperation, it requires regulatory agencies to substitute consultation and active assistance for unilateral action and noninterference.

Positive comity has developed largely in the antitrust community, as an outgrowth of ongoing efforts of EU and US antitrust officials to put their often very rocky relationship on firmer footing. For decades the US policy of extraterritorial enforcement of US antitrust laws based on the direct effect doctrine, even in various modified forms, was met by diplomatic protests, administrative refusals and a growing number of foreign blocking statutes that restricted access to important evidence located abroad or sought to reverse US judgments.[47] The US government gradually began to change course, espousing principles of comity and restraint in congressional testimony and in its international antitrust guidelines.[48]

---

[46] 159 US 113, 163–4 (1895).

[47] Beginning with *United States v. Aluminum Co. of America (Alcoa)*, the Sherman Act was held applicable to foreign conduct that had a direct, substantial, and foreseeable effect on US trade and commerce. 148 F.2d 416, 440–5 (2d Cir. 1945). This 'direct effect' jurisdiction quickly became a source of tension with other states that argued that the United States had no right to assert jurisdiction over persons that were neither present nor acting within US territory. Governments whose nationals and interests were affected by US antitrust law filed diplomatic protests and amicus briefs, refused requests for assistance, invoked national secrecy laws, and eventually began passing blocking laws specifically aimed at the frustration of US antitrust enforcement. Spencer Weber Waller, 'National Laws and International Markets: Strategies of Cooperation and Harmonization in the Enforcement of Competition Law', *Cardozo Law Review*, 18 (1999), pp. 1111, 1113–14; see also Joel R. Paul, 'Comity in International Law', *Harvard International Law Journal*, 32 (1991), pp. 1, 32; Joseph P. Griffin, 'EC and U.S. Extraterritoriality: Activism and Cooperation', *Fordham International Law Journal*, 17 (1994), pp. 353, 377.

[48] Spencer Weber Waller, 'The Internationalization of Antitrust Enforcement', *Boston University Law Review*, 77 (1997), pp. 343, 375. By 1988 the Department of Justice stated that it would only challenge foreign anticompetitive conduct that directly harmed US consumers. Robert D. Shank, 'The Justice Department's Recent Antitrust Enforcement Policy: Toward A "Positive Comity" Solution to International Competition Problems?', *Vanderbilt Journal of Transnational Law*, 29 (1996), pp. 155, 165.

In addition, US regulators began relying less on unilateral state action and more on agency cooperation. In the early 1980s, the United States entered into separate cooperation agreements with the governments of Australia (June 1982) and Canada (March 1984). In both agreements, the parties consented to cooperate in investigations and litigation by the other even when this enforcement affected its nationals or the other party sought information within its territory. In return, the parties agreed to exercise negative comity – to refrain from enforcing competition laws where such enforcement would unduly interfere with the sovereign interests of the other party.[49]

In 1991, the United States executed an extensive antitrust cooperation agreement with the European Community.[50] The agreement contained provisions on notification of enforcement activities, as well as on information-sharing and biannual meetings.[51] Most notably, the agreement was the first to include the principle of positive comity. Article V of the agreement provides that if party A believes that its 'important interests' are being adversely affected by anticompetitive activities that violate party A's competition laws but occur within the territory of party B, party A may request that party B initiate enforcement activities.[52] Thus, government B, in deference to government A, is expected to consider enforcement steps that it might not otherwise have taken.[53]

This notion of positive comity is the converse of the traditional idea of deference, or negative comity. Unlike the earlier agreements concluded by the United States with Australia and Canada, the EC agreement focuses less on protecting the sovereign interests of one

[49] Charles F. Rule, 'European Communities–United States Agreement on the Application of their Competition Laws Introductory Note', *International Legal Materials*, 30 (1991), pp. 1487, 1488. The US signed a comparable agreement with Germany in 1976. See Steven L. Snell, 'Controlling Restrictive Business Practices in Global Markets: Reflections on the Concepts of Sovereignty, Fairness, and Comity', *Stanford Journal of International Law*, 33 (1997), pp. 215, 234.

[50] See 'Agreement Regarding the Application of their Competition Laws, 23 Sept. 1991, E.C.–U.S.', *International Legal Materials*, 30 (1991), p. 1491.

[51] Ibid., pp. 1056–9.

[52] See Griffin, 'EC and U.S. Extraterritoriality', op. cit., p. 376, n. 47.

[53] James R. Atwood, 'Positive Comity – Is It a Positive Step?', in Barry Hawk (ed.), *International Antitrust Law & Policy: Annual Proceedings of the Fordham Corporate Law Institute*, Irvington-on-Hudson, NY, Transnational Juris Publications, 1993, pp. 79, 84.

jurisdiction against the antitrust activities of the other and more on facilitating cooperative and even coordinated enforcement by antitrust authorities.[54] Where deference would tend towards less affirmative enforcement action, positive comity was designed to produce more affirmative enforcement.[55] While the EC–US agreement reflects the increasing trend towards transnational cooperation in antitrust enforcement, the extent of enforcement coordination and information sharing contemplated by the agreement was unprecedented.[56]

In practice, the agreement has spurred an increase in the flow of information between the parties.[57] In addition, there has been increased enforcement of antitrust objectives, both quantitatively and qualitatively.[58] In coordinating their activities, the parties under the agreement work together to minimize the disruption to international trade that multiple uncoordinated investigations might otherwise cause.[59] Merit Janow, reviewing transatlantic cooperation in competition policy, concludes that 'positive comity is an important doctrine and that it can go some way in ameliorating tensions associated with extraterritorial enforcement and in facilitating enforcement cooperation'.[60] At the same time, she advocates taking a step further toward enhanced comity through 'an integrated or work-

[54] See Rule, 'European Communities–United States Agreement', op. cit., p. 1488, n. 49.

[55] See Atwood, 'Positive Comity', op. cit., p. 84, n. 53.

[56] See Rule, 'European Communities–United States Agreement', op. cit., p. 1487, n. 49.

[57] Joseph P. Griffin, 'EC/U.S. Antitrust Cooperation Agreement: Impact on Transnational Business', *Law and Policy in International Business*, 24 (1993), pp. 1051, 1063.

[58] See generally Joel Klein and Preeta Bansal, 'International Antitrust Enforcement in the Computer Industry', *Villanova Law Review*, 41 (1996), pp. 173, 179.

[59] See Rule, 'European Communities–United States Agreement', op. cit., p. 1490, n. 49. This increased efficiency has also proven attractive to businesses themselves. In *United States v. Microsoft Corp.*, after learning that both the Department of Justice and the European Commission were investigating their licensing practices, Microsoft agreed to waive its confidentiality rights under US antitrust law to permit the two authorities to exchange confidential information. See Shank, 'The Justice Department's Recent Antitrust Enforcement Policy', op. cit., p. 179, n. 48.

[60] Merit Janow, 'Transatlantic Cooperation on Competition Policy,' in Simon J. Evenett, Alexander Lehmann, and Benn Steil (eds), *Antitrust Goes Global*, Washington, DC, The Brookings Institution, 2000, pp. 29–56, 51.

sharing approach' between US and EU competition authorities, whereby one or the other would be designated the 'de facto lead agency' in any investigation.[61]

Can positive comity be translated from the antitrust context into a more general principle of governance? Two potential objections arise. First is the concern of many within the antitrust community that positive comity is a label with little content. The second objection is a converse concern that to the extent positive comity works, it assumes enormous trust and close continuing relations between particular national regulatory agencies – factors that cannot be generalized.

The response to both these objections is a simplified and less stringent version of positive comity. As a general principle it need mean no more than an obligation to act rather than merely to respond. In any case in which nation A is contemplating regulatory action and in which nation B has a significant interest in the activity under scrutiny, either through the involvement of its nationals or through the commission of significant events within its territorial jurisdiction, the regulatory agency of nation A, consistent with the dual function of regulatory officials developed above, has a duty at the very least to notify and consult with the regulatory agency of nation B. Nation A's agency must further wait for a response from nation B before deciding what action to take, and must notify nation B's agency of any decision taken.

Even the critics of positive comity acknowledge that, to the extent to which a commitment to positive comity facilitates increased communication and exchange of information between governments, it may have an impact at the margin.[62] This communication and exchange of information in turn lays the foundation for more enduring relationships that ultimately ripen into trust. Thus at a global level, a principle of positive comity, combined with the principle of legitimate difference, creates the basis for a pluralist community of regulators who are actively seeking coordination at least and collaboration at best.

[61] Ibid.
[62] See Atwood, 'Positive Comity', op. cit., p. 88, n. 53.

4 Checks and Balances

Fourth, and for many perhaps first, it is necessary to take a leaf from Madison's book. If, in fact, government networks, or indeed any form of global governance, are indeed to avoid Kant's nightmare of 'soulless despotism', the power of every element of the world order system must be checked and balanced. A system of checks and balances is in fact emerging in many areas, from relations between national courts and supranational courts to the executive of one state challenging the regulatory agency of another in national court. Yet these fragments of evolving experience should be understood and analysed in the context of an affirmative norm of friction and constructive ambiguity in relations among participants in government networks of every kind. The whole should resemble the US Constitution in at least this much – a system of shared and separated powers designed more for liberty than efficiency.

Writing about American federalism, David Shapiro has portrayed it as 'a dialogue about government'.[63] The federal system set forth in the constitution frames a perpetual debate in which 'neither argument – the case for unrestrained national authority or the case against it – is rhetorically or normatively complete without the other'.[64] It is the dialogue itself that is a source both of creative innovation and tempering caution. This description also applies to relations between national courts in EU member-countries and the ECJ, a dialogue that lies at the heart of the EU constitutional order. Their debates over both jurisdictional competence and substantive law are matters of pushing and pulling over lines demarcating authority that are constructed and revised by the participants themselves. Each side is checked less by a specific grant of power intended to act as a check or a balance than by the ability of each side to challenge or refine any assertion of power by the other.

Overall, checks and balances must become an accepted part of a global political arrangement among government institutions. Here again, networks of legislators would be a valuable addition to global government networks – to provide a counterweight, where necessary, to networks of regulators or even judges. Thus, for instance, when a

[63] David L. Shapiro, *Federalism: A Dialogue*, Evanston, IL, Northwestern University Press, 1995, p. 108.

[64] Ibid.

network of securities regulators is promulgating a code of best practices, it is not impossible to imagine a similar code issuing from a network of legislative committees from different nations concerned with the same issues. The determination of what a best practice is and whose interests it is most likely to serve would likely be different. Certainly such a possibility would provide a counterweight to the consensus of professional technocrats.

5 Subsidiarity

The final normative principle necessary to structure a global political process of disaggregated national and supranational institutions is subsidiarity. Subsidiarity is the EU's version of Madisonian checks and balances. The term may be unfamiliar, but the concept is not. It expresses a principle that decisions are to be taken as closely as possible to the citizen.[65] Article V of the Consolidated Treaty Establishing the European Community defines the principle of subsidiarity as the criterion for determining the division of powers between the community and its member states.[66]

Projected onto a global screen, the principle of subsidiarity would reinforce the basic axiom of global governance through government networks: even on a global scale, the vast majority of governance tasks should still be taken by national government officials. Within nation-states, of course, subsidiarity may argue for the exercise of power at a lower level still – at the local or provincial level. Yet, once at the level of the national government, the burden of proof to devolve power up to a regional or global entity will require a demonstration

---

[65] George A. Bermann, 'Taking Subsidiarity Seriously: Federalism in the European Community and the United States', *Columbia Law Review*, 94 (1994), p. 331.

[66] Consolidated Version of the Treaty Establishing the European Community, Art. 5, *Official Journal C 325 of 24 December 2002*. According to the relevant provisions of this Article:

In areas which do not fall within its exclusive competence, the Community shall take action, in accordance with the principle of subsidiarity, only if and insofar as the objectives of the proposed action cannot be sufficiently achieved by the Member States and can therefore, by reason of the scale or effects of the proposed action, be better achieved by the Community. Any action by the Community shall not go beyond what is necessary to achieve the objectives of this Treaty.

that the specific functions needed cannot be adequately provided by national government institutions either coordinating their action or actively cooperating. Finally, within international or supranational institutions themselves, questions of institutional design and allocation of power should depend upon a demonstration of the need for personnel and powers in addition to, or superior to, networks of national government officials.

The value of subsidiarity is that it institutionalizes a system or a political process of global governance from the bottom up. International lawyers, diplomats and global dreamers have long pictured a world much more united from the top down. Even as the need for governance goes global, the ideal location of that governance may well remain local. The principle of subsidiarity requires proponents of shifting power away from the citizen at least to make the case.

To maximize the accountability of the participants in government networks, it would be possible to take a step further and give them a measure of individual, or rather institutional, sovereignty. In a world of disaggregated states, the sovereignty that has traditionally attached to unitary states should arguably also be disaggregated. Taking this step, however, requires a different conception of the very nature of sovereignty. As described in the next section, sovereignty understood as capacity rather than autonomy can easily attach to the component parts of states and includes responsibilities as well as rights.

DISAGGREGATED SOVEREIGNTY

Theorists, pundits and policy-makers all recognize that traditional conceptions of sovereignty are inadequate to capture the complexity of contemporary international relations. The result is a seemingly endless debate about the changing nature of sovereignty – what does it mean? Does it still exist? Is it useful? Everyone in this debate still assumes that sovereignty is an attribute borne by an entire state, acting as a unit. Yet if states are acting in the international system through their component government institutions – regulatory agencies, ministries, courts, legislatures – why shouldn't each of these institutions exercise a measure of sovereignty – sovereignty specifically defined and tailored to their functions and capabilities?

This proposal may seem fanciful, or even frightening, if we think about sovereignty the old way – as the power to be left alone, to exclude, to counter any external meddling or interference. But consider the 'new sovereignty', defined by Abram and Antonia Chayes as the capacity to participate in international institutions of all types – in collective efforts to steer the international system and address global and regional problems together with their national and supranational counterparts.[67] This is a conception of sovereignty that would accord status and recognition to states in the international system to the extent that they are willing and able to engage with other states – engagement that necessarily includes accepting mutual obligations.

Chayes and Chayes begin from the proposition that the world has moved beyond interdependence. Interdependence refers to a general condition in which states are mutually dependent on and vulnerable to what other states do. But interdependence still assumes a baseline of separation, autonomy and defined boundaries. States may be deeply dependent on each other's choices and decisions, but those choices and decisions still drive and shape the international system. For Chayes and Chayes, by contrast, the international system itself has become a 'tightly woven fabric of international agreements, organizations and institutions that shape [states'] relations with one another and penetrate deeply into their internal economics and politics'.[68]

If the background conditions for the international system are connection rather than separation, interaction rather than isolation, and institutions rather than free space, then sovereignty as autonomy makes no sense. The new sovereignty is status, membership, 'connection to the rest of the world and the political ability to be an actor within it'.[69] However paradoxical it sounds, the measure of a state's capacity to act as an independent unit within the international system – the condition that 'sovereignty' purports both to grant and describe – depends on the breadth and depth of its links to other states.

[67] Abram Chayes and Antonia Handler Chayes, *The New Sovereignty: Compliance with International Regulatory Agreements*, Cambridge, MA, Harvard University Press, 1995, p. 4.

[68] Ibid., p. 26. As noted above, Wolfgang Reinicke similarly emphasizes the extent to which globalization, unlike interdependence, penetrates the deep structure and strategic behaviour of corporations and other actors in the international system.

[69] Ibid.

This conception of sovereignty fits neatly with a conception of a disaggregated world order. If the principal moving parts of that order are the agencies, institutions and the officials within them who are collectively responsible for the legislative, executive and judicial functions of government, then they must be able to exercise legislative, executive and judicial sovereignty. They must be able to exercise at least some independent rights and be subject to some independent, or at least distinct, obligations. These rights and obligations may devolve from more unitary rights and obligations applicable to the unitary state, or they may evolve from the functional requirements of meaningful and effective transgovernmental relations. But the sovereignty of 'states' must become a more flexible and practical attribute.

If sovereignty is relational rather than insular, in the sense that it describes a capacity to engage rather than a right to resist, then its devolution onto ministers, legislators and judges is not so difficult to imagine. Judges would respect each other's competence as members of the same profession and institutional enterprise across borders. A fully 'sovereign' court would be entitled to its fair share of disputes when conflicts arise, to negotiate cooperative solutions in transnational disputes, and to participate in a transnational judicial dialogue about issues of common concern. Regulators would be similarly empowered to interact with their fellow regulators to engage in the full range of activities that regulatory networks carry out. And legislators would be directly empowered to catch up.

But if disaggregated state institutions are already engaged in these activities, what difference does it make if they are granted formal capacity to do what they are already doing? The principal advantage is that subjecting government institutions directly to international obligations could buttress clean institutions against corrupt ones and rights-respecting institutions against their more oppressive counterparts. Each government institution would have an independent obligation to interpret and implement international legal obligations, much as each branch of the US government has an independent obligation to ensure that its actions conform to the Constitution. As in the domestic context, either the courts or the legislature would have the last word in case of disputed interpretations of international law, to ensure the possibility of national unity where necessary. In many cases, however, international legal obligations concerning trade, the environment, judicial independence, human rights, arms control and other areas would devolve directly on government institutions charged with responsibility for the issue area in question.

By becoming enrolled and enmeshed in global government networks, individual government institutions would affirm their judicial, legislative, or regulatory sovereignty. They would participate in the formulation and implementation of professional norms and the development of best practices on substantive issues. And they would be aware that they are performing before their constituents, their peers, and the global community at large, as bearers of rights and status in that community.

This idea is not as far-fetched as it may seem. Actual examples already exist or are being proposed. Eyal Benvenisti has raised the possibility of formally empowering sub-state units to enter into agreements.[70] The Princeton Principles on Universal Jurisdiction make the case for establishing clear rules and principles under international law that are directly aimed at national judges, as they are the actual subjects of the international law doctrine. The ambiguity that helps statesmen negotiate treaties is often disastrous for judges, who must actually apply the law.

At first glance, disaggregating the state and granting at least a measure of sovereignty to its component parts might appear to weaken the state. In fact, it would bolster the power of the state as the primary actor in the international system. Giving each government institution a measure of legitimate authority under international law, with accompanying duties, marks government officials as distinctive in larger policy networks and allows the state to extend its reach. If sovereignty were still understood as exclusive and impermeable rather than relational, strengthening the state would mean building higher walls to protect its domestic autonomy. But in a world in which sovereignty means the capacity to participate in cooperative regimes in the collective interest of all states, expanding the formal capacity of different state institutions to interact with their counterparts around the world means expanding state power.

---

[70] Eyal Benvenisti, 'Domestic Politics and International Resources: What Role for International Law?', in Michael Byers (ed.), *The Role of Law in International Politics: Essays in International Relations and International Law*, New York, Oxford University Press, 2000, p. 109.

CONCLUSION

Members of government networks must interact with their foreign counterparts sufficiently transparently to be monitored by ordinary voters; they must give reasons for their actions in terms intelligible to a larger public; and they must be able to formulate arguments in sufficiently general, principled, 'other-regarding' ways to be able to win the day in a process of deliberative decision-making. Operating in a world of generalizable principles, however, requires a baseline of acceptable normative behaviour. The norms I have prescribed ensure wide participation in government networks, seek to preserve local, regional and national autonomy to the extent possible, and guarantee a wide space for local variation, including local variation driven by local and national politics.

At the loftiest level, these principles could be understood as part of a global transgovernmental constitution – overarching values to steer the operation of government networks. Yet the content of these specific principles is less important in many ways than the simple fact that there be principles – benchmarks against which accountability can be measured. Understanding government networks as a form of government, and then holding them to the same standards and subject to the same strictures that we hold all government, will do the rest.

4
Multisectoral Networks in Global Governance: Towards a Pluralistic System of Accountability[1]

Thorsten Benner, Wolfgang H. Reinicke and Jan Martin Witte

MORE THAN 30 YEARS AGO, ONE OF THE PIONEERS OF THE STUDY OF complex interdependence rang the alarm bells decrying 'the striking absence of concern about the implications of the evolving forms of multinational politics for the democratic process'.[2] Now, a generation after the debate on interdependence and well into the second decade of debating globalization, the raves and rants about the 'democratic deficit' of global policy-making are pervasive. The issue has not only provoked the emergence of a true growth industry in political science research; it has also conquered the opinion pages of major international newspapers, and occupies an increasingly prominent spot on the agenda of national and international policy-makers.

While by now there is a sophisticated academic debate on the 'democratic deficit' in global policy-making, all too often contributions to the debate fall short of operationalizing their findings for the daily practice of global governance: what approaches should we use to make global public policy-making more accountable?

This chapter seeks to make a modest contribution to this debate by outlining the elements of a pluralistic system of accountability with regard to one of the most ambitious institutional innovations in global governance: multisectoral public policy networks. Such networks cut across established political and sectoral boundaries. Global public policy networks bring together the public sector

[1] This chapter presents the first results of an ongoing research project on 'Exploring and Analysing the Role of Accountability in Global Governance' undertaken by the Global Public Policy Institute. We gratefully acknowledge the generous support provided by the Fritz Thyssen Foundation.

[2] Karl Kaiser, 'Transnational Relations as a Threat to the Democratic Process', *International Organization*, 25: 4 (1971), p. 715.

(governments and international organizations), civil society and business around issues ranging from corruption, climate change and fighting malaria to environmental and labour standards. Over the past decade, multisectoral networks have grown in number, organizational form and scope. Today, multisectoral networks can be identified in a wide variety of issue areas, involving a broad range of actors from all sectors, raising complex issues regarding their efficiency and effectiveness and, most of all, their legitimacy.

Optimists argue that 'pooling public and private resources in synergetic relationships could improve the overall problem solving capacity and at the same time increase societal participation and control'.[3] In contrast, critics argue that it is questionable whether cooperation between what they regard as 'essentially unrepresentative organizations – international organizations, unaccountable NGOs [nongovernmental organizations] and large transnational corporations' will contribute to promoting effective and legitimate global governance.[4] Others paint a full-blown pessimistic scenario in which globalization 'is leading to a world in which cross-cutting and overlapping governance structures increasingly take private, oligarchic forms' thereby undercutting democracy.[5]

At this stage, however, neither naive optimism nor full-blown pessimism are helpful. Rather, we should aim at a realistic assessment of the conditions under which new forms of networked governance can provide value added by improving global governance. In many cases, networks have developed in response to the failure of traditional governance mechanisms and offered new and alternative ways of getting things done. In addition to careful empirical work there is a need for 'more imagination in conceptualizing, and more emphasis on operationalizing, different types of accountability. It is better to devise pluralist forms of accountability than to bewail the 'democratic deficit'.[6]

---

[3] Klaus Dieter Wolf, *Private Actors and Legitimacy of Governance Beyond the State,* paper prepared for the workshop 'Governance and Democratic Legitimacy', ECPR Joint Sessions, Grenoble, 6–11 April 2001, Darmstadt, TU Darmstadt, 2001, p. 2.

[4] Marina Ottaway, 'Corporatism Goes Global: International Organizations, NGO Networks and Transnational Business', *Global Governance,* 7: 3 (2001), p. 245.

[5] Philip G. Cerny, 'Globalization and the Erosion of Democracy', *European Journal of Political Research,* 26: 2 (1999), p. 2.

[6] Robert O. Keohane and Joseph S. Nye, 'Democracy, Accountability and Global Governance', manuscript, Cambridge, MA, Kennedy School of Government, 2001, p. 8.

It will be crucial to develop appropriate ways and mechanisms to judge the transparency and accountability of new forms of networked governance 'without resorting to the claims of direct democracy or direct domestic analogy'.[7]

We will first analyse the *operational* and *participatory* governance challenges that form the context for the emergence of new forms of networked governance along the public–private frontier. We will then briefly discuss some of the key characteristics, forms and functions of multisectoral networks. In a second step we will, in an ideal-typical fashion, outline the key principles and mechanisms of accountability in multisectoral networks. We argue multisectoral networks should be embedded in a pluralistic system of accountability, making use of a combination of accountability mechanisms on a number of dimensions (actors, process, outcomes). Finally, we will analyse some of the key empirical, conceptual and practical challenges of an evolving agenda of networked governance and accountability and outline the elements of a 'learning model' of accountability in networks.

TRANSFORMING GOVERNANCE ALONG THE PUBLIC–PRIVATE FRONTIER

The 'vessel of sovereign statehood is leaky'[8] and we are faced with a complex and contradictory continuum of global affairs: on the one end the persistence of great power politics, unilateralism or 'multilateralism à la carte' (Richard Haass) and outright state failure, on the other end the emergence of new forms of governance along the public–private frontier. International organizations are caught in the middle trying to reinvent themselves in a changing world. New forms of 'networked governance' at the intersection of the public, private and not-for-profit sectors reflect the transformation of governance in an increasingly interdependent world. They are experiments in dealing with the asymmetries of governance in the age of globalization. We can conceptualize these asymmetries as both an *operational* and a *participatory* governance gap.

[7] Robert O. Keohane and Joseph S. Nye, 'Introduction', in Joseph Nye and John Donahue (eds), *Governance in a Globalizing World*, Washington, DC, Brookings Institution, 2001, p. 36.

[8] Ernst B. Haas, *When Knowledge is Power. Three Models of Change in International Organizations*, Berkeley, University of California Press, 1990, p. 181.

Four asymmetries constitute the operational gap:

First, there is the asymmetry between the territorially bounded nature of the nation-state and the transnational nature of many of today's key problems. The geographic scope of public goods and public bads extends far beyond national borders calling for transnational collective action involving both public and private actors if the present degree of interdependence is to be sustained.

Second, there is a *temporal asymmetry* between the need in a fast-moving global environment to make timely decisions that at the same time also take into account an intergenerational perspective of sustainability. This runs counter to standard decision-making in bureaucracies as well as standard political cycles determined by elections.

Third, the complexity of public policy issues is steadily increasing, contributing to growing knowledge and information asymmetries. Decision-makers in states and international organizations find themselves having to tackle more and more issues that cut across areas of bureaucratic or disciplinary expertise. Decisions made about international trade, for example, often now have profound economic, ecological and security effects, all of which must be considered in the policy debate. Furthermore, entirely new and complex problems have emerged that have not yet been fully understood. As a consequence, there is a need for a more open sourcing of knowledge involving outside experts and stakeholders from academia, civil society and business.

Fourth, there is a striking asymmetry between the 'negative integration' propelled by relatively robust market making agreements (e.g. within the context of the WTO) and efforts at 'positive integration' by way of setting and implementing human rights, environmental and labour standards. This calls for 're-embedding liberalism' at the global level with the help of new governance mechanisms.[9] This growing concern is reflected in the ideological shift away from the 'Washington Consensus' and a greater focus on 'global public goods'.[10]

[9] John Ruggie, 'The Theory and Practice of Learning Networks. Corporate Social Responsibility and the Global Compact', *Journal of Corporate Citizenship,* 5 (2002), pp. 27–36.

[10] Inge Kaul et al. (eds), *Global Public Goods. International Cooperation in the 21st Century,* Oxford, Oxford University Press, 1999.

In addition to the operational gap there is also a dual participatory gap. On the one hand there is a massive asymmetry between those who have access to the advantages of the system of globalization and interdependence and those who are left on the sidelines – massive global inequality and poverty are not only morally non-defendable but also unsustainable from a political-strategic point of view.[11] On the other hand, transnational actors such as nongovernmental advocacy groups demand to be heard in global policy-making. States and international organizations can no longer afford to bypass the concerns of transnational actors who have successfully mobilized around many global issues and have strengthened their bargaining position with significant moral, financial and knowledge resources. At the same time, members of national legislatures are increasingly sidelined by transnational policy-making. Both the operational and participatory governance gaps have prompted the search for alternative governance models that go beyond the purely state-based model and the 'club model' of intergovernmental cooperation. Global public policy networks that bring together state actors, international organizations, civil society and business on an issue-basis have been one of the innovative responses to the perceived need for innovation in governance.

It is important to note that the rise of new forms of cooperation along the public–private frontier does not rest on a simple functionalist argument in which the demand for global governance induced by the operational and participatory gap creates its own supply. As Keohane reminds us: 'Functional solutions to the problem of institutional existence are therefore incomplete. There must be political entrepreneurs with both the capacity and the incentives to invest in the creation of institutions and the monitoring and enforcement of rules'.[12] Institutional innovation is propelled if key players integrate new ideas (e.g. cross-sectoral cooperation) into their arsenal of political strategies. 'Networked governance' can serve as a guiding principle and paradigm for creating 'flexible institutions expanding organizational vision'.[13]

[11] Jeffrey D. Sachs, 'The Strategic Significance of Global Inequality', *Washington Quarterly*, 24: 3 (2001), pp. 187–98.

[12] Robert O. Keohane, 'Governance in a Partially Globalized World', *American Political Science Review*, 95: 1 (2001), p. 4.

[13] Peter M. Haas and Ernst B. Haas, 'Learning to Learn: Improving International Governance', *Global Governance*, 1 (1995), p. 256.

Global Public Policy Networks – Key Features

Most multisectoral networks have emerged over the past decade.[14] Multisectoral networks create bridges on a transnational scale among the public sector (national, regional or state and local governments as well as intergovernmental groups), the private sector and civil society. Networks seek to complement rather than replace traditional governance mechanisms – they are not legislating but help to develop standards and norms, provide global public goods and implement international agreements. They co-exist and co-evolve with other modes of governance: state-centred unilateralism, purely intergovernmental multilateralism, regional integration, private self-regulation.

Global public policy networks come in a wide range of forms and perform a multitude of functions. So far, there is no clear-cut typology of networks. However, it is possible to identify some ideal-typical characteristics of global public policy networks that differentiate these institutional innovations from traditional, hierarchical organizations. Interdependence, flexibility and complementarity are the three most important features of networks that deserve more detailed attention.

Interdependence. Cooperation in networks is based on the premise that none of the groups involved can address the issue at stake by itself. As a result, multisectoral networks create bridges on a transnational scale among the public sector (national, regional or state and local governments, as well as intergovernmental groups), the private sector and civil society that reflect the changing roles and power among those groups (triggered by economic and political liberalization as well as technological change) and that pull their diverse resources together.

Flexibility and openness. Global public policy networks come in various forms and organizational shapes that can also adjust in the process of cooperation. As a result, networks' structures can facilitate constant learning – from both successes and failures.

[14] For the following see Wolfgang H. Reinicke, Francis Deng, Jan Martin Witte and Thorsten Benner, *Critical Choices. The United Nations, Networks, and the Future of Global Governance*, Ottawa, IDRC Publishers, 2000.

Complementarity instead of co-optation. Networks maintain and profit from the diversity of their constituencies. As a result, networks facilitate the negotiation of controversial issues and provide a framework for political discussion and tension. At the same time, they also create the conditions for the combination and coordination of complementary resources.

Networks are therefore mechanisms that facilitate the transfer and use of knowledge and other resources of various actors in the global public policy-making process. They also offer a new mechanism that helps to bridge diverging problem assessments and interest constellations via political debate and mediation.

Over the past years, global public policy networks have developed in a multitude of issue areas. Networks offer negotiation platforms that facilitate the setting of global standards and regulations with the participation of the public and private sectors as well as civil society. They have developed in complex issue areas such as transnational money laundering or global water management (e.g. the World Commission on Dams[15]) and bring together all relevant actors from all sectors in a systematic fashion. Other networks serve primarily as coordination mechanisms that help to bring scarce resources to their most effective use and help provide global public goods. The Global Alliance for Vaccines and Immunization (GAVI) is a case in point. Other networks have sprung up as innovative answers to the challenge of implementing existing international treaties. The Global Environmental Facility (GEF) offers one prominent example. The flexible mechanisms agreed under the Kyoto Protocol for the protection of the global climate – especially the 'Clean Development Mechanism' (CDM) and 'Joint Implementation' (JI) – offer illustrations of the workings and potential significance of such implementation networks.

Global public policy networks have played an instrumental role in placing issues on the global agenda and have thereby created awareness and political capital necessary in pushing problems forward. Many networks have created new venues for participation beyond the closed shops of the 'club model' of international cooperation. At the same time, they raise crucial issues of accountability that need to be addressed.

[15] Sanjeev Khagram, 'Neither Temples nor Tombs: a Global Analysis of Large Dams', *Environment*, 45: 4 (2003), pp. 1–28.

NETWORKED GOVERNANCE AND PUBLIC ACCOUNTABILITY:
KEY PRINCIPLES AND MECHANISMS

How can we conceptualize and operationalize accountability in
global public policy networks? This section lays out the principles of
accountability in networks in an ideal-typical fashion. It offers various
perspectives on the notion of accountability, and reviews the application of accountability mechanisms to the various actors and levels
of governance. It proposes that a 'pluralistic system of accountability' is the most promising way to promote accountability in and of
multisectoral networks.

It is important to note that multisectoral networks and new forms
of public–private governance are meant to complement national
policy-making and international cooperation. Networks help to
negotiate and implement standards, provide global public goods and
help implement intergovernmental treaties – they do not legislate.
Therefore any discussion of accountability in networks can only highlight a limited number of aspects of the overall debate on accountability in global governance. Discussing accountability in networks,
though, is particularly instructive and important for two reasons:
First, it is key to determining under which circumstances networks
can help to improve the effectiveness and legitimacy of global governance and under which circumstances networks might have the
opposite effect. Second, discussing accountability in networks forces
us to think outside the box beyond the conventional mechanisms of
accountability discussed in national and international politics. This,
in turn, might inform the debates on the legitimacy and accountability on other instruments and structures of global governance.

In many respects networks escape traditional mechanisms and
conceptions of accountability. Networks as diffuse, complex and
weakly institutionalized collaborative systems are neither directly
accountable to an electoral base nor do they exhibit clear principal–
agent relationships. Therefore two traditional mechanisms of
accountability are not applicable in networks: electoral accountability and hierarchical accountability.[16] Therefore we need to rely on
alternative mechanisms of accountability. There will be *no single*
mechanism of accountability in networks – we will need to devise a

---

[16] Keohane and Nye, 'Democracy, Accountability and Global Governance', op. cit.,
p. 5.

multi-dimensional system of accountability with multiple alternative mechanisms to improve the accountability of networks.

A Pluralistic System of Accountability: Different Mechanisms

Given the lack of any single clear principal or any one electorate, to whom should networks be accountable? And what are appropriate accountability mechanisms? Using mechanisms of individual accountability alone is not sufficient in complex constructs such as multisectoral networks – we need to complement individual accountability of the participants with mechanisms of 'collective accountability'. Keohane points to the general problems of devising systems of 'collective accountability' in networks: the politics of 'blame avoidance' and the difficulties of assigning responsibilities for failure.[17] A pluralistic system of accountability in networks would rely on checks and balances between different actors and different mechanisms of accountability. The diffusion of power is an important precondition for the efficacy of different forms of accountability in networks.[18]

A number of different accountability mechanisms are of importance in networks:[19]

• *professional/peer accountability*: in networks, participants from a similar sector (e.g., experts, NGOs, business, governments) might be subject to peer accountability by other NGOs, experts, or members of the business community. They might be asked to adhere to professional 'codes of conduct' wherever they exist (see the discussion below on codes of conduct for NGOs);

• *public reputational accountability*: 'naming and shaming' is important in this context – actors in networks are accountable to the public for their actions and face reputational costs or can reap reputational benefits;

• *market accountability*: participants in networks who are also market participants might be rewarded/punished by other market

---

[17] Robert O. Keohane, 'Political Accountability', draft paper, Duke University, 2002, p. 12.

[18] Keohane and Nye, 'Democracy, Accountability and Global Governance', op. cit., p. 5.

[19] See Keohane, 'Political Accountability', op. cit., for an overview of different accountability mechanisms.

participants/consumers for their actions – this might be the case in
networks where market actors play important roles;
• *fiscal/financial accountability*: networks and their participants have
to account for the use of funds in the network – here we have something close to a principal–agent relationship between agent (network
participants) and principals (donors);
• *legal accountability*: network participants and networks themselves
(in case they have a full status as 'legal persons') need to justify their
actions. However, this mechanism is expected to be of minor importance in networks.
Reputational accountability is of prime importance for guaranteeing
accountability in and of networks. 'Naming and shaming' is a key
strategy in this context – one that often works well if the credibility
of a company, a brand, a government, an individual or a civil society
organization is on the line. Since not only information but also sanctions have to be part of our understanding of accountability, the loss
of credibility is one of the most effective negative sanctioning mechanisms to further accountability in and of networks. Of course this
mechanism will not work with 'rogue actors' that do not care about
their reputation, e.g. companies not putting a premium on developing and maintaining a brand. However, these companies are also
unlikely to engage in multisectoral networks in the first place.

Accountability in Networks: Actors, Process, Outcomes

The previous section introduced a number of mechanisms that can
enhance the accountability of various forms of governance. Multisectoral networks can be conceptualized along three dimensions:
actors, processes and outcomes. All three dimensions need to be
reviewed critically with regard to the level and significance of
accountability. This section analyses how and to what extent the
various notions of accountability discussed above are of relevance to
the various actors and levels of governance.

Accountability of actors. Networks can only be as legitimate as the actors
involved. If the actors in networks do not live up to basic criteria of
accountability and transparency, the network itself cannot either.
Therefore it is of foremost importance to ensure the *individual*
accountability of participants in networks. In this context peer

accountability and public reputational accountability are the most important mechanisms.

How can we put these two mechanisms to work? Transparency is key here. Internal procedures and structures have to be open to scrutiny.[20] This applies to government agencies, international organizations, corporations, foundations as well as NGOs. Information on the internal division of responsibilities, voting rules and procedures and most of all on funding (sources and spending patterns) are crucial in this context. The internet offers a powerful medium with which such information can be made widely available and thereby enhance the ability to identify wrongful behaviour.

Often NGOs themselves form advocacy coalitions and networks that then in turn participate in multisectoral networks. While some NGO (network)s regularly question the legitimacy of global policy processes and the actors involved, their own accountability has come under attack. These new demands for transparency about legitimacy and representation are emerging from within NGO networks and most prominently from NGO critics.[21] Summarizing the results of a long-term research project on the rise of NGOs, Florini emphasizes the critical importance of promoting transparency in the work of NGOs.[22] As Florini points out, many civil society organizations still do not provide sufficient information about their operations, funding sources and expenditures. Given the rise of GONGOs, BONGOs and DONGOs (NGOs organized by governments, business and donors), financial accountability is a particularly important element.[23]

Certification, self-regulation and codes of conduct are additional possible ways to ensure greater transparency.[24] Edwards suggest that

[20] Michael Zürn, 'Democratic Governance Beyond the Nation-State: The EU and Other International Institutions', *European Journal of International Relations*, 6: 2 (2000), p. 206.

[21] Paul J. Nelson, 'Agendas, Accountability, and Legitimacy among Transnational Network Lobbying the World Bank', in Sanjeev Khagram, James V. Riker and Kathryn Sikkink (eds), *Restructuring World Politics. Transnational Social Movements, Networks, and Norms*, Minneapolis, University of Minnesota Press, 2002, p. 150.

[22] Ann Florini, 'Lessons Learned', in Ann Florini (ed.), *The Third Force. The Rise of Transnational Civil Society*, Washington, DC, Carnegie Endowment for Peace, 2001, p. 237.

[23] Kathryn Sikkink, 'Restructuring World Politics. The Limits and Asymmetries of Soft Power' in Khagram, Riker and Sikkink, *Restructuring World Politics*, op. cit., p. 312.

[24] Michael Edwards, *NGO Rights and Responsibilities. A New Deal for Global Governance*, London, Foreign Policy Centre, 2000, p. 30.

at the international level the United Nations could 'set and monitor standards for NGO involvement across all international institutions, and . . . keep track of the large number of different codes of conduct and structures for participation that will probably evolve'.[25] A better and most likely more effective approach might be to use the model of the Global Reporting Initiative (which seeks to provide a common umbrella for different approaches of social and environmental reporting of companies) and extend it to NGO certification. Social and environmental reporting mechanisms themselves are important additional sources for information on businesses.

Companies are also important players in networks. Similar to the number of transnational NGOs, companies have reorganized themselves into truly transnational players. Companies have played significant roles in networks with their accountability being one of the most difficult and contested issues at stake. By their very nature, companies are not democratically organized. Even though the age of shareholder capitalism has brought some mechanisms of public control and election to the modern corporation, in essence companies are guided by individual leaders and board rooms. That is why many have questioned the right of companies to sit at the negotiation table. The debates surrounding the role of business in the UN's Global Compact is just one prominent example.

At the same time, however, the social and environmental reporting movement of the past two decades has created significant opportunities for individuals to retrieve detailed information about the behaviour, the 'good' or 'bad' citizenship of at least the largest corporations. The Global Reporting Initiative (GRI)[26] estimates that at least 2,000 companies worldwide voluntarily report information on their economic, environmental, and social policies, practices and performance. Through their global reorientation and their activities in developing countries, these companies are under increasing public scrutiny. An infinite number of codes of conduct, social and environmental reporting mechanisms has sprung up during recent years trying to establish benchmarks for good corporate citizenship and that seek to enhance the accountability of firms not only vis-à-

[25] Ibid., p. 31.
[26] For more information see www.globalreporting.org.

vis their customers but also vis-à-vis the public at large.[27] These reporting requirements and the voluntary implementation of codes of conduct present one important instrument with which the individual accountability of companies has been strengthened considerably. The future will show whether the consolidation of reporting criteria and codes of conduct will add to a more level playing field and improved reporting.

On the one hand greater transparency of individual actors will allow for greater public scrutiny of network participants. On the other hand (in the absence of any attempts at collusion) peer accountability might also be an important mechanism: given the reputational risks associated with being involved in a network each participant will want to make sure to have sufficient information on the bona fide qualities of the other participating actors.

While it is true that networks can only be as legitimate as the actors involved, engaging in networks might have positive feedback effects on the accountability of individual actors: they might be more in the spotlight (e.g. companies involved with the Global Compact or other initiatives on corporate social and environmental reporting) and the public will want to know more about them, forcing them to live up to higher standards of transparency.

Process. Networks are process-oriented forms of governance. Therefore, thinking about the accountability of networks also requires a thorough examination of their process dimension. Again transparency is key for the mechanisms of reputational, financial and peer accountability to work. The selection process needs to be transparent and individual actors need to live up to high standards of transparency (see previous section). The criteria for identifying and selecting participants (e.g. competence, representation) should be openly communicated and applied consistently. Reputational accountability is an important mechanism for the selection of participants. Consider for example the United Nations: for the UN, a significant reputational risk 'is associated with selecting an inappropriate private sector partner or partnership activity, or being

---

[27] For an overview see Ariane Berthoin Antal, Meinolf Dierkes, Keith MacMillan and Lutz Marz, *Corporate Social Reporting Revisited. WZB Discussion Paper FS II 02-105*, Berlin, WZB, 2002.

perceived to do so by key stakeholders, and undermining the credibility and reputation of the United Nations body in question, or the entire United Nations system'.[28] Furthermore, there need to be clear terms of engagement in terms of common goals and guidelines for cooperation, clear timetables and decision-making procedures.

A broad sourcing of knowledge and positions is also helpful. While there are limits to including actors into the 'core' of a network, additional broad consultations with a variety of stakeholders can help to ensure a broad sourcing of openness about consultations and debates in networks. These consultations should be open and transparent and the results should be made available to the public. Transparency about sources and uses of funding is another key element. Sources and uses of funding in networks need to clearly documented and available to the public. Making use of new technologies (e.g. consultations via email, making information available on websites) is an important element but certainly not a panacea to the problems of process accountability. Certainly making information available online can greatly facilitate access to crucial information on accountability. However, virtual consultations cannot substitute for face-to-face interaction and discussions. It is important to ensure that cooperation in networks does not lead to collusion. A measure of competition and mutual checks and balances is healthy for accountability.[29]

Outcomes. While the accountability of the actors and the process cover what is often referred to as 'input legitimacy', networks also have to account for their outcomes ('output legitimacy'). Since networks do not legislate the outcomes of networks (e.g. standards which are proposed) are not legally binding in a traditional 'hard law' sense. So for negotiation networks to make a difference they in many ways need to rely more on the persuasiveness of their results as judged by the participants and outside actors.

Accountability for outcomes in networks has a number of dimensions: it is crucial to re-embedding the results e.g., by discussing recommendations in national legislatures, promoting the application of

---

[28] Jane Nelson, *Cooperation Between the United Nations and all Relevant Partners, in Particular the Private Sector*, report of the Secretary-General, A 56/323, New York, United Nations, 2001, p. 24.

[29] Keohane and Nye, 'Introduction', op. cit., p. 35.

proposed standards by the network participants themselves. (Re)embedding networks also refers to greater involvement of national legislators. Among others, Anne-Marie Slaughter has emphasized the importance of including national legislators in transnational policy-making.[30] Independent evaluations can help to assess the process and outcomes of a network with a special focus on accountability, and with time-bounded enterprises can do so at the end of the duration (e.g., the independent assessment of the World Commission on Dams conducted by the World Resources Institute[31]) or at different stages of the network cycle so that the results are constantly monitored.

Certainly there can be no one-size-fits-all accountability system. Different types of networks might choose different systems of accountability, placing differential weights on individual elements and mechanisms of accountability. Whereas in negotiation networks a premium might be placed on transparency and outside access to information, coordination networks that collaboratively deal with very substantial outside contributions might put a special focus on the use of funding from donors. It is clear, however, that transparency in its many facets has to be the central element of any system of accountability for multisectoral networks.

As the previous section has demonstrated, conceptually there are a number of mechanisms for promoting accountability in and of multisectoral networks. However, it is ultimately an empirical question of whether global public policy networks provide value added, that is, make a difference in terms of greater efficiency, effectiveness and (our prime concern in this paper) accountability of global public policy-making. Here it important to stress that the empirical basis is still very weak. Evidence so far is largely impressionistic rather than living up to strict and sound social scientific methodology. Very few of the studies available put a particular emphasis on accountability.[32] There is a fairly strong selection bias in the studies available and a

[30] See Anne-Marie Slaughter, 'Building Global Democracy', *Chicago Journal of International Law*, 1: 2 (2002), pp. 79–96.

[31] See Navroz K. Dubash, Mairi Dupar, Smitu Kothari and Tundu Lissu, *A Watershed in Global Governance. An Independent Assessment of the World Commission on Dams*, Washington, DC, World Resources Institute, 2001.

[32] For a notable exception see Klaus Dingwerth, *Globale Politiknetzwerke und ihre demokratische Legitimation. Eine Analyse der World Commission on Dams. Global Governance Working Paper No. 6*, Potsdam, Global Governance Project, 2003.

tendency to focus on the success of multisectoral cooperation. In this context, we need to compare the effectiveness and accountability of networks with alternative institutional mechanisms in the same issue areas (e.g., intergovernmental regimes).

Moreover, according to a number of observers much of the work on 'networked governance' (although at times dealing with issues that are part of the development agenda) has an inherent OECD bias: multisectoral cooperation presupposes a significant degree of pluralism and a relative separation of public and private actors.[33] So far we lack conclusive empirical evidence on how the approach can work in some developing country settings where the basics of sound governance systems are missing.

One important aspect needs to be taken into account: When evaluating mechanisms to improve the legitimacy of global governance, it is important to choose the right yardstick. All too often, critics condemn the 'undemocratic' mechanisms and structures of global governance by comparing current practice in global governance with an ideal-type national democracy. However, at least since Dahl's famous study of 'polyarchy', we know that such ideal-type democracies have never existed in practice.[34] There are a number of similarities to 'networked governance' here – networked governance does not pretend to organize a perfectly democratic process at the transnational level. The ideal of democracy is hard, if not impossible, to implement at the national level in its purest form. Given the imperfections of the 'club model' of international cooperation and the far from perfect nature of democracy at the national level, the record of multisectoral networks might be viewed in a different light. As Sikkink points out, it is the existing degree of democracy in international institutions and in international governance against which networks should be evaluated.[35]

---

[33] See Andreas Nölke, 'Regieren in transnationalen Politiknetzwerken? Kritik postnationaler Governance-Konzepte aus der Perspektive einer transnationalen (Inter)-Organisationssoziologie', *Zeitschrift für Internationale Beziehungen*, 7: 2 (2000), pp. 331–58.

[34] Robert A. Dahl, *Polyarchy: Participation and Opposition*, New Haven, Yale University Press, 1971.

[35] Sikkink, 'Restructuring World Politics', op. cit., p. 315.

PROMOTING INNOVATION AND LEARNING: EVOLVING AGENDA OF
NETWORKED GOVERNANCE

Global public policy networks can serve as crucial catalysts promoting much-needed innovations in global governance in order to
address both the operational and participatory deficits. A 'utopian
realism' (Giddens)[36] should inform the further development of
the networked governance approach. 'Utopian', in the sense that
networked governance can help to broaden the horizon of policy
options promoting the 're-invention of our political traditions for a
global, as well as local, age' that David Held is demanding.[37] 'Realist',
in the sense that we need a sober assessment of the conditions under
which networks can provide value added by addressing both the
operational and participatory governance gaps. The lack of a sober
assessment will necessarily lead to 'network fatigue' resulting from
unfulfilled expectations. Talk about 'state failure', 'market failure'
and 'regime failure' would be quickly complemented by talk about
'network failure'. This in turn might lead to an overly rash dismissal
of the evolving 'networked governance' approach.

Critics argue that a lot of the literature on global governance treats
'governance as a neutral concept in which rational decision-making
and efficiency in outcomes, not democratic participation, is privileged'.[38] By further conceptualizing and operationalizing a pluralistic system of accountability, researchers and practitioners of global
governance can demonstrate that global governance taken seriously
cannot constitute itself as a technocratic approach. Problems of effectiveness, accountability and legitimacy are interlinked.

Promoting Research

A promising research agenda around 'networked governance' has to
draw creatively on a variety of approaches from different disciplines.

---

[36] See Anthony Giddens, *The Consequences of Modernity*, Cambridge, Polity Press,
1990.
[37] David Held, *Democracy and the Global Order. From the Modern State to Cosmopolitan
Governance*, Cambridge, Polity Press, 1995.
[38] Richard Higgott, 'Contested Globalization: the Changing Context and Normative Challenges', *Review of International Studies*, 26: 1 (2000), p. 142.

For the international relations discipline in particular, this holds promise for conceptual innovation beyond the 'either/or' of the prevailing 'paradigmatic' divides. The core of literature from international relations should certainly be one part of this agenda. In particular, more recent research on the role of international regimes in global governance could critically inform a new research agenda on networked governance. Studies on regime creation and regime effectiveness have made considerable progress in analysing the sources and dynamics of international cooperation but need to move further beyond a state-centric approach and simple two-level games. As networks have a strong cognitive dimension, the literature on the role of learning, norms and ideas in international relations will play a key role. The sociological and policy science literature on the prospects and pathologies of networks is similarly resourceful and instructive. Furthermore, research on the linkages between organization and regime theory, complexity theory and international law should inform the multidisciplinary research work. Including insights from political philosophy and public administration research will be beneficial for future work on governance and accountability. Future research on multisectoral networks and other forms of 'networked governance' can yield important insights into the changing role of states, international organizations, multinational companies and transnational civil society organizations. It presents a chance to move away from the orthodoxies of entrenched approaches and often anaemic debates, towards a creative interdisciplinary stance that invites conceptual experiments while at the same time maintaining a high degree of policy relevance by cross-fertilizing practice and theorizing.

Further research will need to answer the questions of how their record in terms of effectiveness and accountability compares to other governance mechanisms in different issue areas. Further research should also yield insights on best practices of promoting the accountability of new forms of networked governance. Here it is important to build on first efforts to measure accountability in global governance such as the 'Global Accountability Report'.[39]

---

[39] Hetty Kovach et al., *Power without Accountability? The Global Accountability Report 1*, London, One World Trust, 2003.

Experimentation and Learning

There is no one-size-fits-all approach to promoting public accountability of multisectoral networks. What we need is a pluralist system of accountability with a set of clearly defined general principles and mechanisms that at the same time allow for flexible operationalization. In this sense, networked governance is best conceptualized as a learning model. More sharing of experience on innovating governance is needed. Creating a learning network linking practitioners and academics can help to identify lessons learned and best practices on networks and accountability. A 'clearing house' could help to disseminate lessons learned and lead to a more standardized 'accountability audit' of different forms of global governance.

To use the potential of networks more effectively in the future, governments, international organizations, companies and NGOs face an extensive reform agenda. Promoting changes in organizational culture is one of the most important elements of the reform agenda. Today, transparency and 'interface skills' are of crucial importance: actors in networks need to be able to mediate between different sectors and actors as well as between different levels of organizations – local, regional, national, global.

In order to succeed in improving the prospects for global governance, two aspects are crucial. One the one hand we need to make sure that actual action on global governance lives up to the grandiose rhetoric that can often emanate from the corridors of power and the major institutions. We need to take G8 countries, the leaders of the World Bank and the UN as well as representatives of multinational companies at their word. Taking the recent G8 pledge to 'promote innovative solutions based on a broad partnership with civil society and the private sector'[40] seriously means investing *real* resources in new forms of networked governance in order to tackle the most pressing challenges from security to health and the environment in an efficient and accountable manner.

On the other hand we need stronger societal involvement: global governance is bound to fail without strong societal backing and

---

[40] G8 communiqué, Genoa, 22 July 2001 http://www.g7.utoronto.ca/g7/summit/2001genoa/finalcommunique.html.

involvement.[41] Right now, 'global governance' is a rather abstract and arcane issue with the term itself not lending itself to easy popularization in public debates. All too often in political debates on global issues oversimplifying and parochial notions of the 'national interest' remain unquestioned. In order to move beyond the parochialism of many policy debates we need an active public involved global public policy-making.[42] If global public policy networks manage to live up to basic standards of accountability, they can help to promote public participation and involvement in the debates around the crucial issues on the global governance agenda.

[41] See Michael Zürn, *Regieren jenseits des Nationalstaats. Globalisierung und Denationalisierung als Chance*, Frankfurt am Main, Suhrkamp, 1998.

[42] As Karl Kaiser pointed out more than 30 years ago: 'Only an active society which is "aware, potent and committed", not blindly active but responsive to essential human values and publicly active, can function as an effective counterforce to national and international technocracies and preserve, if not rebuild, a working democratic system.' (Kaiser, 'Transnational Relations', op. cit., p. 719).

5
Civil Society and Democratically Accountable Global Governance

Jan Aart Scholte

IN A DEMOCRACY, GOVERNORS ARE ANSWERABLE TO THE GOVERNED for their actions and omissions. When democratic authorities perform well, they warrant their public's support. However, when they err, rulers owe affected citizens apologies, explanations, compensations and possible resignations. When the damage of misguided governance is particularly severe, the public in a democracy may remove the responsible persons from office or even shut down the agency in question. In this way democracy is a continual correction of mistakes.

Unfortunately, little democratic accountability has operated in respect of contemporary global governance arrangements. The past 150 years have seen an unprecedented proliferation and growth of suprastate laws and institutions with transplanetary coverage. However, these regulatory instruments have included only weak, if any, formal accountability mechanisms. The leaderships of the organizations have not been subject to direct popular election. Nor has any global governance institution had a democratically appointed legislative arm. Citizens have in most cases been unable to take global authorities to court for redress. Most global governance arrangements have also lacked ombudspersons and formal external policy evaluation mechanisms, though the Bretton Woods institutions have over the past decade taken some modest steps in this respect.

True, a notional accountability chain does connect voters via national parliaments and national governments to global governance organizations, but the links have in practice been very weak. National political parties have rarely addressed global governance issues with any prominence in election manifestos and debates. A few exceptions aside, national parliaments have exercised only occasional and mild if any oversight over most suprastate regulatory bodies. In addition, many disillusioned citizens have concluded that the very system of parliamentary politics does not offer adequate channels to make their democratic voice heard, as reflected in low voter turnouts and widespread cynicism about professional politicians. In any case, relationships between national governments and global governance agencies have mainly flowed through unelected technocrats who lack any direct connection with citizens. Moreover, governments have on the whole intervened with global governance institutions only in respect of broad policy lines, leaving the suprastate bodies considerable unchecked prerogative in operational activities. In short, then, the conventional statist formula of democratic accountability does not suffice in relation to present-day expanded global governance.

In this unhappy situation, some citizens have looked to civil society activity as a way to obtain greater democratic accountability from United Nations (UN) agencies, multilateral financial institutions, the World Trade Organization (WTO), and various private global regulatory arrangements that have emerged in recent decades. The hope and expectation is that civil society associations – like business forums, community organizations, faith-based groups, labour unions, nongovernmental organizations (NGOs), professional bodies, think tanks and more – could bring greater public control to global governance.

This chapter explores these possibilities in three main steps. The first section below reviews the growth of civil society engagement of global governance. The second part elaborates on four general ways that civil society associations have promoted increased accountability in global governance. The third section identifies six broad circumstances that have affected (and often limited) the extent of civil society achievements in this area. That six-fold diagnosis can, in the conclusion of the article, suggest ways to enhance the future contributions of civil society groups to global democracy.

The analysis presented here draws on eight years of observations of civil society involvement in an incipient global polity.[1] Much of that research has focused more particularly on civil society activities in respect of the International Monetary Fund (IMF) and the

---

[1] J. A. Scholte, 'Global Civil Society', in N. Woods (ed.), *The Political Economy of Globalization*, London, Macmillan, 2000, pp. 173–201; J. A. Scholte, 'Civil Society and Governance in the Global Polity', in M. Ougaard and R. A. Higgott (eds), *Towards a Global Polity*, London, Routledge, 2002, pp. 145–65; J. A. Scholte, 'Civil Society and Democracy in Global Governance', *Global Governance*, 8: 3 (2002), pp. 281–304.

broader governance of global finance.[2] More recently, discussions with some 350 civil society actors in seven countries across the world have included considerable attention to issues of accountability in global governance.[3]

These various investigations have suggested that civil society associations do indeed offer significant possibilities to increase democratic accountability in global regulatory arrangements. This is especially important since, as noted above, other accountability mechanisms for global governance are at present so weak and un-likely to improve substantially in the short and medium term. This is not to say that all civil society activities inherently and automati-cally enhance democratic accountability in global regimes. Nor is it to suggest that civil society initiatives are the only or a complete way to make global authorities more answerable to their publics. But it is to affirm that civil society contributions in this regard are con-siderable and worth fostering further.

CIVIL SOCIETY AND GLOBAL GOVERNANCE

This is not the place for lengthy ponderings on definitions of civil society.[4] Suffice to say that the term has historically carried multiple and sometimes blatantly contradictory meanings. Thus current usages by, say, the CIVICUS World Alliance for Citizen Participation and the World Bank diverge considerably from Lockean, Kantian, Hegelian and Gramscian formulations. The issue is not to determine a definitive definition, but rather to craft a concept of civil society that is intellectually and politically relevant to the context at hand.

[2] R. J. O'Brien, A. M. Goetz, J. A. Scholte and M. A. Williams, *Contesting Global Governance: Multilateral Economic Institutions and Global Social Movements*, Cambridge, Cambridge University Press, 2000, ch. 5; J. A. Scholte, *Civil Society Voices and the International Monetary Fund*, Ottawa, North-South Institute, 2002; J. A. Scholte with A. Schnabel (eds), *Civil Society and Global Finance*, London, Routledge, 2002. See also J. A. Scholte, 'The WTO and Civil Society', in B. Hocking and S. McGuire (eds), *Trade Politics: International, Domestic and Regional Perspectives*, 2nd edn, London, Routledge, 2003, pp. 146–61.

[3] J. A. Scholte, *Democratizing the Global Economy: The Role of Civil Society*, Coventry, Centre for the Study of Globalisation and Regionalisation, 2003.

[4] Cf. J. L. Cohen and A. Arato, *Civil Society and Political Theory*, Cambridge, MA, MIT Press, 1992.

In relation to contemporary world politics, civil society might be conceived as a political space where voluntary associations seek, from outside political parties, to shape the rules that govern one or the other aspect of social life. Civil society groups bring citizens together non-coercively in deliberate attempts to mould the formal laws and informal norms that regulate social interaction. Although in practice civil society arenas cannot be wholly separated from official and commercial spheres, veritable civil society associations do not pursue for themselves public office or pecuniary gain.

Given their aim to influence social rules, civil society activities unfold in close relation to a governance apparatus. In earlier times, governance effectively came down to government, and civil society organizations operated almost entirely in relation to the state. However, today's world exhibits more polycentric governance, where substate (local and provincial) and suprastate (regional and global) agencies exist alongside – and with some autonomy from – national states. Civil society associations have therefore predictably redirected some of their attention from states to other sites of governance, including global regulatory institutions.

Civil society engagement of global governance is now part of the daily fare of politics.[5] For example, so-called 'anti-globalization' protests have railed against the IMF, World Bank and WTO, while many business forums and think tanks have suggested milder reforms of the global economic architecture. Human rights advocates have campaigned for a permanent International Criminal Court. Peace groups have pushed for enhanced global regimes of arms control and conflict management. Women's associations have promoted increased gender sensitivity across the whole of global governance. Environmental movements have argued for tighter global regulation

---

[5] Cf. T. G. Weiss and L. Gordenker (eds), *NGOs, the UN, and Global Governance*, Boulder, CO, Rienner, 1996; P. Willetts (ed.), *'Conscience of the World': The Influence of Non-Governmental Organisations in the UN System*, Washington, DC, Brookings Institution, 1996; J. A. Fox and L. D. Brown (eds), *The Struggle for Accountability: The World Bank, NGOs and Grassroots Movements*, Cambridge, MA, MIT Press, 1998; J. W. Foster with A. Anand (eds), *Whose World Is It Anyway? Civil Society, the United Nations and the Multilateral Future*, Ottawa, United Nations Association in Canada, 1999; O'Brien et al., *Contesting Global Governance*, op. cit.; A. M. Florini (ed.), *The Third Force: The Rise of Transnational Civil Society*, Washington, DC, Carnegie Endowment for International Peace, 2000; M. Edwards and J. Gaventa (eds), *Global Citizen Action*, Boulder, CO, Rienner, 2001; *Global Civil Society Yearbook*, Oxford, Oxford University Press, 2001–3.

of various ecological conditions. Trade unions have urged greater adherence to global labour standards. Health and development groups have called for more effective global arrangements in respect of transworld diseases like HIV/AIDS and malaria. Other NGOs have espoused revisions in the global communications regime so as to bring greater digital inclusion and media diversity across the world. Networks of religious revivalists have pressed for spiritual renewal in the global order. Still other civil society organizations have addressed global governance arrangements in respect of children, consumer protection, corruption, cultural preservation, education, food security, humanitarian relief, intellectual property, migration, refugees, sports, tourism and more.

Most global governance agencies have now devised mechanisms of one kind or another to engage (at least to some extent) with these initiatives from civil society associations. Most global regulatory institutions have developed elaborate websites and upgraded other public communications to address civil society audiences. Most have also increased their release of information to civil society circles in the name of 'transparency'. Most have made arrangements to include civil society groups in their conferences and workshops. Many have arranged briefings and other events specifically for civil society organizations. Many have appointed civil society liaison officers who regularly attend civil society venues. Many have adopted formal guidelines for staff engagement with civil society organizations.[6] Some have set up civil society advisory bodies and have formalized civil society involvement in their policy-making processes.

Thus, for example, the IMF circulates a quarterly *Civil Society Newsletter* to well over 1,000 recipients. The World Bank maintains publicly accessible information centres in many of its resident missions across the planet. Each UN global summit (Beijing, Cairo, Johannesburg, Monterrey, etc.) includes a parallel civil society forum. The Non-Governmental Liaison Service (NGLS) serves

[6] Cf. S. Cleary, *A Handbook for Working with Civil Society*, New York, United Nations Development Programme, 1996; United Nations General Assembly, 'Arrangements and Practices for the Interaction of Non-Governmental Organizations in All Activities of the United Nations System. Report of the Secretary-General', Doc. A/53/170, 10 July 1998; World Bank, *Consultations with Civil Society Organizations: General Guidelines for World Bank Staff*, Washington, DC, World Bank, 2000; IMF, 'Guide for Staff Relations with Civil Society Organizations', 2003 (at www.imf.org).

sixteen global governance institutions in the UN family. The International Labour Organization (ILO) has involved representatives of trade unions and employers' associations in its Assembly for over 80 years, while in June 2003 the Director-General of the WTO established an Informal NGO Advisory Body.[7] At the same time the UN Secretary-General convened a Panel of Eminent Persons on United Nations Relations with Civil Society to propose improvements in this area.[8] Today it is a rare global governance agency that, like the Bank for International Settlements, has given no significant attention to relations with civil society associations. Even the privately run Internet Corporation for Assigned Names and Numbers (ICANN) has maintained discussions with civil society groups such as Computer Professionals for Social Responsibility (CPSR).[9]

To be sure, these arrangements by global governance bodies have had various shortcomings. Most of the measures for civil society liaison are quite new, and most global civil servants are inexperienced in executing them. On the whole, transworld regulatory institutions have so far treated contacts with civil society associations as a secondary priority, and inputs from these citizen groups have not been fully integrated into policy processes. In general global governance agencies have tended to reach mainly Northern, urban, elite, English-speaking civil society professionals, failing to engage wider (and often more marginalized) constituencies. And clumsy handling of exchanges with civil society organizations has sometimes unhelpfully disrupted relations between global governance bodies and their member governments.

Nevertheless, transworld governance agencies have in recent years increasingly taken proactive steps to engage with civil society associations, recognizing that these relationships can yield important gains. For example, civil society organizations can serve as significant agents of public education, countering widespread ignorance about global governance. In addition, inputs from civil society groups can bring helpful information and insights to policy processes, including data

[7] Author's communications with Ricardo Meléndez-Ortiz, Executive Director of the International Centre for Trade and Sustainable Development and Hans-Peter Werner, External Relations Officer of the WTO, June 2003.

[8] *UN News*, 3 June 2003, at www.globalpolicy.org/ngos/int/un/access/2003/0604panel.htm.

[9] See www.cpsr.org.

and perspectives that are missing in official circles. Discussions with civil society bodies can also provide global governance agencies with an important gauge of the political viability of existing and contemplated policy measures. And, so many people presume, well-conducted relationships with civil society associations could enhance the democratic legitimacy of global governance arrangements with increased public participation and public accountability.

CIVIL SOCIETY CONTRIBUTIONS TO ACCOUNTABLE GLOBAL GOVERNANCE

On many occasions civil society associations have indeed made global authorities more publicly answerable for their projects, programmes and overall policy approaches. Civil society organizations have elicited this greater accountability in four main ways: by increasing the public transparency of global governance operations; by monitoring and reviewing global policies; by seeking redress for mistakes and harms attributable to global regulatory bodies; and by advancing the creation of formal accountability mechanisms for global governance. Examples of important contributions can be cited under each of these four headings. That said, the overall achievements of civil society advocacy in furthering the democratic accountability of global governance have remained relatively modest to date. There is much potential – and need – to do more in this area.

Transparency

It is well-nigh impossible to hold governors to account if their governance is invisible to constituents. If regulatory operations are to be subject to effective public scrutiny, then they must be open to public view. Citizens need to be aware who is governing them, towards what objectives, with what decisions, by what processes and using what resources. Only then can people have adequate grounds to judge the performance of the rules and rulers that govern them. Public transparency is therefore a crucial precondition for effective democratic accountability.

A number of civil society associations have provided a significant democratic service by pressing global governance agencies to undertake greater public disclosure about their work. For example, civil society activists have urged the institutions to increase their public visibility with brochures, annual reports, websites, exhibitions, speeches, media appearances, etc. In addition, certain civil society associations have campaigned for the governing bodies to release key policy and project documents, so that citizens can better analyse circumstances and choices for themselves.

For example, in 1997 pressure from the Brazil Network on Multi-lateral Financial Institutions (Rede Brasil) ensured that the World Bank's Country Assistance Strategy for Brazil was published and also translated into Portuguese.[10] The following year civil society organizations in Canada and France made public the previously secret text of a Multilateral Agreement on Investment (MAI) that was being negotiated through the Organization for Economic Cooperation and Development (OECD).[11] Also thanks largely to pressure from civil society groups, the Paris Club (an intergovernmental forum to regulate problems related to bilateral debts) opened a public website in 2001.[12] Before the Quebec Summit of the Americas civil society groups, led by the Hemispheric Social Alliance (HSA), pursued a yearlong 'liberate the text' campaign, which insisted that authorities should publish the negotiating document for the Free Trade of the Americas Agreement (FTAA) so that the terms would be open for public discussion. Governments finally relented just prior to the conference in April 2001. Other associations like the Toronto-based Maquila Solidarity Network (MSN) have pressed globally operating firms to disclose more, and more readily comprehensible, information about their product sourcing and labour practices.

As the MSN example illustrates, civil society groups have sometimes also stressed the need for *effective* transparency. It is one thing to release information into the public domain; it is another to make that information understandable to all affected people. So some civil

[10] M. Chiriboga, 'Latin American NGOs and the IFIs: The Quest for a South-Determined Agenda', in Scholte with Schnabel, *Civil Society and Global Finance*, op. cit., pp. 35–6; author's interviews with civil society practitioners in Brazil, January 2002.

[11] E. Smythe, 'State Authority and Investment Security: Nonstate Actors and the Negotiation of the Multilateral Agreement on Investment at the OECD', in R. A. Higgott et al. (eds), *Nonstate Actors and Authority in the Global System*, London, Routledge, 2000, pp. 74–90.

[12] www.clubdeparis.org/en/index.php.

society advocates have urged global governance agencies to make themselves truly visible to laypersons. For example, budgets need to be presented in ways that are easily followed. Published statements about policies need to be free of technical terms, obscure acronyms, professional jargon and other specialized vocabulary that can both confuse and alienate the general public. These civil society groups have argued that documents should be translated into the relevant languages and that hard copies need to be made available for people who lack internet access. In other words, various civil society associations have pressed that 'transparency' should go beyond rhetoric and lip service to be democratically meaningful.

Policy Monitoring and Review

Once policy practices are publicly visible, civil society associations are in a position to advance democratic accountability in global governance through watchdog and evaluation activities. For example, advocates can check to see that authorities comply with their constitutions, official resolutions and public declarations. In this vein a global civil society network called Social Watch has since 1995 tracked progress (or otherwise) towards reaching the goals of UN summits on poverty eradication and gender equality.[13] Across the world, human rights groups have monitored governments' compliance with UN human rights conventions, sometimes submitting to UN commissions parallel reports that challenge official accounts of the situation in the country.

In addition, civil society organizations have undertaken countless studies to document the consequences of various global governance policies. A number of these investigations have uncovered shortfall, error, incompetence and harm. For instance, in the late 1990s hundreds of civil society associations joined with the World Bank in a Structural Adjustment Policy Review Initiative (SAPRI) to assess the effects of macroeconomic reforms in eight countries.[14] Research by civil society groups in many countries has also put a critical spotlight on the previously little-questioned Trade-Related Intellectual Property Rights (TRIPS) Agreement of the WTO. Civil society advocates

[13] www.socwatch.org.uy.
[14] www.saprin.org/.

across the world have exposed detrimental consumer, labour and environmental practices of under-regulated global businesses. Studies by women's organizations have highlighted gender implications of various global governance arrangements that the authorities themselves have tended to overlook. Likewise, civil society investigations have documented country, class, race, age and other social inequalities that global regimes have often inadequately addressed or even compounded.

Civil society associations have in addition alerted the public to ethical lapses in the operations of global governance. For example, the Uganda Debt Network has monitored the government's Poverty Action Fund to watch that officials do not misuse IMF/World Bank debt relief monies that have been earmarked for primary education, sanitation, etc.[15] Another civil society initiative, Global Forest Watch, has since 1997 tracked illegal logging and its impacts on local populations in ten countries across the world, thereby performing a monitoring function that some governments have neglected.[16]

Pursuit of Redress

Civil society organizations have also provided channels through which citizens – in principle from any country, culture or social sector – can seek the correction of mistakes in global governance. In this regard civil society groups have pressed to have rules changed, officials replaced, institutions reconstructed and reparations paid. The associations concerned have taken grievances about global governance to auditors, ombudspersons, parliaments, courts and the mass media. For instance, groups in the global black people's movement have pursued reparations for historical crimes of colonialism against people of colour. This issue figured prominently in the NGO Forum at the UN's World Conference on Racism in Durban in 2001. Géledes, a black women's association in São Paulo, has prepared a case on this matter to present before the Inter-American Court of Human Rights.

---

[15] www.udn.or.ug/; author interviews in Uganda, November 2001 and August–September 2003.
[16] www.globalforestwatch.org/.

In addition, certain civil society activists have staged symbolic public 'trials' with informal 'tribunals' as a way to call global governance authorities to task. For example, the Permanent Peoples' Tribunal (PPT), created in 1979 by the Lelio Basso International Foundation, has publicly examined various cases against global corporations, the IMF and the World Bank.[17] Similarly, an International People's Tribunal on Debt was held at the 2002 World Social Forum (WSF) in Porto Alegre.

As well as such largely symbolic exercises, civil society groups have in some cases helped to exact corrective actions from global governance agencies. For example, NGOs have halted several World Bank-funded dam constructions or obtained better compensation arrangements for people adversely affected by these projects.[18] In addition, pressure from advocacy groups has on different occasions elicited measures to compensate vulnerable circles for, say, the removal of subsidies in IMF-supported macroeconomic reforms.

Promoting Formal Accountability Mechanisms

Civil society associations have also sought to improve democratic accountability in global governance by urging the creation and use of formal mechanisms to monitor and control the agencies concerned. In this vein a number of civil society organizations have urged local, national and regional elected assemblies to undertake more scrutiny of global governance institutions. For example, in response to a campaign from some 40 civil society groups, the French government has since 1999 submitted a publicly available annual report on its activities in the Bretton Woods institutions to the National Assembly in Paris.

Certain civil society activists have also campaigned for the establishment of official policy assessment mechanisms for global governance institutions. For instance, pressure from civil society groups

---

[17] www.grisnet.it/fib/tribu%20eng.html; 'When People Judge: The Permanent Peoples' Tribunal', *Corporate Watch*, 11 (Summer 2000).

[18] L. Udall, 'The World Bank and Public Accountability: Has Anything Changed?', in Fox and Brown, *The Struggle for Accountability*, op. cit., pp. 391–436; S. Khagram, 'Toward Democratic Governance for Sustainable Development: Transnational Civil Society Organizing around Big Dams', in Florini, *The Third Force*, op. cit., pp. 83–114.

was instrumental in the creation of an Inspection Panel for the World Bank in 1994 and an Independent Evaluation Office for the IMF in 2001.[19] Subsequently a number of civil society associations have also actively monitored and contributed inputs to these review mechanisms. In addition, civil society associations in many if not most countries across the world have promoted ideas and practices of corporate social responsibility (CSR) as a voluntary accountability regime for companies, in particular those that operate globally. The many civil society groups that have promoted CSR schemes include the Instituto Ethos in Brazil, the Conference Board of Canada, the Forum for Responsible Investment in France, and the Social Venture Network in Thailand.

In short, various civil society efforts have sought to advance democratic accountability in global governance, at a time when few other actors have concertedly pursued this goal. Civil society associations have highlighted and righted some wrongs as a result. However, much more could and should still be done on each of the four lines just reviewed. An important step in building more democratic global governance is therefore to encourage further civil society activities in the area of accountability promotion.

CHALLENGES

At least six general issues need to be addressed if civil society associations are more fully to realize their potentials as promoters of democratic accountability in global governance. These challenges concern resources, networking, official attitudes, the mass media, political culture and the democratic accountability of civil society organizations themselves. Depending on how they play out in particular contexts, these six influences can either create significant opportunities or present formidable difficulties for the democratization of global governance through civil society actions.

---

[19] Fox and Brown, *The Struggle for Accountability*, op. cit.; A. Wood and C. Welch, *Policing and Policemen: The Case for an Independent Evaluation Mechanism for the IMF*, London and Washington, DC, Bretton Woods Project and Friends of the Earth–US, 1998.

Resources

Accountability promotion requires resources. Research and advocacy on global governance cannot be accomplished without funds, staff, premises, equipment and supplies. In the words of an activist who has taken the cause of Toronto's urban poor to the United Nations, 'to build democracy you need time, space and resources, but we often have none of these'.[20]

Transworld civil society advocacy in particular demands significant means. True, global internet communications have become relatively inexpensive for many associations, but other groups (especially in marginalized parts of world society) lack computers or face high user charges. Meanwhile air travel, conference calls and translation services remain costly for all. Thus intensive transworld activism – which is often necessary to address issues of global governance effectively – is generally only available to well-endowed organizations. As one community activist in eastern Uganda has noted, 'It is hard for a rural woman to go to the global village.'[21]

Some civil society groups that address global governance matters have enjoyed relatively ample resources and therefore greater possibilities to extract accountability from the agencies concerned. These fortunate bodies include certain think tanks like the Brookings Institution, business associations like the World Economic Forum (WEF), NGOs like Oxfam, and faith-based organizations like the Roman Catholic Church. Regrettably, if predictably, the better endowed civil society associations have resided mainly in privileged quarters of world society: Northern countries, professional classes, English speakers, etc.

However, the exceptions highlight the rule that most civil society engagement of global governance has occurred on a shoestring. The great majority of community associations, NGOs, religious groups and trade unions have operated with small budgets and limited long-term financial security. Even some business forums (especially among small entrepreneurs) and think tanks (especially in the South) have led a precarious existence. These organizations have

---

[20] Josephine Grey, Low Income Families Together, during a discussion with the author in Toronto, May 2002.

[21] Zainab Wambedde, Mental Health Uganda, during a discussion with the author in Mbale, September 2003.

had only a few staff specifically dedicated to global governance issues and have often relied heavily on voluntary and low-paid labour. Exacerbating these resource difficulties, most civil society associations that deal with global governance issues are relatively young. Having been newly established in the past two decades, if not the last few years, these groups have as yet had little time to build up assets or institutional experience. And lots do not survive. Indeed, in many parts of the world a substantial proportion of registered civil society organizations are moribund.

Of course, the provision of adequate resources for civil society activities is by itself no guarantee of enhanced democratic accountability in global governance. Indeed, eagerness to obtain funds has led some civil society associations to compromise their autonomy. These co-opted organizations become voices of – rather than watchdogs over – official agencies, political parties and powerful individuals in global governance. However, dubious politics around some resource provision to civil society groups does not alter the fact that adequate resources are a precondition for effective accountability initiatives.

Networks

Resource shortages for civil society activity to further accountability in global governance can often be partly alleviated when associations collaborate in networks.[22] A civil society organization that is weak in isolation can become stronger through cooperation with other groups. For example, networking through Transparency International since 1993 has lent considerable added strength to dozens of national campaigns to increase openness and reduce corruption in the global economy.

Most civil society networking occurs among similar types of groups. Thus trade unions have cooperated with other trade unions, for instance, in the International Confederation of Free Trade Unions (ICFTU) and the World Confederation of Labour (WCL). Likewise, human rights organizations have joined forces with each

[22] On civil society networks, see M. Keck and K. Sikkink, *Activists beyond Borders: Advocacy Networks in International Politics*, Ithaca, NY, Cornell University Press, 1998; S. Khagram, J. V. Riker and K. Sikkink (eds), *Restructuring World Politics: Transnational Social Movements, Networks, and Norms*, Minneapolis, University of Minnesota Press, 2002.

other in the International Federation of Human Rights (IFHR), consumer advocates have come together in Consumer International (CI), and so on.

However, accountability in global governance can also be promoted through networks that encompass several sectors of civil society. For example, NGOs, religious groups, trade unions and business forums have teamed up to advocate reconsideration of official policies on poor country debts. Cross-sectoral networks can be particularly helpful in strengthening the position of subordinated populations, for instance, when black movements combine efforts with women's movements. The World Social Forum, launched in 2001, has been particularly effective in this respect.

The WSF illustrates another especially fruitful form of civil society networking with respect to global governance matters, namely transborder cooperation among associations in different countries. In particular, South-North and South-South coalitions have often strengthened the position of weak civil society groups in poor countries. Thus local civil society actors in India had greater effect in demanding accountability from Union Carbide for the Bhopal disaster of 1984 when they collaborated with sympathizers across the world.

Of course civil society networks can be problematic. For one thing, effective networking requires resources that many associations do not have. In addition, networks often lack clearly established procedures to formulate and execute joint positions, so that collective decision-taking among the participating groups can be cumbersome and confused. Moreover, members of a civil society network invariably have to negotiate differences – sometimes quite considerable divergences – regarding priorities, analyses, strategies and tactics. Such negotiations can become all the more difficult in cross-sectoral and transborder advocacy networks, where cultural diversity may generate major communications difficulties. Indeed, in some contexts like contemporary Russia, collaborating with allies abroad has provoked governing circles and the general public to have considerable distrust of many NGOs. Furthermore, like any other political entity, civil society networks to one degree or another involve power hierarchies and internal power struggles that can undermine efforts at cooperation. However, civil society associations that successfully address the challenges of networking can greatly enhance their impacts on accountability in global governance.

Official Attitudes

In addition to how they connect with each other, the ability of civil society associations to promote democratic accountability in global governance also depends considerably on their relationships with ruling authorities. On the one hand, if global regulators are know-ledgeable about civil society groups and eager to involve them in policy processes, then the chances that civil society activities can generate greater public accountability are much enhanced. On the other hand, if global regulators are ignorant about civil society organizations, averse to engage with them, and reluctant to allow them political space generally, then the prospects for democratization of global governance via voluntary collective citizen action are substantially weakened.

One significant indicator of official attitudes is the formal position that global governance institutions accord to civil society organizations. Depending on their nature, official rules of engagement can have either enabling or disabling effects for civil society activities. For example, the charters of the UN and the WTO specifically sanction relations with civil society bodies, while the constitutions of the IMF and the OECD lack such a provision. The United Nations Development Programme (UNDP) has published guidelines for relations with civil society associations, while the Bank for International Settlements (BIS) has never even formally recognized the existence of interlocutors in civil society. The World Bank has created a number of joint committees with civil society practitioners, while the Group of Eight (G8) has never contemplated such a thing.

The ways that staff of global governance institutions apply the rules and procedures for interactions with civil society groups makes a difference, too. Unsympathetic officials have ignored, belittled or obstructed civil society efforts to bring greater accountability to global regimes. In these negative scenarios, authorities have treated contacts with civil society groups as a public relations exercise and have only sought views from sympathetic civil society actors. In contrast, other officials have seriously tried to expand space for all sorts of civil society inputs to global governance and to respond concretely to civil society critiques of global governance policies and processes. Positively inclined global authorities have taken multiple initiatives to maintain channels of communication with civil society groups and to publicize research and demands from civil society within the global institution. To date, however, no global governance agency has systematically trained its professional staff in relations with civil society groups or made good performance in civil society liaison a significant criterion for staff evaluation and promotion.

Also important are the attitudes that states adopt towards civil society contacts with global governance bodies. Some governments have taken a relaxed position towards direct links (that is, bypassing the state) that civil society associations in their country might maintain with global regulatory institutions. However, other governments have opposed such relations as an attack on state sovereignty and have discouraged or actively blocked these relationships. A number of governments in the South have also objected when civil society groups (especially those based in or funded from the North) have lobbied for policies (e.g. on social and environmental clauses) that those governments underplay or reject.

Mass Media

Along with the approach of official circles, circumstances in the mass media have also significantly broadened or restricted the possibilities for civil society associations to bring greater accountability to global governance. When newspapers, magazines, radio, television, websites, CD-ROMs, etc. give considerable publicity to matters of global regulation, civil society campaigns for greater accountability can more readily attract a large and informed audience. However, if mass media communications mainly ignore global governance, publics are correspondingly less receptive to civil society initiatives on this subject, and the authorities feel less pressure to respond.

In addition to the quantity of attention, the quality of mass media coverage of global governance also makes a difference to civil society work. In positive situations, the press offers clear, detailed, probing and nuanced reporting on global regimes, and civil society associations can build on sound public understanding to pursue demands for accountability. In many other contexts, however, mass media treatments of global governance are muddled, careless, superficial and sensationalized. On these occasions the mass media are sooner a hindrance than a help to serious civil society campaigns. Moreover, mass media reporting about global governance has sometimes lacked a sharp critical edge that would enhance civil society efforts to promote public accountability. Indeed, much of the contemporary mass media are themselves powerful global actors with vested interests in the status quo. Such mass media organs can have limited concern to encourage accountability, particularly to weaker sectors of society. It seemed telling that, for example, mainstream media gave almost no space to representatives of Southern governments and civil society groups to explain their positions at the Cancún Ministerial Conference of the WTO in 2003. Meanwhile, alternative media that open more critical channels have generally struggled at the margins in most parts of today's world, if indeed they exist at all.

Apart from coverage of global governance in general, the quantity and quality of press treatment of civil society initiatives more specifically can also help or hinder accountability campaigns. On the positive side, public visibility through the mass media has allowed a number of civil society initiatives to gain large audiences and increased followings. In particular, newspapers and television have substantially raised the profile of the so-called 'anti-globalization movement' since the so-called 'Battle of Seattle' in late 1999. In contrast, however, the WSF has thus far failed to gain headlines in most of the world press, even though this initiative has attracted tens of thousands of participants for several years running. Nor have the mainstream media given much attention to the day-to-day work of civil society associations, that is, outside the limelight of periodic street demonstrations. In addition, many journalists have oversimplified and caricatured civil society positions on globalization, for example, by suggesting that 'NGOs are against trade'. Hence the mere fact of mass media attention is not necessarily a plus for civil society efforts to enhance accountability in global governance. The quality of coverage also matters.

Political Culture

A fifth key circumstance shaping the effectiveness of civil society activity as a means to obtain more democratically accountable global governance is political culture, that is, the established ways that questions concerning the acquisition, allocation and exercise of power are handled in a given social context. For example, some countries, regions or sectors of society might have long-standing rituals of citizen mobilization and a deeply embedded democratic political culture. In contrast, other sites have few such habits. Thus in Canada civil society groups could obtain taxpayer funds to bring scores of dissidents from Latin America to the People's Summit that challenged the FTAA meeting in Quebec. However, in terms of political culture such a scenario was unthinkable when Qatar hosted the Doha Ministerial Conference of the WTO later that year.

So the structural relationship between state and civil society has, depending on the context, discouraged or encouraged organized citizen action for democratic accountability in global governance. The authoritarian heritage of tsarist and communist regimes has done much to keep civil society at bay in contemporary 'democratic' Russia. Patrimonial relations have made business and labour associations largely tools of state in Brazil and Egypt. The historical succession of pre-colonial kingdoms, colonial rule and Idi Amin has tended to make most civil society groups in Uganda endure pains of structural adjustment in silence.[23] In contrast, rulers in liberal orders have usually treated critical monitoring of regulatory bodies by self-generated civil society associations as a normal and expected part of politics. Indeed, global governance bodies that are dominated by liberal states have generally accepted civil society activism in principle, even if these multilateral agencies have not always dealt with it comfortably in practice.

The political culture of citizenship in a given context also matters for the chances that civil society will bring greater democratic accountability to global governance. Some political cultures are marked by a strong tradition of citizen activism, while others are defined by deference towards governing authorities. More recently, a culture of consumerism and entertainment has lured many people – including younger generations in particular – away from active citizenship. Likewise, an environment of pervasive cynicism about politics can greatly discourage citizen activism through civil society associations. Indeed, in contexts where citizens tend to regard all governance as corrupt, many people may look sceptically on the motives of civil society organizations as well, doubting that civil society could be a space where persons of integrity could pursue public interests.

Another problem of political culture – one that poses particular difficulties for civil society work on global governance – are

[23] Discussion with Nduhukhire Owa Mataze, Uganda Martyrs University, Nkozi, 3 September 2003.

nationalist, statist and territorialist mindsets. In many contexts across the contemporary world, people retain deep-seated habits of conceiving of the political arena solely in terms of the territorial national state. Indeed, some political environments are marked by strong isolationist tendencies. Clearly civil society associations that work on global governance issues have greater struggles to attract attention and support to the extent that their publics are not accustomed to think globally about politics.

Civil Society Accountability

Finally there is the accountability of civil society groups themselves. Just like the global governance agencies that they may critique, civil society groups have an obligation to answer to stakeholders for their actions and omissions.[24] In the words of one veteran civil society campaigner at the United Nations, 'If civil society organizations are going to deal with democracy issues, then they also have to have a self-critical reflection on how they work themselves.'[25] Or, as another democracy advocate has put it, 'When you point a finger you need to do it with a clean hand'.[26]

Regrettably, most civil society groups have operated very limited and unimaginative accountability mechanisms in relation to their own activities. At best, the organizations have tended to have no more than loose oversight by a board (often composed largely of friends, who are in some cases paid), periodic elections of officers (with low rates of participation and sometimes dubious procedures),

---

[24] Cf. M. Edwards, *NGO Rights and Responsibilities: A New Deal for Global Governance*, London, Foreign Policy Centre, 2000; L. D. Brown et al., 'Civil Society Legitimacy: A Discussion Guide', in L. D. Brown (ed.), *Practice-Research Engagement and Civil Society in a Globalizing World*, Cambridge, MA, Hauser Center for Nonprofit Organizations, Harvard University, 2001, pp. 63–79; H. Slim, 'By What Authority? The Legitimacy and Accountability of Non-Governmental Organisations', paper for the International Conference on Global Trends and Human Rights – Before and After September 11, Geneva, 10–12 January 2002; M. Edwards and A. Fowler (eds), *The Earthscan Reader on NGO Management*, London, Earthscan, 2002.

[25] John Foster, North-South Institute, in discussion with the author in Ottawa, May 2002.

[26] Perry Arituwa, Uganda Joint Christian Council, in discussion with the author in Kampala, August 2003.

occasional general meetings (with sparse attendance), minimalist reports of activities (that few people read) and summary financial records (which often conceal as much as they reveal). Such pro forma accountability mainly addresses the bureaucratic requirements of governments and donors. It does not actively engage the association's stakeholders or promote genuine organizational learning. Thus – in civil society just as much as in governance and market circles – formal accountability may fall well short of effective accountability.

Worse still, some civil society players in global politics have not met even minimal standards of accountability. Such groups lack a clear constituency and operate without any public mandate. Their leadership is self-elected and stays in office indefinitely. They rarely if ever consult their supposed constituents. They do not report publicly on their activities. They lack rigorous financial monitoring. They offer aggrieved parties no channels for complaint and redress. Hence one hears cynical talk of MONGOs (My Own NGOs), BRINGOs (Briefcase NGOs), come-and-gos, self-serving religious and trade union elites, etc.

Moreover, many civil society practitioners have expressed scepticism about the need to develop their accountability. They do not see how demonstrations of accountability are related to their mission. They perceive only risks and no returns in the exercise. They regard it as an overly expensive undertaking. And they argue that the 'real' accountability problems lie with actors other than themselves – like global governance agencies.[27]

Neglect of their own accountability can greatly compromise the potentials of civil society associations to democratize global governance. For one thing, unaccountable civil society organizations generally fail to correct shortcomings in their performance and thereby underachieve. In addition, unaccountable civil society bodies can lose moral credibility and indeed can give the whole sector a bad name. Unaccountable civil society actors can also reflect and reinforce low democratic standards in society at large.

Moreover, accountability shortfalls can be politically costly to civil society work. Again and again, authorities have seized upon issues of accountability to reject the legitimacy of civil society associations.

[27] L. Jordan, 'The Importance of Rights to NGO Accountability', draft paper, August 2003.

Many politicians, officials, business leaders, journalists and academics have asked why unaccountable civil society actors should have the right to influence the course of globalization. In this light, civil society organizations need to become more accountable if they wish to retain and expand their involvement in and impact on global governance.

Fortunately an increasing number of civil society associations have in recent years begun pursuing innovative initiatives to develop their own accountability. In this vein, for example, the NGO Steering Committee of the United Nations Commission on Sustainable Development created an elaborate self-regulatory framework for promoting accountable civil society involvement in UN work on environment and development, although that process became increasingly burdensome and fractious until it collapsed in 2001.[28] With more success the Canadian Council for International Co-operation has overseen a self-regulatory Code of Ethics for its members since 1995.[29] The Philippine Council for NGO Certification has developed a highly rigorous scheme of nonofficial oversight for civil society in that country.[30] In 1999 scores of civil society associations in India formed a Credibility Alliance that promotes guidelines for 'minimum norms', 'desirable norms' and 'good practices'.[31] Under its strategy 'Fighting Poverty Together' (1999–2003), ActionAid has given particular attention to developing NGO accountability to poor people themselves.[32] Similarly, the Humanitarian Accountability Project (HAP) started in 2000 has given special attention to raising NGO accountability to the recipients of international emergency relief.[33] Thus their own accountability has become a notable governance concern for many civil society organizations, although much more remains to be done in this area.

[28] F. Dodds, 'From the Corridors of Power to the Global Negotiating Table: The NGO Steering Committee of the Commission on Sustainable Development', in Edwards and Gaventa, *Global Citizen Action*, op. cit., pp. 203–13.

[29] www.ccic.ca.

[30] www.pcnc.com.ph.

[31] http://credibilityalliance.org/; presentation by Anil Singh of the Voluntary Action Network India at Sawarung/Ford Foundation conference on NGO accountability, Bandung, January 2003.

[32] J. Chapman and A. Wameyo, 'Monitoring and Evaluating Advocacy: A Scoping Study', ActionAid, January 2001.

[33] www.hapgeneva.org/.

CONCLUSION

The preceding analysis suggests that civil society associations can make important contributions to greater democratic accountability in global governance. Already these activities have reached a notable scale, and considerable opportunities exist to broaden them further. Moreover, accountability through civil society interventions is a fairly immediately available way forward, inasmuch as it requires no major constitutional reorganization of global regulatory arrangements.

On the other hand, as elaborated in the third section above, civil society enhancement of democratic accountability in global governance does not occur automatically and on the contrary faces multiple challenges. Some of the difficulties (like official attitudes and political culture) relate to the environment of civil society work, while others (accountability within civil society) lie with the associations themselves. Thus civil society is not an easy answer to the global accountability problem. Nor can organized voluntary citizen action be expected to secure accountability in global governance on its own, without concurrent interventions from parliaments, judiciaries, official expert evaluations and the mass media.

Improvements in a number of areas are required if civil society contributions to accountability in global governance are to be maximized. Funders need to commit more resources to these activities, particularly to those associations that give voice to marginalized groups in world society such as underclasses, people of colour, rural populations and women. Civil society organizations need more fully to exploit the possibilities of networks, especially links across countries and across sectors. Official quarters need to make themselves more amenable to civil society inputs, by improving both the institutional mechanisms and the attitudes that they bring to consultations. The mass media need to raise both the quantity and the quality of their coverage of civil society and global governance. All parties need to resist forces of political culture that discourage active, critical civil society engagement of global regulatory structures. And civil society associations need to attend more rigorously to their own accountability, especially towards subordinated social circles that have had so little say in global governance to date.

6
Transnational Corporations and Public Accountability

Mathias Koenig-Archibugi[1]

THE ROLE OF TRANSNATIONAL CORPORATIONS (TNCS) IN THE GLOBAL economy has increased considerably during the second half of the twentieth century. Their activities have grown at a much faster pace than world output, and during the 1990s the stock of foreign direct investment (FDI) has almost quadrupled, from $1.7 trillion in 1990 to $6.6 trillion in 2001.[2] UNCTAD estimates that today there are about 64,000 TNCs, with about 840,000 foreign affiliates. These affiliates account for about 54 million employees, but the economic importance of international production is even higher when non-equity relationships such as subcontracting and licensing are considered.

What TNCs do (or do not do) affects the lives of a substantial share of the world's population. This impact can take many forms: for instance, the dissemination of new technologies and management practices changes production methods and performances of domestic industries; extractive activities can change the lives of local communities; and local affiliates of TNCs can be agents of cultural change in host societies. Because of their size and capacity to transcend national boundaries, TNCs have traditionally been a reason for concern on the part of important social and political groups, notably trade unions and socialist, traditionalist and nationalist parties. The governments of recently de-colonized countries perceived TNCs as potential or actual agents of a neo-colonialist project aiming at exploiting national resources without adequate compensation and at interfering in the political process of the newly inde-

[1] I am grateful to Daniele Archibugi and David Held for their comments on previous drafts. I am responsible for any mistake. The financial support of the Rockefeller Foundation is gratefully acknowledged.

[2] UNCTAD, *World Investment Report 2002: TNCs and Export Competitiveness*, Geneva, United Nations, 2002.

pendent states. During the 1990s, the economic and political significance of TNCs has brought them once again into the spotlight of public attention. Anti-corporate activism has become a mass movement again, with campaigners forming networks at the same global level as the activities of the TNCs they target. This is a serious challenge for TNCs, since it may trigger a reversal of the trend towards a business-friendly political climate that has dominated policymaking in developed and developing countries since the early 1980s.

At the heart of this challenge is the issue of accountability. Because of their often huge economic clout and their capacity for global mobility, corporations are widely perceived as capable of evading public control and getting away with behaviour that harms employees, consumers, vulnerable communities or the environment. 'Economic globalization' is considered responsible for altering the balance of power between citizens and corporations in favour of the latter, thus reversing in part the achievements of the struggles for the democratization of national politics and societies in developed countries and for national self-determination in the developing world. 'Globalization means that it is more difficult for national governments to hold corporations accountable than in the past.'[3]

This chapter considers the issue of public accountability of TNCs in the light of the experiences of the past 30 years. The next section discusses briefly the problem of accountability of corporations in general. The second section examines the accountability gaps that are particularly severe as a result of the transnational reach of TNCs. The third section looks at existing attempts to close these gaps, including intergovernmental cooperation, business 'self-regulation' and initiatives that involve nongovernmental organizations and supranational agencies in defining standards of conduct for companies and monitoring their compliance; it will also try to assess to what extent these initiatives are able to close the accountability gaps generated by transnationalized production.

---

[3] Robert O. Keohane, 'Global Governance and Democratic Accountability', in David Held and Mathias Koenig-Archibugi (eds), *Taming Globalization: Frontiers of Governance*, Cambridge, Polity Press, 2003, pp. 130–57; 146.

CORPORATIONS: HOW ARE THEY ACCOUNTABLE TO WHOM FOR WHAT?

Most generally, 'an accountability relationship is one in which an individual, group or other entity makes demands on an agent to report on his or her activities, and has the ability to impose costs on the agent'.[4] Somewhat more specifically, accountability is frequently defined as applying to situations in which an agent 'is held to answer for performance that involves some delegation of authority to act'.[5] Directors of corporations are certainly meant to be accountable in this sense, since their authority in the organization is the result of a formal act of delegation by the shareholders. It might be less obvious why corporations should be accountable to the general public, since no delegation of authority seems to occur between them. However, the granting of charters and legal personality to collective financial entities by the state was prompted at least in part by the benefits that the separation of personal finances and business finances were expected to bring to the broader public, especially in relation to major ventures, such as the opening of new commercial trade routes, the building of railways and ships, and large industrial projects.[6] Corporations are not 'natural entities', but creatures of legislation. The idea that corporations should have a special duty of accountability to the wider public is therefore justified in light of their owners' enjoyment of limited liability.

In addition, influential strands in democratic theory hold that delegation of authority is not the only reason why one actor can legitimately demand accountability from another actor. The fact that a person or community is substantially affected by the actions of an individual or organization may, under certain circumstances, justify the establishment of a relationship of accountability between them.[7] In the words of Robert Keohane, 'internal accountability' to those

---

[4] Ibid., p. 139.

[5] Barbara S. Romzek and Melvin J. Dubnick, 'Accountability', in Jay M. Shafritz (ed.), *International Encyclopedia of Public Policy and Administration*, Boulder, Westview Press, 1998, quoted in Robert D. Behn, *Rethinking Democratic Accountability*, Washington, DC, Brookings Institution, 2001, p. 4.

[6] John Braithwaite and Peter Drahos, *Global Business Regulation*, Cambridge, Cambridge University Press, 2000, pp. 146–56.

[7] David Held, *Democracy and the Global Order*, Cambridge, Polity Press, 1995.

who delegate power to and support an agent may be insufficient and need to be complemented by mechanisms of 'external accountability' to the wider circle of persons who are affected by the agent's decisions and actions. Because of their central role in modern economies, corporations are prime targets for demands for increased public accountability. In the national context, the social groups formulating these demands have been mainly the labour movement, consumers' associations, women's movements, environmentalists, and sometimes the general public, especially after dramatic events and accidents. As a result of these various demands, in the national contexts corporations are typically involved in a complex set of accountability relationships.

Accountable to whom? – Corporations are variously accountable to their owners, creditors, employees, customers, other corporations (through business associations) and to the general public through state institutions – legislatures, bureaucracies and courts. Internal accountability, as defined by Keohane, is usually stronger than external accountability, and within companies the accountability to shareholders is stronger than accountability to other groups with institutionalized relationships to the executive directors, notably the employees.[8] However, even the strength of internal accountability should not be overestimated. Susan Strange notes that 'The multiple accountability of CEOs to shareholders, banks, employees, suppliers and distributors, not to mention strategic allies, means that like renaissance Princes, they can usually divide and rule.'[9]

How are they accountable? – Mechanisms of accountability vary, but two aspects are crucial to all accountability relationships: the flow of information to the principals and other stakeholders about the decision-makers' actions, and the capacity of stakeholders to impose

---

[8] Indeed, for many democratic theorists the main accountability deficit afflicting the large corporation is the insufficient accountability of managers towards the employees. See, for instance, Robert Dahl, *A Preface to Economic Democracy*, Berkeley and Los Angeles, University of California Press, 1985.

[9] Susan Strange, *The Retreat of the State: The Diffusion of Power in the World Economy*, Cambridge, Cambridge University Press, 1996, p. 197.

sanctions on the agents.[10] On the one hand, stakeholders must possess certain types of information (provided by the agent or third parties such as external auditors or 'watchdog' associations) to exercise accountability, notably information about formal decision-making procedures, actual decision-making processes, various outputs (including compliance with regulations, financial management, etc.), the outcomes expected by decision-makers and the actual outcomes of the activities of the organization. On the other hand, stakeholders must be able to punish decision-makers if their performance is unsatisfactory. Depending on the kind of stakeholder/principal and on the circumstances, this punishment can consist of removal from the job, reduction of powers and competences (i.e. redefinition of mandate), withdrawal/non-renewal of the licence to operate, termination of financial support or service provision, infliction of financial penalties (e.g., tort law), loss of reputation and prestige, loss of customers and market share, or criminal prosecution.

Accountable for what? – Different categories of principals may have different goals, and a principal might want the agent to pursue several goals at the same time. For instance, shareholders might want directors to increase dividends *and* refrain from 'unethical' investments, the employees might want to be given high salaries *and* pleasant working conditions, and so on. Similarly, state institutions hold companies accountable for their compliance with a diverse range of regulations. These regulations aim to protect various stakeholders: investors and creditors (accounting practices and financial probity), workers (minimum wage, trade union organization, health and safety in the workplace), consumers (competition laws, product safety, particularly regarding food and drugs) and the public at large (environmental, tax and criminal law).

TRANSNATIONAL CORPORATIONS AND ACCOUNTABILITY GAPS

Companies are accountable to the general public mainly through the governments of the countries where the companies conduct their

---

[10] James G. March and John P. Olsen, *Democratic Governance*, New York, Free Press, 1995, pp. 162–7.

activities. This is at least the 'standard' situation. It corresponds to the assumption, common to most democratic thought of the nineteenth and twentieth centuries, that the relationship between political decision-makers and the recipients of political decisions is 'symmetrical' and 'congruent'.[11] This assumption may be justified to most activities of most companies. However, it can become quite problematic in the case of TNCs. The congruence between the two sides of the accountability relationship can be put into question by the mismatch between the growing integration of world markets and the fragmented character of world politics. The globalization of economic activity breeds the potential for 'accountability gaps'[12] that would not occur, or be less severe, in a world of closed economies.

Pointing at accountability gaps does not imply that TNCs should be thought of as 'footloose' entities that are able to evade any constraint. The ability to withhold territorial access remains a crucial resource of states in dealing with TNCs and other transnational actors.[13] However, transnationalized production challenges the standard model of public accountability of corporations through governmental regulation and supervision. Broadly speaking, there are four sources of accountability gaps in the relationship between TNCs and citizenries: the collusion between government officials and the directors of TNCs; the consequences of regulatory competition; the problem of weak and collapsed states; and subversive activities by TNCs.

Collusion Between Government Officials and Transnational Corporations

Collusive behaviour can range from relatively benign forms, such as the provision of campaign money in exchange for privileged access to decision-making, to severe forms of corruption that distort

[11] Held, *Democracy and the Global Order*, op. cit., p. 224.

[12] On accountability gaps see Keohane, 'Global Governance and Democratic Accountability', op. cit., p. 142.

[13] Stephen D. Krasner, 'Power Politics, Institutions, and Transnational Relations', in Thomas Risse-Kappen (ed.), *Bringing Transnational Relations Back In: Non-State Actors, Domestic Structures and International Institutions*, Cambridge, Cambridge University Press, 1995, pp. 257–79.

substantially the political process and its outcomes. Certainly, collusion between public officials and business is not unique to the relationship between TNCs and host governments – also domestic companies engage in collusive practices. But collusion involving TNCs, especially with authoritarian governments in developing countries, may have a particularly detrimental effect on the prospects of effective mechanisms of accountability.

Several commentators are concerned that TNCs are attracted by countries in which democratic rights are curtailed, and that their presence in the country prolongs authoritarian rule.[14] While it is true that wages tend to be lower under authoritarian regimes than they are in democratic countries,[15] the evidence suggests that, on the whole, democratic political systems tend to attract more FDI inflows than their authoritarian counterparts.[16] But this certainly does not rule out that in specific situations, the collaboration between a government and a TNC makes the latter less accountable to the citizens of the host country. The risk of harmful collusion is especially strong with regard to companies that extract natural resources in developing countries.[17] In this sector more than others, TNCs may take investment decisions with little regard to the vital interests of local communities and at the same time provide the government with resources – royalties and tax revenues – that are vital for maintaining the political status quo. During the 1990s, Shell came under intense pressure to review its collaboration with the Nigerian government, in the light of severe human rights abuses linked to its use

[14] Keohane and Ooms remarked that foreign investment has a right-wing bias and that under some circumstances it may 'bolster the position of a government, strengthening its support among key elites and reducing the necessity to satisfy nonelite demands', Robert O. Keohane and Van Doorn Ooms, 'The Multinational Firm and International Regulation', *International Organization*, 29: 1 (1975), pp. 169–209; 180.

[15] Dani Rodrik, 'Democracies Pay Higher Wages', *Quarterly Journal of Economics*, 14: 3 (1999), pp. 707–38.

[16] Nathan Jensen, 'Democratic Governance and Multinational Corporations: Political Regimes and Inflows of Foreign Direct Investment', *International Organization*, 57: 3 (2003), pp. 587–616.

[17] Debora Spar, 'Foreign Investment and Human Rights', *Challenge*, 42: 1 (1999), pp. 55–80; Darryl Reed, 'Resource Extraction Industries in Developing Countries', *Journal of Business Ethics*, 39 (2002), pp. 199–206.

of Nigeria's oil resources.[18] In the 1980s, stopping foreign investment in South Africa was seen by anti-apartheid activists as an important means for pressing the government towards political reforms.[19]

Regulatory Competition

Until the 1970s, the governments of developing countries had an ambivalent attitude towards foreign investment. The concern was that, left to themselves, TNCs might exploit the resources of the host countries without giving much in return. Foreign investment was thus subject to a wide range of restrictions and requirements related to profit repatriation, technology transfer, exports, domestic participation, the local content of products and other aspects of TNC activity.[20] This has changed in the meantime and today most governments accept that it is not in their interest to exclude their countries from access to global technologies and global markets – and consequently from the TNCs that facilitate this access.[21] The prevailing view is that FDI is beneficial to developing countries,[22] and most of them have enacted regulatory changes aimed at attracting foreign capital.

[18] Human Rights Watch, *The Price of Oil: Corporate Responsibility and Human Rights Violations in Nigeria's Oil Producing Communities*, New York, Human Rights Watch, 1999, available at http://www.hrw.org/reports/1999/nigeria/index.htm (accessed 2 October 2003).

[19] John M. Kline, 'Business Codes and Conduct in a Global Political Economy', in Oliver F. Williams (ed.), *Global Codes of Conduct: An Idea Whose Time Has Come*, Notre Dame, University of Notre Dame Press, 2000, pp. 39–56.

[20] Michael Hansen, 'Environmental Regulation of Transnational Corporations: Needs and Prospects', in Peter Utting (ed.), *The Greening of Business in Developing Countries: Rhetoric, Reality and Prospects*, London and New York, Zed Books, 2002.

[21] Raymond Vernon, *In the Hurricane's Eye: The Troubled Prospects of Multinational Enterprises*, Cambridge, MA, Harvard University Press, 1998, p. 61. The range of policy responses to technological change is examined by Danicle Archibugi and Simona Iammarino, 'The Policy Implications of the Globalisation of Innovation', *Research Policy*, 28 (1999), pp. 317–36.

[22] Econometric studies suggest that FDI inflows contribute to long-term economic growth. Robert E. Lipsey, 'Inward FDI and Economic Growth in Developing Countries', *Transnational Corporations*, 9: 1 (2000), pp. 67–95; Eduardo Borensztein, Jose De Gregorio and Jong-Wha Lee, 'How Does Foreign Direct Investment Affect Economic Growth?', *Journal of International Economics*, 45 (1998), pp. 115–35. These studies also suggest that the impact of FDI on growth is marginal in countries with low levels of education, but becomes stronger as the level of schooling increases.

The ability of multinational corporations to choose in which juris-diction to locate their activities, however, affects the capacity of gov-ernments to hold them accountable for their social, environmental and fiscal performance. Internationally mobile capital is a scarce good,[23] and governments have incentives to engage in competition for investment by lowering taxation and social and environmental standards or by refraining from enforcing the standards that formally exist. Regulatory competition impairs the accountability relationship between governments and TNCs, since it induces the principal to relax its demands on the agent and to abstain from punishment for fear that the agent will move to the jurisdiction of another principal. In a sense, the TNCs' opportunities for 'exit' turn the accountabil-ity relationship upside down by making governments accountable to TNCs, or at least by increasing the bargaining power of TNCs vis-à-vis the governments.

An extreme interpretation of these developments holds that 'not much remains of the accountability of market forces to political con-straints'.[24] But this view underestimates some important resources held by governments. First, once foreign investment decisions are implemented, reversing them is often costly for companies, and gov-ernments have additional means to 'lock' them in – the extreme case being expropriation.[25] Through their power over territory, states can control investment flows.[26] Second, governments control resources – infrastructures, human capital, legal systems, natural resources, etc.

[23] From the perspective of countries, capital has strong characteristics of a common pool resource, i.e. it is rival in consumption and non-excludable. This should make 'competitive extraction' the dominant mode of appropriation. See Alkuin Kölliker, 'Competing for International Economic Commons: Towards a Collective Goods Theory of Regulatory Competition', paper presented at the ECPR Joint Sessions, Edinburgh, 28 March–2 April 2003.

[24] Strange, *The Retreat of the State*, op. cit., p. 197.

[25] Indeed, expropriation and nationalization were a common risk associated with foreign investment, especially in Latin America and in oil-exporting countries. See Vernon, *In the Hurricane's Eye*, op. cit.

[26] Geoffrey Garrett, 'The Causes of Globalization', *Comparative Political Studies*, 33: 6/7 (2000), pp. 941–91. But the importance of this factor for the bargaining power of states depends to a large extent on what is produced (e.g., mining, garments, banking): 'If production can take place in any one of a number of countries, the ability to grant entry to any one country will not be worth much'. Krasner, 'Power Politics, Institutions and Transnational Relations', op. cit., p. 275.

– that companies need for their activities and that are not easily reproduced.[27]

The available evidence seems to indicate that, on the whole, OECD countries are able to resist the downward pressure of competitive regulation.[28] But fiscal, social and environmental 'races to the bottom' are a serious risk in the developing world. The picture is mixed. For instance, sometimes TNCs bring advanced environmental processes to their foreign plants even when host countries do not mandate them.[29] But in other cases TNC choose production locations with an eye to taking advantage of lax environmental regulation and enforcement, with governments of host countries 'occasionally pointing to the feebleness of their environmental regulations as a selling point in initially attracting them'.[30] Even though a 'pollution haven' strategy may be unable to attract large amounts of inward investment, dramatic episodes such as the Bhopal catastrophe show the risk involved in lax standards and enforcement.[31] Also tax policies are affected, since governments offer subsidies and tax exemptions to TNCs for the sake of job creation and technology transfer,[32] while the mere threat of exit allows them to elicit concessions from their host governments.[33] In most cases, 'the perception of more mobile production may be more important than the actual behaviour of business'.[34]

[27] Geoffrey Garrett, *Partisan Politics in the Global Economy*, Cambridge, Cambridge University Press, 1998.

[28] In particular, international capital mobility does not seem to have pushed down capital taxation or forced governments to move to less progressive forms of taxation. Geoffrey Garrett and Deborah Mitchell, 'Globalization, Government Spending and Taxation in the OECD', *European Journal of Political Research*, 39 (2001), pp. 145–77; Duane Swank, *Global Capital, Political Institutions, and Policy Change in Developed Welfare States*, Cambridge, Cambridge University Press, 2002.

[29] Braithwaite and Drahos, *Global Business Regulation*, op. cit., pp. 267–70.

[30] Vernon, *In the Hurricane's Eye*, op. cit., p. 58.

[31] Hansen, 'Environmental Regulation of Transnational Corporations', op. cit., p. 171. In 1984 an accident at a subsidiary of the US company Union Carbide killed several thousand people in Bhopal, India.

[32] Vernon, *In the Hurricane's Eye*, op. cit., pp. 30–7.

[33] Ibid., p. 39. Moreover, through transfer pricing, companies are able to move their global profits to less demanding jurisdictions. Similarly, they can protect shareholders from liability in different countries by creating separate legal entities.

[34] David Held, Anthony McGrew, David Goldblatt and Jonathan Perraton, *Global Transformations*, Cambridge, Polity Press, 1999, p. 269.

State Weakness and Breakdown

Host governments might be unable to act effectively as agents of accountability between TNCs and citizens because of the lack of material and organizational resources for policy formulation and implementation. Often the problem is limited to the possession of inadequate administrative and technical capabilities. For instance, transnational food corporations have exploited the weaknesses of public health systems in some developing countries to engage in dangerous marketing practices of breast-milk substitutes.[35] But sometimes the problem emerges in an extreme form when countries are affected by large-scale violence and civil war. While most multinational corporations have no interest in entering or remaining in these countries, a few companies may have reason to stay and take advantage of the situation. In recent years, the case of multinational corporations trading in rough diamonds and minerals in Congo and other conflict zones has been particularly prominent.[36] Corporations might collude with one of the conflict parties and prolong the conflict as a result of their financial support. In some cases, corporations may fuel the conflict directly by providing arms to the fighting parties.[37] Under these conditions, any normal relationship of accountability breaks down.

Political Subversion

Finally, TNCs may try to avoid public accountability by promoting the overthrow of the government that is supposed to hold them

[35] S. Prakash Sethi, *Multinational Corporations and the Impact of Public Advocacy on Corporate Strategy: Nestle and the Infant Formula Controversy*, Boston, Dordrecht and London, Kluwer Academic Publishers, 1994; Judith Richter, *Holding Corporations Accountable: Corporate Conduct, International Codes, and Citizen Action*, London and New York, Zed Books, 2001.

[36] Panel of Experts on the Illegal Exploitation of Natural Resources and Other Forms of Wealth in the Democratic Republic of the Congo, *Report*, Transmitted by the UN Secretary-General to the UN Security Council on 12 April 2001, available at: http://www.un.org/News/dh/latest/drcongo.htm (accessed 2 October 2003).

[37] In addition, TNCs of mercenaries participate in combat operations. See Christopher Cooker, 'Outsourcing War', in Daphné Josselin and William Wallace (eds), *Non-State Actors in World Politics*, Basingstoke, Palgrave, 2001, pp. 189–202.

accountable. Such actions are comparatively rare, but episodes such as the involvement of the United Fruit Company in the Guatemalan coup d'état of 1954 and ITT's machinations against Salvador Allende's government in Chile contributed to the widespread perception of TNCs as a potential threat to national sovereignty and democracy.[38] Like the other sources of potential accountability gaps, this risk is more serious in developing countries than in developed countries.

GLOBALIZED ACCOUNTABILITY MECHANISMS

Since the activities of TNCs span several jurisdictions, they have more opportunities to evade demands for accountability or to engage in collusive behaviour with unaccountable governments than other organizations. This is made easier by their sheer economic size. In principle, governments are able to impose substantial restrictions on the mobility of companies, but this could involve considerable economic and social costs and ultimately not bring an improvement in the citizen's ability to hold decision-makers accountable. The accountability gaps brought about by TNCs are all the more serious as trade unions, which in industrialized countries have traditionally been the main countervailing power to business interests, find it difficult to cooperate effectively with one another at the transnational level.[39]

This section presents an overview of the attempts, initiated by governments, international organizations, nongovernmental organizations (NGOs), advocacy groups and business groups themselves, to establish mechanisms of accountability that would operate at the same global scale as the activities of TNCs. A crucial distinction is that between mandatory and voluntary mechanisms. A fully mandatory mechanism operates in the same way as national legislation: it sets precise rules of conduct, creates obligation and creates

---

[38] Some of these episodes are narrated by Daniel Litvin, *Empires of Profit: Commerce, Conquest and Corporate Responsibility*, New York and London, Texere, 2003.

[39] Daphné Josselin, 'Back to the Front Line? Trade Unions in a Global Age', in Josselin and Wallace, *Non-State Actors in World Politics*, op. cit., pp. 169–86.

mechanisms for adjudication and enforcement.[40] Some forms of international regulation might consist of 'softer' rather than 'hard' law, but they could still be considered mandatory. By adhering to voluntary mechanisms of accountability, on the other hand, companies commit themselves to disclose their activities and thus make it easier for consumers, investors and other stakeholders to assess their social and environmental performance and make their choices accordingly. In voluntary mechanisms, sanctions are essentially informal and decentralized. Also voluntary mechanisms are a matter of degree: independent institutions that formulate the rules that may be adopted by companies, monitor their compliance and report violations of commitments to the public all reduce the 'voluntarism' of standard-setting and certification. The distinction between mandatory and voluntary is best thought of not as a dichotomy, but as the ends of a continuum displaying decreasing degrees of corporate discretion.

The trend of transnational accountability mechanisms has to some extent mirrored the changes in national regulatory environments. In most countries, heavy regulation until the 1970s has been supplanted by deregulatory policies during the 1980s. Similarly, the emphasis of the international debate in the 1970s was mainly on the creation of mandatory frameworks for TNC regulation, whereas the debates of the 1980s and 1990s were mostly about corporate self-regulation. More recently, co-regulation through multi-stakeholder partnerships has received much attention.

Intergovernmental Cooperation

Unlike trade and finance, multinational corporations and foreign investment are not governed by a coherent international regime.[41] This absence is due mainly to a fundamental disagreement about the prime objective of such a regime: should it protect foreign investment from discriminatory policies of governments, or should it curb the power of multinational corporations for the sake of national

[40] On the concepts of precision, obligation and adjudication, see Judith L. Goldstein, Miles Kahler, Robert O. Keohane and Anne-Marie Slaughter (eds), *Legalization and World Politics*, Cambridge, MA, and London, MIT Press, 2001.

[41] Held et al., *Global Transformations*, op. cit., p. 257. See also Keohane and Ooms, 'The Multinational Firm', op. cit.

economic sovereignty? This question prevented the emergence of a comprehensive global regulatory framework for over 30 years.[42] It is notable that this outcome was not intended by the architects of the international economic order after the Second World War. The Havana Charter granted to the International Trade Organization some competences over the policies of governments towards TNCs as well as the conduct of TNCs themselves. What is remarkable is that the provisions concerning host-nation policies were weaker than those regulating restrictive business practices on part of TNCs. This asymmetry was due to concerns about restrictive practices, and specifically about international cartels, that stemmed from the inter-war experience. The opposition of business actors to these provisions was a contributing factor in the failed ratification of the charter.[43]

The debate about international regulation of TNCs resurged in the late 1960s. Developing countries requested the adoption of an international code of conduct for TNCs, whereas most developed countries were either opposed or indifferent. The aims of the developing country governments were economic (the increase of their bargaining power vis-à-vis foreign investors) as well as political (the prevention of anti-governmental activities by TNCs). A few international arrangements emerged from these debates: the United Nations set up a Centre on Transnational Corporations (UNCTC), which drafted a code of conduct for TNCs in 1978 and revised it in later years (the code was never adopted); the OECD issued a set of Guidelines for Multinational Enterprises in 1976; the International Labour Organization (ILO) issued the Tripartite Declaration of Principles Concerning Multinational Enterprises and Social Policy in 1977; UNCTAD formulated a code on restrictive business practices and a code on technology transfer, which were adopted by the UN General Assembly in 1980. None of these initiatives was of much consequence to the actual regulation of TNCs.

The efforts of developing countries to establish international rules for TNCs subsided in the 1980s, as a result of their changed attitude towards foreign investment. Almost all of them altered their public

---

[42] Paz Estrella Tolentino, 'Transnational Rules for Transnational Corporations: What Next?', in Jonathan Michie and John Grieve Smith (eds), *Global Instability: The Political Economy of World Economic Governance*, London, Routledge, 1999, pp. 171–97.

[43] Edward M. Graham, 'Should there be Multilateral Rules on Foreign Direct Investment?', in John H. Dunning (ed.), *Governments, Globalization, and International Business*, Oxford, Oxford University Press, 1997, pp. 481–505; 484.

policies so as to attract rather than control foreign investment.[44] The great majority of regulatory reforms aimed at making the domestic investment climate more favourable to inward FDI.[45] Similarly, negotiations on international arrangements regarding investment continued throughout the 1990s, but these aimed at providing a framework for the liberalization of investment rules and mechanisms for investor protection rather than putting constraints on TNCs. This was evident in the Multilateral Agreement on Investment (MAI) negotiated at the OECD and in the discussions within the GATT/WTO context.[46] While several global intergovernmental agreements regulate specific aspects of foreign investment,[47] regional arrangements (NAFTA, EU) and bilateral treaties are still the main source of rules and standards on international investment. Governments that accede to these multilateral and bilateral agreements limit their own freedom of action with regard to foreign investors and thus may reduce their capacity to hold corporations accountable in specific circumstances.

International regulation of TNCs is less developed than norms about foreign investor protection and property rights. Environmental NGOs tried to include strong norms about TNC

[44] Vernon, *In the Hurricane's Eye*, op. cit., p. 31.

[45] See the annual overviews in the World Investment Reports issued by UNCTAD.

[46] Sol Picciotto and Ruth Mayne (eds), *Regulating International Business: Beyond Liberalization*, Basingstoke, Macmillan, 1999. US business groups favoured negotiations within the OECD instead of the WTO as a way to sidestep opposition by developing countries, who would be presented with a *fait accompli* and invited to accept the rules. See Andrew Walter, 'Unraveling the Faustian Bargain: Non-State Actors and the Multilateral Agreement of Investment', in Josselin and Wallace, *Non-State Actors in World Politics*, op. cit., pp. 150; 159.

[47] Tolentino, 'Transnational Rules', op. cit., lists 27 intergovernmental instruments concerning TNCs adopted between 1948 and 1998. The UN estimates that at least 35 international regulatory instruments, such as the Basle Convention on hazardous waste to the Montreal Protocol on ozone-depleting substances, constrain the activities of TNCs; but the effectiveness of international environmental law vis-à-vis TNCs is limited by its fragmented character and by the failure of many host countries to ratify the relevant agreements. Hansen, 'Environmental Regulation of Transnational Corporations', op. cit., pp. 172 and 183, n. 12. With regard to labour and other human rights, the (limited) role of the UN agencies in holding corporations accountable is reviewed by David P. Forsythe, *The Political Economy of Human Rights: Transnational Corporations*, Human Rights Working Papers, 2001, available at http://www.du.edu/humanrights/workingpapers/index.html.

responsibilities for sustainable development in the final documents of the 1992 UN Conference on Environment and Development in Rio de Janeiro, but their efforts were largely unsuccessful, not least because of the major role of the Business Council for Sustainable Development in shaping the chapter on business in Agenda 21.[48] Business groups succeeded in presenting self-regulation as an effective alternative to 'command-and-control' approaches. After Rio, some NGOs and transnational advocacy networks continued to consider mandatory regulation as the only effective way to hold companies accountable for their environmental performance, but an increasing number of NGOs were willing to engage with companies and help shift the self-regulatory trend towards forms of 'multistakeholder' co-regulation.[49]

Intergovernmental regulation of TNCs was hindered by conflicts of interest between states. The history of the attempts at creating an intergovernmental regulatory framework for TNCs essentially confirms a hypothesis formulated by Keohane and Ooms almost 30 years ago: 'We can only expect extensive international regulation on a global scale where the principal issues pit the state against the enterprise, rather than state against state with the enterprise only as a willing or unwilling intermediary'.[50]

Voluntary Mechanisms

In the past few years, an increasing number of TNCs decided to participate in voluntary institutions designed to enhance their public accountability. These decisions resulted from a number of considerations, whose weight depended on the circumstances. The most common reasons for action were: the concern that the business might lose customers and investors as a consequence of negative publicity; the hope to gain new customers and investors by

[48] Hansen, 'Environmental Regulation of Transnational Corporations', op. cit., pp. 164–6. Ian H. Rowlands discusses under which conditions TNCs are particularly influential in his 'Transnational Corporations and Global Environmental Politics', in Josselin and Wallace (eds), *Non-State Actors in World Politics*, op. cit., pp. 133–49.

[49] Simon Heap, *NGOs Engaging with Business: A World of Difference and a Difference to the World*, Oxford, INTRAC, 2000; Peter Newell, 'Campaigning for Corporate Change: Global Citizen Action on the Environment', in Michael Edwards and John Gaventa (eds), *Global Citizen Action*, London, Earthscan, 2001, pp. 189–201.

[50] Keohane and Ooms, 'The Multinational Firm', op. cit., p. 184.

projecting an image of corporate responsibility; the prevention of court litigation; the prevention of state regulation; and the improvement of the morale and loyalty of employees. In general, corporations whose reputation is at risk because of the activities of consumer and advocacy groups may prefer to submit to institutionalized mechanisms of accountability rather than to be exposed to unpredictable and uncontrollable punishment in the marketplace. Moreover, an important incentive is the prevention of more stringent national and international regulation, especially in the wake of major disasters such as the Chernobyl accident in 1986 and Exxon Valdez oil spill in 1989.[51]

Voluntary mechanisms are mostly based on communicating to interested parties that the firm complies with certain procedural or substantive standards of conduct. This involves two steps.[52] In the first step, the standards must be formulated and made public. There are essentially three types of standards:[53] 1) process standards, which specify procedural rules such as the establishment of management systems and platforms for stakeholder consultation; 2) performance standards, which specify what companies should do or not do; and 3) certification standards, which define how compliance with process and performance standards should be monitored and certified. The second step consists in certifying that a company complies with the standards. Certification can involve several activities: internal audits, annual reports of social and environmental performance, third-party inspections and auditing, and verification (when an independent authority re-examines a prior monitoring activity).

Standards can be set internally by each company, collectively by the corporations of a certain industry or economic sector, or by external third-party entities. Similarly, compliance can be certified through a purely internal audit process (self-certification), by industry associations, or by external monitoring and certification agents. Different combinations of these functions are possible: for instance,

[51] Mathias Koenig-Archibugi, 'Mapping Global Governance', in David Held and Anthony McGrew (eds), *Governing Globalization: Power, Authority and Global Governance*, Cambridge, Polity Press, 2002, pp. 46–69; 62.

[52] Gary Gereffi, Ronie Garcia-Johnson and Erika Sasser, 'The NGO-Industrial Complex', *Foreign Policy*, 125 (2001).

[53] See Malcolm McIntosh, Ruth Thomas, Deborah Leipziger and Gill Coleman, *Living Corporate Citizenship*, Harlow, FT Prentice Hall, 2003. These authors add foundation standards to this list.

standards may be set by an individual company but certification might be conducted by a third party.[54]

Internal standards and certification. – Many TNCs have adopted company codes of conduct and/or publish reports on their social and environmental performance in addition to their financial reporting.[55] In the case of exclusively internal standard-setting and certification, companies decide the norms to be incorporated in their codes of conduct, and compliance with those rules is monitored through internal procedures. Essentially, companies ask interested parties to trust the adequacy and accuracy of these internal rule-making and monitoring procedures. From the point of view of public accountability, purely internal certification raises two problems. The first problem is that unilateral codes frequently ignore key concerns of stakeholders;[56] moreover, even those directly affected (such as workers) often do not know how to use the code to express complaints.[57] The second problem is that self-certification is usually not sufficient to provide reliable information about compliance when, on balance, deception or lax enforcement would be advantageous to the firm.[58] Considering also that many companies – especially smaller companies[59] – are not interested in adopting codes of conduct,

[54] Ronie Garcia-Johnson, 'Multinational Corporations and Certification Institutions: Moving First to Shape a Green Global Production Context', paper for presentation at the International Studies Association Convention, 20–4 February 2001, p. 12.

[55] OECD, *Codes of Corporate Conduct – An Expanded Review of Their Contents*, Paris, OECD, 2000; Ans Kolk, Rob van Tulder and Carlijn Welters, 'International Codes of Conduct and Corporate Social Responsibility: Can Transnational Corporations Regulate Themselves?', *Transnational Corporations*, 8: 1 (1999), pp. 143–80; Rhys Jenkins, Ruth Pearson and Jill Seyfang (eds), *Corporate Responsibility and Labour Rights: Codes of Conduct in the Global Economy*, London, Earthscan, 2002; Rhys Jenkins, 'Corporate Codes of Conduct: Self-Regulation in a Global Economy', in UNRISD (ed.), *Voluntary Approaches to Corporate Responsibility*, Geneva, UN Non-Governmental Liaison Service, 2002, pp. 1–59.

[56] Jenkins, 'Corporate Codes of Conduct', op. cit., p. 38; Peter Utting, 'Regulating Business via Multistakeholder Initiatives: a Preliminary Assessment', in UNRISD, *Voluntary Approaches to Corporate Responsibility*, op. cit., pp. 61–130; 70.

[57] Ibid., p. 71.

[58] Very few company codes include provisions for independent monitoring. See OECD, *Codes of Corporate Conduct*, op. cit., p. 35, and Kolk et al., 'International Codes of Conduct', op. cit., p. 168.

[59] Jenkins, 'Corporate Codes of Conduct', op. cit., p. 20.

company codes of conduct have serious deficiencies as mechanisms of accountability.

Sectoral standards and certification. – In some cases, projecting an image of high standards and accountability can be a source of competitive advantage for corporations. Most of the time, however, standards are mainly a source of costs for the companies that actually implement them, and thus compliant companies are interested in levelling the playing field by extending standards to other companies in the same industry. Moreover, what one company does may affect the reputation of other companies in the same industry.[60] High-standard companies are thus likely to promote the creation and enforcement of sector-wide codes of conduct. But such codes also can be useful to other companies in the sector because they can reduce uncertainty about which rules and regulations should be followed and increase the information about what other companies in the sector are doing.

Sectoral codes of conduct are common especially in sectors where the risk of damaging the collective reputation of the whole industry is particularly high. This can be a consequence of the inherent risks associated with the industry's operations, as in the case of the World Association of Nuclear Operators, the Responsible Care programme of the chemical industry, and the Guidelines for Good Manufacturing Practice of the pharmaceutical industry;[61] or it can be a consequence of the vulnerability to negative reactions by consumers, which persuaded industry groups such as the World Federation of Sporting Goods Industry and the British Toy and Hobby Association to develop codes of conduct for their associated companies. Similarly, the diamond industry has reacted to campaigns about 'blood diamonds' from conflict zones by creating a World Diamond Council that developed a code of conduct for its members. Also the International Federation of Organic Agriculture Movements (IFOAM) exercises a form of collective self-regulation.

From the point of view of public accountability, sectoral codes are an improvement on company codes, but are not without their

---

[60] Garcia-Johnson, 'Multinational Corporations', op. cit., p. 8.

[61] Virginia Haufler, *A Public Role for the Public Sector: Industry Self-Regulation in a Global Economy*, Washington, DC, Carnegie Endowment for International Peace, 2001; Karsten Ronit and Volker Schneider, 'Global Governance through Private Organizations', *Governance*, 12 (1999), pp. 243–66.

problems. Hansen has pointed at the crucial problem of inclusiveness: 'Standards and guidelines such as the ICC Business Charter for Sustainable Development or the environmental management standards issued by the ISO are, for all practical purposes, initiated, drafted and adopted by OECD-based companies for OECD-based companies. LDCs [less developed countries], consumer groups and environmental NGOs have little influence on these activities.'[62] Another problem is that 'industry associations are reluctant to punish noncomplying members or make public their violations'.[63] A systematic evaluation of the Responsible Care initiative suggests that any programme without third-party monitoring and sanctions for non-compliance is likely to be ineffective.[64] Sectoral codes are not really able to assuage concerns about the performance of TNCs, pointing to the inherent limitations of mechanisms of accountability that are designed and managed by business actors themselves.

External standards and certification. – Collaborating with other companies in the same sector solves some of the credibility problems of unilateral codes and reporting, since sectoral associations can exercise a degree of surveillance to prevent damages to the collective reputation of the industry. But neither the formulation nor the monitoring of sectoral codes is truly independent of company interests, creating doubts as to whether the accountability gap has really been closed. In order to improve the public acceptance of standards and the credibility of monitoring, companies are increasingly willing to collaborate with other actors, notably with NGOs and in some cases with intergovernmental organizations (IGOs) and government agencies. In many areas, self-regulation is giving way to co-regulation, as NGOs, IGOs and government agencies are willing to take a role in the promotion and management of voluntary accountability schemes. It has been often the case that NGOs decided to support voluntary schemes after realizing that the prospects of mandatory social and environmental regulation at the international level were

---

[62] Hansen, 'Environmental Regulations of Transnational Corporations', op. cit., p. 177.

[63] Haufler, *A Public Role for the Public Sector*, op. cit., p. 33.

[64] Andrew King and Michael Lenox, 'Industry Self-Regulation without Sanctions: The Chemical Industry's Responsible Care Program', *Academy of Management Journal*, 43: 4 (2000), pp. 698–716.

poor. 'As NGOs experienced repeated defeats in international arenas, they put more energy and resources into developing non-governmental programs.'[65] Many NGOs consider co-regulation a second best solution.

So-called 'multi-stakeholder' initiatives are often seen as an effective way to address the accountability gap of TNCs.[66] Some proponents hail them as 'third way' between government regulation and corporate self-regulation.[67] Some multi-stakeholder initiatives are limited to the standard-setting phase, while others include monitoring, certification and verification. A prominent example of the former type is the Global Reporting Initiative (GRI). The GRI, a collaborating centre of the UN Environment Programme, involves companies, corporations, NGOs, accountancy organizations, business associations and research institutes and aims to increase the credibility, consistency and comparability of corporate reporting on social and environmental issues. GRI creates process standards (Sustainability Reporting Guidelines) and keeps a record of the companies that have adopted them, but is not involved in monitoring or verifying compliance. The multi-stakeholder organization Social Accountability International (SAI) focuses on working conditions and performs a broader range of functions: it develops and updates the SA8000 performance standard based on ILO conventions, it trains and accredits independent auditors, it verifies public reports, and it publicizes a list of SA8000 certified facilities. The Fair Labor Association involves leading US apparel companies, universities and NGOs and its tasks include the development of an industry code of conduct, the accreditation of independent monitors, the facilitation of remediation in cases of non-compliance and the publication of instances of non-compliance and remediation.[68] Other initiatives in which civil society organizations participate actively in the design and implementation of codes and standards are the Forest Stewardship Council, the Marine Stewardship Council, the Ethical Trading

[65] Tim Bartley, 'Certifying Forests and Factories: States, Social Movements, and the Rise of Private Regulation in the Apparel and Forest Products Fields', *Politics and Society*, forthcoming.

[66] See also the chapters by Thorsten Benner, Wolfgang Reinicke and Jan Martin Witte and by Thomas Risse in this volume.

[67] Utting, 'Regulating Business', op. cit., p. 66.

[68] Kimberly Ann Elliott and Richard B. Freeman, *Can Labor Standards Improve Under Globalization?*, Washington, DC, Institute for International Economics, 2003.

Initiative and the Global Alliance for Workers and Communities. UN agencies participate in a number of them. In those initiatives, especially when they are initiated by NGOs, civil society organizations function as 'accountability entrepreneurs', bent on exploring new ways to improve the social and environmental performance and public accountability of business in light of the inadequacy of state action.

The Global Compact proposed by UN Secretary-General Kofi Annan is a prominent multi-stakeholder initiative that gained much attention since it was launched in 2000.[69] It cannot be described as an accountability mechanism, however, as its aim is to generate 'shared understandings' about how companies can help promoting UN principles within corporate domains. The architect of the Global Compact, John Gerard Ruggie, describes it as a 'social learning network'.[70] It does not contemplate the possibility of sanctions for companies or verification of their statements.[71] As the reputational risk associated with unfulfilled commitments within the Global Compact framework increases, however, the initiative might evolve into a multi-stakeholder accountability system.

External standard-setting and certification has clear advantages over unilateral or sectoral measures in terms of improving the public accountability of companies. It limits the discretion of companies with regard to what they can and cannot do and makes it likelier that a broader range of interests and concerns are taken into account in the definition of standards. Furthermore, external certification

[69] John Gerard Ruggie, 'Taking Embedded Liberalism Global: The Corporate Connection', in David Held and Mathias Koenig-Archibugi (eds), *Taming Globalization: Frontiers of Governance*, Cambridge, Polity Press, 2003; McIntosh et al., *Living Corporate Citizenship*, op. cit., pp. 125–217. The Global Compact is strongly criticized by Kenny Bruno and Joshua Karliner, *Earthsummit.biz: The Corporate Takeover of Sustainable Development*, Oakland, CA, Food First Books, 2002.

[70] Ruggie, 'Taking Embedded Liberalism Global', op. cit., p. 113. On the possibility of persuasion and learning in international affairs see the article by Thomas Risse in this issue.

[71] The then Secretary-General of the International Chamber of Commerce, Maria Livianos Cattaui, stated that 'Business would look askance at any suggestion involving external assessment of corporate performance, whether by special interest groups or by U.N. agencies', 'Yes to Annan's "Global Compact" If It Isn't a License to Meddle', *International Herald Tribune*, 26 July 2000, quoted by Bruno and Karliner, *Earthsummit.biz*, op. cit., p. 53.

provides information about compliance that can be substantially more credible and reliable than self-certification, especially if it involves key stakeholder groups. However, the capacity of multi-stakeholder initiatives to ensure accountability has limits. First, independent auditing may be performed in an inadequate way.[72] Second, the very pluralisms of many multi-stakeholder initiatives can lead to damaging conflicts between different intermediaries in accountability relationships, for instance between NGOs and trade unions. Third, multi-stakeholder initiatives frequently have a narrow sectoral focus and have not expanded (yet) into domains where they would be particularly required.[73] Fourth, many companies choose not to participate in partnerships, sometimes reaping free-rider benefits from the initiatives.[74] This problem is exacerbated by the fact that the participating companies may not be those for which regulation would be most necessary,[75] and that 'lower profile competitor firms may largely avoid the cost of both compliance and public criticism'.[76] The non-universal participation in voluntary schemes is their most serious shortcoming together with a fifth problem: the lack of enforcement mechanisms other than negative publicity for non-compliant companies. This problem, of course, is common to all voluntary approaches to corporate responsibility.[77] Negative publicity may work as an instrument of accountability,[78] but it suffers from the

[72] Dara O'Rourke, 'Monitoring the Monitors: A Critique of Corporate Third-Party Labour Monitoring', in Jenkins, Pearson and Seyfang, *Corporate Responsibility and Labour Rights*, op. cit.

[73] Utting, 'Regulating Business', op. cit., p. 82.

[74] Ruth Mayne, 'Regulating TNCs: The Role of Voluntary and Governmental Approaches', in Picciotto and Mayne, *Regulating International Business*, op. cit., p. 247; Ronnie D. Lipschutz and Cathleen Fogel, '"Regulation for the Rest of Us?" Global Civil Society and the Privatization of Transnational Regulation', in Rodney Bruce Hall and Thomas J. Biersteker (eds), *The Emergence of Private Authority in Global Governance*, Cambridge, Cambridge University Press, 2002; Utting, 'Regulating Business', op. cit., p. 80.

[75] Hansen, 'Environmental Regulation of Transnational Corporations', op. cit., p. 177; interview, Anti-Slavery International.

[76] Kline, 'Business Codes and Conduct', op. cit., p. 42.

[77] It should be noted, however, that US courts are examining cases in which companies are accused by consumers of misrepresenting working conditions in their supply chains in promotional material.

[78] Especially since the internet has intensified what Debora Spar calls the 'spotlight' phenomenon. Spar, 'Foreign Investment and Human Rights', op. cit.

fact that the people who are able to punish companies (e.g. consumers in rich countries) are frequently not the same people whose interests the codes are supposed to protect (e.g. workers and communities in developing countries). This absence of congruence in the accountability relationship[79] may lead to the underprovision of sanctions or to the use of sanctions that may be counterproductive (e.g. consumer boycotts). In addition, even if a substantial proportion of consumers and investors were willing to hold companies accountable for their behaviour abroad, they face serious collective action problems when it comes to applying sanctions.

If sanctioning is a problem for voluntary accountability mechanisms, it would be wrong to assume that sanctions are all that matter in inducing companies to improve their social and environmental performance. Research in global standard-setting has stressed the importance of 'webs of dialogue' in ensuring compliance with existing standards as well as promoting their 'continuous improvement'.[80] 'Globalized rules and principles can be of consequence even if utterly detached from enforcement mechanisms.'[81] To institutionalize such a web of policy dialogue and to promote the 'global public domain' is clearly the intention of the architects of the Global Compact. However, in these cases the progress and 'ratcheting-up' of business self-regulation does not necessarily occur as a result of the operation of accountability mechanisms.

CONCLUSION

The globalization of production exacerbates accountability gaps in the relationship between citizens and corporations. Some of these gaps stem from the difficulties that governments have in holding TNCs accountable under conditions of sustained capital mobility and opportunities for jurisdictional 'exit'. Other gaps stem from the difficulties that citizens have in holding their government accountable when it colludes with, and receives support from, economically robust corporations – and TNCs tend to be robust in comparison to

[79] Held, *Democracy and the Global Order*, op. cit.

[80] Braithwaite and Drahos, *Global Business Regulation*, op. cit., p. 615. On the role of persuasion and learning in transnational relations see the article by Thomas Risse in this issue.

[81] Ibid., p. 10.

many host countries. Finally, sometimes governments are too weak to function as effective links in the accountability chain between citizens and companies. All these accountability gaps are particularly worrying in developing countries.

On the whole, the problem might not be as severe as asserted by some anti-corporate activists. Most governments still possess impressive resources that can be used in their interactions with corporations, most of all their control over access to territory. Furthermore, the trend towards the democratization of national political systems enhances the influence of ordinary citizens on social and economic policies, including those affecting the operations of TNCs. Notwithstanding these countervailing trends, the power of large corporations is rightly perceived as a reason for concern by many citizens and political groups in the developing and the developed world. On balance, FDI may be beneficial to home and host countries, but the risk of socially and environmentally irresponsible behaviour by companies (especially in extractive industries) warrants concerted efforts to close the gaps in public accountability.

Currently, voluntary mechanisms for corporate accountability are in greater favour than mandatory mechanisms, especially among business representatives (not surprisingly) but also among many representatives of civil society, who see multi-stakeholder initiatives and certification institutions as a promising way to steer business behaviour towards greater social and environmental responsibility. However, 'certification remains a blunt and imperfect tool for augmenting the accountability of global firms'.[82] Several NGOs turned to these institutions after experiencing disappointment with intergovernmental forums. It may well be possible that dissatisfaction with voluntary initiatives will boost demands for a binding international legal framework that is agreed on and enforced by states. A renewed emphasis on mandatory mechanisms is evident in the current dispute about the norms on TNC responsibilities that have been adopted by a UN panel of independent experts in August 2003.[83]

[82] Gereffi et al., 'The NGO-Industrial Complex', op. cit.

[83] *Norms on the Responsibilities of Transnational Corporations and Other Business Enterprises with Regard to Human Rights*, UN Doc. E/CN.4/Sub.2/2003/12/Rev.2 (2003), approved by the UN Sub-Commission on the Promotion and Protection of Human Rights on 13 August 2003, available at http://www1.umn.edu/humanrts/links/norms-Aug2003.html (accessed 2 October 2 2003).

These norms bring together a range of obligations drawn from existing international human rights, labour and environmental conventions, and are widely regarded as a first step towards binding regulation and monitoring of TNC activities by UN bodies, backed by national enforcement. Leading human rights NGOs have celebrated the norms, whereas the main global business organizations – notably the International Chamber of Commerce and the International Organization of Employers – have condemned them for embodying a 'legalistic' approach to corporate responsibility. The norms will be debated by government representatives in the UN Commission on Human Rights in March 2004, and a fierce battle between business associations and NGOs can be expected.

This and other ongoing controversies suggest that, ultimately, the establishment of effective mechanisms for holding TNCs accountable may depend on the success of large-scale reforms of international institutions and the redefinition of their mandate. 'Robust' accountability mechanisms require state action, but this action is likely to remain problematic if international governance is not democratized. Where executive multilateralism has failed, societally-backed multilateralism may succeed.[84]

---

[84] See the chapters by Michael Zürn and David Held in this volume.

7
Global Governance and Legitimacy Problems

Michael Zürn

THERE ARE TWO SIDES TO THE CONCEPT OF 'LEGITIMACY'. FROM A normative perspective it refers to the validity of political decisions and political orders and their claim to legitimacy. From a descriptive perspective, in contrast, the focus is on the societal acceptance of political decisions and political orders as well as the belief of the subjects of rule in legitimacy. In this contribution I will argue, on the basis of this distinction, that the removal of numerous decisions from the circuit of national and democratic responsibility gives rise to normative problems, which in turn lead to growing acceptancy problems and resistance to global governance.

In *normative terms*, there is broad agreement that currently the functioning of international institutions such as the WTO or the UN does not meet democratic standards. Acknowledged democratic deficits include the lack of identifiable decision-makers who are directly accountable for wrong decisions made at the international level, as well as the inscrutability of international decision-making processes and thus the advantage the executive decision-makers have over others in terms of information. Furthermore, particularly the prime actors in international politics, such as multinational business and the superpowers, are at best only accountable to a fraction of the people affected by their activities. Moreover, most deficits cannot easily be remedied, since democratic majority decisions depend – *in descriptive terms* – at least partially on a political community built on trust and solidarity. The absence so far of a fully developed transnational political community is incongruous with the existence of transnational social spaces, and poses a congruency problem that cannot easily be overcome. The majority of analyses of international institutions in terms of their legitimacy problems have focused on these questions.[1]

---

[1] See, e.g., R. A. Dahl, 'A Democratic Dilemma: System Effectiveness versus Citizen Participation', *Political Science Quarterly*, 109: 1 (1994), pp. 23–34; D. Held, *Democracy*

From the descriptive perspective – that is, with regard to societal acceptance – the democratic deficit of international institutions was for a long time regarded as a purely academic problem. This has changed over the past few years. There have been massive protests, sometimes violent, at major meetings of international institutions, for instance in Seattle and Genoa, but also at EU summit talks, as in Nice or Gothenburg. Furthermore, there has been an increase in right-wing populist tirades against the EU and other international institutions. Objections by national parliaments, in particular by the US, to international agreements are also on the increase.

The aim of this chapter is to demonstrate that the normative legitimacy deficits of international institutions are in fact increasingly generating problems with respect to societal acceptance. I shall do this by taking up and substantiating in four steps Lipset's hypothesis that in modern societies, empirical belief in the legitimacy of an institution closely depends on the normative validity of a political order.[2] The first step comprises an outline of the institutional dynamic of the international political order since the Second World War. The argument states that this order has been so successful and dynamic that it enabled globalization and thus undermined its own foundations. In a second step I shall discuss the new quality of international institutions that have emerged in this context over the past two decades, giving rise to the term *global governance*. It will be argued that the rising need for enlarged and deepened international cooperation in the age of globalization led to the establishment of new international institutions with specific features. As a result the intrusiveness of those new international institutions into national societies has increased dramatically. The third step will then be to offer an explanation as to how and why the quality of these new international institutions is leading to problems of societal acceptance. I will especially point out that the decision-making mode of 'executive multi-

and the Global Order. From the Modern State to Cosmopolitan Democracy, Cambridge, Polity Press, 1995; D. Archibugi, D. Held and M. Koehler (eds), *Re-imaging Political Community. Studies in Cosmopolitan Democracy*, Cambridge, Polity Press, 1998; F. W. Scharpf, *Governing in Europe*, Oxford, Oxford University Press, 1999; M. Zürn, 'Democratic Governance Beyond the Nation-State. The EU and Other International Institutions', *European Journal of International Relations*, 6: 2 (2000), pp. 183–221.

[2] S. M. Lipset, *Political Man. The Social Bases of Politics*, London, Melbourne and Toronto, Heinemann, 1960, p. 77.

lateralism' is not any more able to provide legitimacy for the new, more intrusive international institutions. The need for new forms of legitimation and the resistance against global governance dominated by executive multilateralism is described as an expression of *reflexive denationalization*. Fourthly, and lastly, I shall reflect on how such an explanation can be tested empirically in further research.

The hypothesis that the normative deficits of international institutions inhibit their social acceptability brings us to the conclusion that if we are to continue to enjoy the benefits of multilateralism – the fundamental principle of the vast majority of international institutions since 1945 – it must have the backing of transnational society and the respective national societies. Although multilateralism – in functional terms – seems to be more necessary than ever in a globalized or denationalized world, it currently appears to be in a legitimacy crisis. Multilateralism must therefore be reshaped to meet the challenges of an increasingly denationalized world. Without radical reform, conventional multilateralism will fail to fulfil the growing societal demands for legitimacy.

THE VIRTUES AND INSTITUTIONAL DYNAMICS OF EXECUTIVE MULTILATERALISM

States were never able to achieve all their political goals without taking the activities of other states into account. After all, states only actually became states by being acknowledged as such by other states, and the territorial integrity of a state was unquestionably influenced by the expansionary plans of neighbouring states. In this sense, the *interdependence of states* is a constitutive characteristic of the modern state system.

With the spread of industrialization in the nineteenth century, this interdependence extended into the economic, and thus societal, sphere. For a long time, the international system of states was unable to cope with the interdependence of societies and the increase of transborder externalities. The crises to which European states were particularly susceptible from the 1870s until the mid-twentieth century were always triggered, or at least exacerbated, by external forces. Economic historians have convincingly demonstrated, for example, that the world economic crisis of 1929 was not a direct consequence of the so-called Black Friday, but was in fact brought about by the reaction of the major trading nations to the sudden fall in stock-market prices. All the economically important states reacted by increasing their customs tariffs and devaluing their currencies so as to protect their own individual economies from the crisis. As a result, world trade broke down completely, paving the way for the Great Depression.[3]

It is only since the end of the Second World War, however, that the western world has been able to turn economic interdependence to their advantage. This success can be attributed to the international institutions established after the Second World War under the leadership of the US, and of which the economic institutions were of particular significance.[4] Notably, the international trade regime – GATT – and the regimes for regulating currency and financial affairs created an institutional framework without which the worldwide postwar economic boom would not have been possible. The principle behind these international institutions was summed up in the term *embedded liberalism*.[5] This term describes a fundamental orientation towards free trade and open borders while at the same time resting firmly embedded within the context of national political systems which are able to absorb the shocks and irregularities of the world market. Embedded liberalism facilitated relatively unrestrained economic trade among all industrial countries, but still left room for different national political and societal structures. In this way, corporatist welfare states were able to coexist quite happily alongside liberal, Anglo-Saxon systems and Eastern Asian state-oriented societies and economies. International institutions thus established a form of *international governance* which enabled national governance

---

[3] Cf. especially C. P. Kindleberger, *The World in Depression. 1929–1939*, Berkeley, University of California Press, 1973 and B. Eichengreen, *Vom Goldstandard zum Euro. Die Geschichte des internationalen Währungssystems*, Berlin, Klaus Wagenbach, 2000.

[4] See R. O. Keohane, *After Hegemony: Collaboration and Discord in the World Political Economy*, Princeton, Princeton University Press, 1984.

[5] See J. G. Ruggie, 'International Regimes, Transactions, and Change: Embedded Liberalism in the Postwar Economic Order', in S. D. Krasner (ed.), *International Regimes*, Ithaca, NY, Cornell University Press, 1983, pp. 195–231 and J. G. Ruggie, 'Trade, Protectionism and the Future of Welfare Capitalism', *Journal of International Affairs*, 48: 1 (1994), pp. 1–12.

to function effectively, and initially even led to an extension of state activities. As trade barriers fell, the states established welfare systems to offset or at least cushion the undesired domestic effects of free trade. The concept of embedded liberalism is thus not only an expression of the compatibility of free trade and welfare statism, but it also points to a positive and very close relation between the two: those national economies which are most integrated in the international market are typically governed by states with particularly extensive welfare systems.[6]

The term embedded liberalism also highlights the essence of this institutional arrangement, i.e., a certain combination of liberalized international markets and national state intervention into the market. Embedded liberalism was engendered by a distinctive method of international decision-making and thus also contains a procedural component that I suggest we call *executive multilateralism*. The term is used to describe a decision-making mode in which governmental representatives (mainly cabinet ministers) from different countries coordinate their policies internationally, but with little national parliamentary control and away from public scrutiny. On the one hand, multilateralism refers to a decision-making system that is open to all states involved, includes a generalized principle of conduct, creates expectations of diffuse reciprocity and is seen as indivisible.[7] On the other hand – and this aspect was neglected for a long time – multilateralism after the Second World War was heavily executive-centred, since the rules of embedded liberalism were negotiated and implemented nationally without the contribution of the legislatures and without the systematic incorporation of national or transnational societal actors. Embedded liberalism hovered in a sphere beyond the reach of the normal democratic channels of influence in a democratic welfare state. Of course, embedded liberalism also had its domestic bridgeheads, but these were more or less exclu-

---

[6] Cf. e.g., D. Rodrik, *Has Globalization Gone too Far?*, Washington, DC, Brookings Institution, 1997; E. Rieger, and S. Leibfried, *Limits to Globalization*, Cambridge, Polity Press, 2002, and, as early as 1984, P. J. Katzenstein, *Corporatism and Change. Austria, Switzerland, and the Politics of Industry*, Ithaca, NY, and London, Cornell University Press, 1984. See D. Cameron, 'The Expansion of the Public Economy, *American Political Science Review*, 72: 4 (1978), pp. 1243–61.

[7] J. G. Ruggie, 'Multilateralism. The Anatomy of an Institution', *International Organization*, 46: 3 (1992), pp. 561–98; 571.

sively economic interest groups, whereas the national publics were completely excluded from decision-making.[8]

Post-Second World War international economic institutions were extremely successful. They supported stable growth in the western industrial societies for almost 30 years; they promoted the integration of the world economy and thus strengthened the role of export-oriented industries within the national political systems; and they helped to prevent the spiralling of protectionism and devaluation during economic recessions. Furthermore, these institutions facilitated the growth of democratic welfare states, through which almost half of the gross national product in some western European countries is channelled. From the perspective of international relations theory, these success stories are historic milestones. International cooperation, prosperity and democracy reinforced each other and led to a period of extreme stability and peace among democratic welfare states.[9]

However, the international economic institutions were too successful in some respects. Embedded liberalism gained a momentum of its own, precipitating an ever-expanding liberalization and accelerating technological progress, which between them had a catalytic effect on the most recent period of accelerated globalization, or rather, societal denationalization,[10] toppling the pillars of the national interventionist state. *Societal denationalization*, seen as a process in which the boundaries of social transactions increasingly

[8] Cf. also R. O. Keohane and J. S. Nye Jr., 'Introduction', in J. S. Nye and J. Donahue (eds), *Governance in a Globalizing World*, Washington, DC, Brookings Institution, 2000, pp. 1–41; 26, who liken international politics to a club in which cabinet ministers negotiate behind closed doors without informing outsiders about the negotiation process.

[9] Cf. B. Russett and J. R. Oneal, *Triangulating Peace. Democracy, Interdependence, and International Organization*, New York, W. W. Norton, 2001; E. D. Mansfield, H. V. Milner and B. P. Rosendorff, 'Why Democracies Cooperate More: Electoral Control and International Trade Agreements', *International Organizations*, 56: 3 (2002), pp. 477–513, and J. C. Pevehouse, 'Democracy from the Outside-In? International Organizations and Democratization', *International Organization*, 56: 3 (2002), pp. 515–49.

[10] See M. Zürn, *Regieren jenseits des Nationalstaates. Denationalisierung und Globalisierung als Chance*, Frankfurt am Main, Suhrkamp, 1998, and M. Beisheim, S. Dreher, G. Walter, B. Gregor, Bernhard Zangl and M. Zürn, *Im Zeitalter der Globalisierung? Thesen und Daten zur gesellschaftlichen und politischen Denationalisierung*, Baden-Baden, Nomos, 1999.

transcend national borders,[11] has challenged the capacity of national policies to bring about desired social outcomes. The effectiveness of state policies comes under pressure in those issue areas in which the spatial scope of national regulations does not extend as far as the real boundaries of transactions. In particular, the potential of effective national market intervention and social welfare programmes is challenged by the rapid increase in direct investments and highly sensitive financial markets. Moreover, some national defence or deterrence measures no longer seem to be effective against many new security threats from outside, be it of a military, ecological or even 'cultural' nature. The paradox of post-war liberalism is therefore that it has ruined its own shock-absorbers. The capacity of an individual nation-state to intervene into market processes in order to cushion the undesired effects is challenged.

Such challenges facing nation-states in their endeavours to achieve their governance goals do not, however, directly translate into the 'fall' or 'retreat of the nation-state'. The challenges are serious, yet the outcome is largely determined by political responses to them, and not the challenges themselves. Governments and other political organizations can respond to the challenges of globalization in a number of different ways. The establishment of international institutions is probably the most frequent response. It can be stated, therefore, that embedded liberalism has a dynamic of its own: the growing numbers of international institutions since the Second World War has made national borders less significant for societal transactions (societal denationalization), and this in turn has led to an increase in the number and political scope of international institutions (political denationalization). While initially it was primarily the economic policy areas that were coordinated through the Bretton Woods institutions, in the course of political denationalization international institutions have meanwhile become involved in a whole range of conceivable policy areas. And while initially the international institutions still allowed the national political systems a large degree of autonomy, they now, in the age of political denationalization, penetrate deeply into the national systems. It is this institutional dynamic, as I shall proceed to argue, that puts the establishment of an expedient political order onto the international political agenda.

[11] The boundaries of social transactions are 'the place where there is some critical reduction in the frequency of a certain type of transaction' (K. W. Deutsch, *Nationalism and its Alternatives*, New York, Knopf, 1969, p. 99).

THE NEW QUALITY OF INTERNATIONAL INSTITUTIONS

In what way do the quantity and quality of international institutions reflect this dynamic? What characterizes the institutional dynamic described above? A first measure of the extent of this institutional dynamic is the growth in numbers of international governmental agreements that exist. Indeed, there was a linear increase from less than 15,000 in 1960 to well over 55,000 in 1997.[12] A similar growth rate is measured in the annual ratification of multilateral treaties.[13] These remarkable growth rates, which rank closely behind those of central globalization indicators and far surpass growth rates in national legislation, lie especially in the areas of international economic and international environmental policy,[14] but there has also been substantial growth in other areas, such as security or human rights policy.[15] These figures speak for themselves. What is more, the increase in international agreements is accompanied by a growing intensity in transgovernmental relations[16] through the building up of networks among various national state authorities such as regulatory bodies, courts, executive bodies and also, increasingly, legislatives in different countries. In fact, Anne-Marie Slaughter deems this development to be the crucial step towards the emergence of a new world order.[17]

[12] The data is taken from the World Treaty Index Research Programme; University of Washington.

[13] C. Hirschi, U. Serdült and T. Widmer, 'Schweizerische Außenpolitik im Wandel', *Schweizerische Zeitschrift für Politikwissenschaft*, 5: 1 (1999), pp. 31–56; 40.

[14] Since the beginning of the 20th century the number of newly concluded multinational environmental treaties and agreements has increased steadily. While up until the 1970s an average of five agreements were concluded every five years, this figure has increased five-fold since the 1980s (Beisheim et al., *Im Zeitalter der Globalisierung?*, op. cit. p. 351). The development of new international economic treaties and agreements reveals a very similar pattern (ibid., p. 353).

[15] For a survey, see ibid.

[16] See also R. O. Keohane and J. S. Nye, 'Transgovernmental Relations and International Organizations', *World Politics*, 27: 1 (1974), pp. 38–62, who introduced the term 'transgovernmental relations', and R. Cox, 'Global Perestroika', in R. Miliband and L. Panitch (eds), *New World Order*, London, Merlin Press, 1992, pp. 26–45; 30, who emphasized the significance of such networks in his work.

[17] A. M. Slaughter, 'The Real New World Order', *Foreign Affairs*, 76: 5 (1997), pp. 183–97; 190.

As well as the growing quantity of international and transgovern-mental agreements, a second measure of institutional dynamic is the new quality of international governance. This development becomes manifest when one contrasts the typical traditional multilateral insti-tutions of *embedded liberalism* with the new international institutions in the age of denationalization. The GATT regime is a good example of a traditional international institution. Its form of regulation has three distinctive features:

• the *states* are the ultimate and exclusive *addressees* of the regulation. They are issued with directives not to increase customs tariffs or to apply them in a discriminating way. The objective of the regulation is therefore to influence state behaviour in order to solve the problem in question;

• such regulations take effect at the borders between states, and in this sense they primarily constitute a form of *interface management*, regulating the transit of goods and bads out of one national society into another;

• there exists a relatively high degree of *certainty* as to the effects of such regulations. The actors are able to make relatively precise, empirically sound predictions about the economic consequences of their tariffs.

In today's age of societal denationalization and globalization, inter-national institutions have different features. International regimes for overcoming global environmental problems are typical examples here.

• The ultimate *addressees* of regulations issued by international institutions are largely *societal actors*. While the states act as interme-diaries between the international institutions and the addressees, it is ultimately societal actors such as consumers and businesses who have to alter their behaviour in order, say, to reduce CO_2 or CFC emissions;[18]

• the new international institutions are no longer merely concerned with interface management. The reduction of pollutants requires regulations that take effect behind the national borders, within the national societies. In this sense, the international climate regime reg-

---

[18] See E. A. Parsons, 'Protecting the Ozone Layer', in P. M. Haas, R. O. Keohane and M. A. Levy (eds), *Institutions for the Earth: Sources of Effective International Environ-mental Protection*, Cambridge, MA, MIT Press, 1993, pp. 27–73.

ulates behind-the-border issues, but the new international trade regime, with its focus on the prohibition of subsidization and overcoming discriminatory product regulations, has also developed in this direction.[19] Equally, the measures of the Security Council of the United Nations have for some time now increasingly been directed at intrastate rather than interstate wars;[20]

• international institutions today are for the most part concerned with finding solutions to *highly complex problems*. There is therefore a high degree of uncertainty as to the ecological and economic consequences of, say, a particular climate regime. The same is true of other environmental regimes, but also financial agreements and regulations on product safety as well as security issues.[21]

Of course, in order to successfully tackle highly complex behind-the-border issues with societal actors as the ultimate addressees, these new kinds of international institutions require a more sophisticated institutional design. The conventional international obligation not to increase import duties on certain goods is, in retrospect, in many ways a very simple form of regulation. By contrast, the obligation to reduce CO_2 emissions by 30 per cent has much broader ramifications. As the ultimate addressee of the regulation is not the state, but societal actors (such as the car industry and car drivers), the reduction of CO_2 is not simply a matter of volition on the part of the executive. Unlike most other international regimes, its failure is even possible if the signatory governments have the full intention to reduce CO_2 emissions. Substantial financial, administrative and technological resources are needed to fulfil such an obligation. What is more, monitoring compliance in behind-the-border issues such as these is significantly more difficult than in at-the-border issues. In addition, the problem itself is so complex that discussions about an appropriate form of regulation are permanently overshadowed by questions as to the real causes and the actual degree of global warming.

---

[19] See M. Kahler, *International Institutions and the Political Economy of Integration*, Washington, DC, Brookings Institution, 1995.

[20] B. Zangl and M. Zürn, *Frieden und Krieg. Sicherheit in der nationalen und postnationalen Konstellation*, Frankfurt am Main, Suhrkamp, 2003, ch. 8.

[21] B. Koremenos, C. Lipson and D. Snidal, 'The Rational Design of International Institutions', *International Organization*, 55: 4 (2001), pp. 761–99.

Against this background we can formulate the hypothesis that *to the same degree that there is a growth in modern international institutions with the new type of regulation described above, there will be a growth in demand for new types of supranational and transnational institutional features.*[22] According to the quasi-functional version of rationalist regime theory, one can expect this demand to be fulfilled to a certain degree[23] even if this has unintended side-effects on the national sovereignty of the states involved.[24] This hypothesis requires some clarification. Let us begin with the dependent variable, i.e. the notion of 'supranational and transnational institutional *features*'. 'Supranationality' here refers to a certain degree of autonomy of the international institutions vis-à-vis the nation-states involved. International norms are thus given a certain priority over national regulations.[25] Similarly, 'transnational' features of international institutions are those in which non-state, private actors get involved for the purposes

[22] These hypotheses follow a logic according to which the design of international institutions is largely determined by the underlying cooperation problem. See now Koremenos, Lipson and Snidal, 'The Rational Design of International Institutions', op. cit., and also L. Martin, 'Interests, Power, and Multilateralism', *International Organization*, 46: 4 (1992), pp. 765–92; M. Zürn, *Interessen und Institutionen in der internationalen Politik. Grundlegung und Anwendungen des situationsstrukturellen Ansatzes*, Opladen, Leske & Budrich, 1992 and M. Zürn, 'Assessing State Preferences and Explaining Institutional Choice. The Case of Intra-German Trade', *International Studies Quarterly*, 41: 2 (1997), pp. 295–320 for a theoretical elaboration of this perspective.

[23] See Keohane, *After Hegemony*, op. cit.

[24] See especially A. M. Burley and W. Mattli, 'Europe before the Court: A Political Theory of Legal Integration', *International Organization*, 47: 1 (1993), pp. 41–76 and K. Alter, *Establishing the Supremacy of European Law. The Making of an International Rule of Law in Europe*, Oxford, Oxford University Press, 2001, for convincing accounts of how the European Court of Justice – the best example of a supranational component within the overall institutional concept of the EU – was not the outcome of an intergovernmentally desired decision, but the unintended outcome of a number of developments.

[25] A. Moravcsik differentiates between 'pooled sovereignty', where governments aim to make future decisions by majority within the context of an international institution, and 'delegated sovereignty', where supranational actors are authorized to make certain decisions themselves, regardless of interstate objections or unilateral vetos (A. Moravcsik, *The Choice for Europe. Social Purpose and State Power from Messina to Maastricht*, Ithaca, NY, Cornell University Press, 1998, p. 67). See also A. Bogdandy, *Supranationaler Föderalismus als Wirklichkeit und Idee einer neuen Herrschaftsform. Zur Gestalt der Europäischen Union nach Amsterdam*, Baden-Baden, Nomos, 1999, for a constructive use of the term supranationality.

of self-regulation.[26] These definitions build on a differentiation between primarily supranational or transnational institutions on the one hand and supranational or transnational features within more comprehensive institutions on the other. Hence, international institutions that are essentially controlled by national governments may also have supranational or transnational components. Whether an international institution is intergovernmental, supranational or transnational is therefore not a question of either/or, it is a question of degree.

The theoretical grounds for the hypothesis also require clarification. Functionalist explanations generally tend to be afflicted by severe inadequacies and are not seldom – and rightly so – regarded with scepticism.[27] It should therefore be noted that the hypothesis presented here is not an explanation of the development of an individual international institution. It rather points to a trend by which a growing demand is sometimes fulfilled, as one might expect, but without necessarily assuming that demand is automatically met by supply. An explanation of how individual institutions developed must also take into account the interests, ideals and power resources of the actors involved. What is more, the hypothesis is not based on structuralist functionalism, according to which functions are defined in terms of the requirements of a self-reproducing system. Rather, quasi-functionalism points to a micromechanism – namely, the assumed rationality of the actors – which connects supply and demand. In this sense, the hypothesis formulated here is comparable with the statement that in a heavy snowfall in November, an

[26] On national self-regulation cf. e.g., R. Mayntz and F. W. Scharpf (eds), *Gesellschaftliche Selbstregelung und politische Steuerung,* Frankfurt am Main and New York, Campus, 1995, and E. Ostrom, *Governing the Commons. The Evolution of Institutions for Collective Action,* Cambridge, Cambridge University Press, 1990. A. Cutler, V. Haufler and T. Porter (eds), *Private Authority and International Affairs,* Albany, NY, SUNY Press, 1999; A. Héritier (ed.), *Common Goods. Reinventing European and International Governance,* Lanham, MD, Rowman & Littlefield, 2002, and R. Higgot, G. Underhill and A. Bieler (eds), *Non-State-Actors and Authority in the Global System,* London, Routledge, 2000, are important contributions on transnational self-regulation.

[27] The discussions of Jon Elster, in particular J. Elster, *Making Sense of Marx,* Cambridge, Cambridge University Press, 1985, ch. 1, and Jon Elster, *Sour Grapes. Studies in the Subversion of Rationality,* Cambridge, Cambridge University Press, have contributed here. Cf. also a summary and in the context of international politics, Zürn, *Interessen und Institutionen in der internationalen Politik,* op. cit, pp. 40–62.

increased demand for winter tyres can be expected. This mechanism is based on the assumption of the self-interest of the actors (and not the systemic requirements of road traffic), and makes no claims to be a complete explanation for each individual choice. It therefore acknowledges that the purchase of winter tyres requires sufficient financial resources, the anticipation of further snowfalls in the near future, etc.

Now why do the new quantity and quality of international institutions lead to a relative rise in supranational and transnational institutional features? The answer lies in three different mechanisms:

• a high density of international institutions increasingly gives rise to collisions between different international regulations as well as between national and international ones. In such cases a supranational arbitration body is a sensible means of settling differences.[28] The dispute settlement procedure of the WTO for instance decides in case of a collision between WTO rules and domestic regulations, as well as in case of collision between environmental and trade goals, for instance with reference to the *Codex Alimentarius*.[29] Furthermore, the increased complexity also gives rise to a greater need for independent dispute settlement bodies. The quantitative growth and the growing complexity of international institutions thus leads to an increased need for supranational components;[30]

• the significance of independent supranational and transnational institutional features also increases as the numbers of regimes grow that are concerned with behind-the-border issues and specify societal actors as the ultimate addressees. In such cases verification

[28] See especially K. W. Abbott and D. Snidal, 'Hard and Soft Law in International Governance', *International Organization*, 54: 3 (2000), pp. 421–56, J. McCall Smith, 'The Politics of Dispute Settlement Designs. Explaining Legalism in Regional Trade Pacts', *International Organization*, 54: 1 (2000), pp. 137–80, and other contributions to the special issue of *International Organization* on legalization, 54: 3 (2000).

[29] Collisions between different international regulations are, with the exception of the European Court of Justice and the International Court of Justice, not settled with the help of courts that are independent of specific regimes. Most dispute settlement bodies are associated with one specific international regime, but in fact settle disputes that take place at the borders between different regulatory areas.

[30] Correspondingly, in the 1990s alone, 40 new arbitration procedures were introduced (C. Romano, 'The Proliferation of International Judicial Bodies: The Pieces of the Puzzle', *New York University Journal of International Law and Politics*, 31: 4 (1999), pp. 709–51; 723–8).

problems become more complicated. The more difficult compliance and monitoring become, the greater the need for supranational and transnational agents to gather and provide reliable information on compliance rates.[31] Hence, many international secretariats have the assignment to gather information about rule-compliance and, at the same time, transnational NGOs – such as for instance Amnesty International – are most active in this area;

• finally, the growing need for international institutions to gather and distribute impartial knowledge and information on complex international problems also strengthens the trend towards supranationalization and transnationalization.[32] The conferences and institutes created by the UN Environmental Program are good examples of this development.

These hypotheses can be summarized as follows: if, for the effectiveness of an international institution, an institutional design is required that comprises

• quasi-judicial dispute settlement bodies;
• independent monitoring bodies;
• and international agents for the collection and distribution of knowledge;

then there will be an increased share of supranational and transnational features of international institutions.

There has therefore developed a dense network of international regulations and organizations of unprecedented quality and quantity. In the age of denationalization, these new international institutions are far more intrusive than the conventional international institutions.[33] The democratic decision-making processes within

---

[31] See the contributions in D. G. Victor, K. Raustiala and E. B. Skolnikoff (eds), *The Implementation and Effectiveness of International Environmental Commitments: Theory and Practice*, Cambridge, MA, MIT Press, 1998.

[32] See especially the work of Peter M. Haas: P. M. Haas, *Saving the Mediterranean. The Politics of International Environmental Cooperation*, New York and Oxford, Columbia University Press, 1990, and P. M. Haas, 'Introduction: Epistemic Communities and International Policy Coordination', *International Organization*, 46: 1 (1992), pp. 1–35.

[33] See also N. Woods and A. Narlikar, 'Governance and the Limits of Accountability: The WTO, the IMF, and the World Bank', *International Social Science Journal*, 53: 170 (2001), pp. 569–83, who discuss the 'new intrusiveness' of international economic institutions particularly in the context of increased conditionality of granting credit and the increased sanctioning possibilities of international rules.

Table 1
New and Old Institutions

	International institutions in the age of embedded liberalism	International institutions in the age of denationalization	Regulatory problem	Institutional solution
Number of international regulations	Few	Many	→ Collisions with other regulations	→ Incentive for transnational or supranational adjudication
Addressees of the regulations	States	Societal actors	→ Compliance monitoring	→ Incentive for transnational or supranational monitoring bodies
Locus of intervention	State borders	Behind-the-border issues	→ Compliance monitoring	→ Incentive for transnational or supranational monitoring bodies
Degree of complexity of regulation	Low	High	→ Knowledge problems	→ Incentive for transnational or supranational knowledge agencies

nation-states are thus losing their anchorage. They are superseded by organizations and actors who indeed are mostly accountable to their national governments one way or another, but at the same time quite remote and inaccessible for the nationally enclosed addressees of the regulations in question. Given the extent of the intrusion of these new international institutions into the affairs of national societies, the notion of 'delegated, and therefore controlled authority' in the principal and agent sense[34] no longer holds. At best, the agents – the new international institutions with transnational and supranational institutional features – are answerable to a few governments, but not to all the societies into which they intrude, and certainly not to a transnational society.

DEFIANCE IN THE FACE OF UNINTENDED POLITICAL DENATIONALIZATION

Whereas traditional institutions used to be seen as an international complement to a dominantly national paradigm, today's international institutions are an expression of political denationalization. The transformation process itself can be separated into different stages. The first stage is marked by the emergence of a trend towards supranationalization and transnationalization as the more or less *unintended, indirect outcome* of the sum of deliberate political responses to perceived functional demands on international institutions as a result of societal denationalization. In the second stage, the process becomes *reflexive*. When society and political actors begin to comprehend the changes outlined above, they begin to reflect on the features of a legitimate and effective political order beyond national borders. This is where issues of transboundary identity and transboundary ethics are taken on board in their deliberations. The increasing commitment to improve the living conditions of people of other nationalities and race living in other countries thousands of miles away,[35] as well as the debate over European identity and

---

[34] See the article by Miles Kahler in this issue.

[35] See M. Keck and K. Sikkink, *Activists Beyond Borders: Advocacy Networks in International Politics*, Ithaca, NY, Cornell University Press, 1998 and T. Risse, A. Jetschke and H. P. Schmitz, *Die Macht der Menschenrechte. Internationale Normen, kommunikatives Handeln und politischer Wandel in den Ländern des Südens*, Baden-Baden, Nomos, 2002.

European democracy[36] are the first signs of this reflexive stage in the transformation process. In this reflexive stage, the intergovernmental processes that allowed for liberalization and internationalization begin to turn against themselves. At this point, borders lose their normative dignity and, increasingly, universalistic political concepts are developed.[37] The connection between increasing integration and the expansion of the application of the principle of justice was pointed out quite early on by Charles Beitz in his cosmopolitan theory of politics following John Rawls.[38] As a result of this process, denationalization becomes reflexive, and thus politicized. At the same time, the politicization of international politics harbours the potential for resistance to political denationalization, which increases the need – both from a normative and descriptive perspective – for the legitimation of such international institutions.

Reflexive denationalization can be seen as part of the broader process of reflexive modernization.[39] The unintended side-effects of decisions taken in the context of modernization lead in this view to such a radicalization of modernization that an adequate reaction to the consequences within the old system is not possible. According to Beck, it is the inner dynamic of modernization itself that leads to a self-transformation – an independent, unintended and largely unnoticed, reflex-type of transition. In this sense, reflexive thus means self-transformation through self-confrontation. In other words, it concerns – so to speak – the after-effects of processing the side-effects. Concomitant to this process is the politicization of pre-

[36] Cf. the contributions in B. Kohler-Koch and R. Eising (eds), *The Transformation of Governance in the European Union*, London, Routledge, 1999, and M. T. Greven and L. W. Pauly (eds), *Democracy Beyond the State? The European Dilemma and the Emerging Global Order*, Lanham, MD, Rowman & Littlefield, 2000.

[37] See e.g., A. Linklater, *The Transformation of Political Community: Ethical Foundations of the Post-Westphalian Era*, Columbia, SC, University of South Carolina Press, 1998 and R. Schmalz-Bruns, 'Deliberativer Supranationalismus. Demokratisches Regieren jenseits des Nationalstaates', *Zeitschrift für Internationale Beziehungen*, 6: 2 (1999), pp. 185–244.

[38] C. R. Beitz, *Political Theory and International Relations*, Princeton, Princeton University Press, 1979, p. 165.

[39] See U. Beck and W. Bonß, *Die Modernisierung der Moderne*, Frankfurt am Main, Suhrkamp, 2001; U. Beck, A. Giddens and S. Lash, *Reflexive Modernization. Politics, Tradition and Aesthetics in the Modern Social Order*, Cambridge, Polity Press, 1997, and U. Beck, *World Risk Society*, Oxford, Blackwell, 1999.

viously unpolitical issues and debates on political institutions, and not just on the right policies. To put it differently, 'in the age of globalization, the political did not die, it just migrated'.[40]

The ecological consequences of industrial modernity and the concept of 'risk society' originally served as a model for the concept of 'reflexive modernization'.[41] But the history and dynamic of the Bretton Woods institutions can also be seen in the same light, both in substantial and in procedural terms. The steady progression of liberalization has severed it from its national roots. As John Ruggie put it: 'by lowering and eliminating point-of-entry barriers to the flow of economic transactions and by encouraging cross-border corporate ties and market forces, governments have also inadvertently undermined the efficacy of some of their standard policy tools of managing the consequences of liberalization'.[42]

From a procedural point of view, the steady expansion of international institutions through supranationalization and transnationalization led to growing problems concerning the acceptance of executive multilateralism as a decision-making mechanism. The further international institutions intervene in formerly national issues, the more they will be confronted with questions regarding their legitimacy. In this sense, political denationalization has become a reflexive process, creating its own potential for resistance. At the same time, this resistance accelerates political denationalization in certain respects, since the critical movements themselves are an expression of political denationalization. They use the internet for internal communication, the global mass media to transport their message and they aim at re-regulating financial markets.

The politicization of world politics has led to a questioning of the formerly strict demarcation line between national and international politics. In this way transnational protests as exemplified in Seattle 1999, and the rise of resistance against international institutions within national political systems can be explained as part of the process of reflexive denationalization. Seen thus, however, reflexive denationalization is not only an obstacle to international

---

[40] U. Beck, *Macht und Gegenmacht im globalen Zeitalter. Neue weltpolitische Ökonomie*, Frankfurt am Main, Suhrkamp, 2002, p. 364.

[41] See U. Beck, *Risikogesellschaft. Auf dem Weg in eine andere Moderne*, Frankfurt am Main, Suhrkamp, 1986.

[42] Ruggie, 'Trade, Protectionism and the Future of Welfare Capitalism', op. cit., p. 8.

institution-building, but also a building block for a new world order of legitimate global governance.

ON THE EMPIRICAL TESTING OF THE HYPOTHESIS

In good social science, theoretical reflections are complemented with methodically sound empirical analyses. It should be possible to derive falsifiable hypotheses from the theoretical reflections and test them empirically. The theoretical argumentation put forward here comprises two substantial empirical implications. Firstly, it should be possible to provide evidence that there has in fact been a growth in the quantity of international institutions and at the same time a qualitative trend towards a supranationalization and transnationalization of international institutions. Although there is undoubtedly need for additional research in this area, the evidence presented here should suffice for the time being, for the clearly more contested issue is the second empirical implication that the trend towards a supranationalization and transnationalization of international institutions is resulting in a legitimacy crisis for global governance.[43]

How can this part of the argument be empirically tested? What observations bear out this statement? There are two hypotheses in particular which appear to be testable derivations from the general argument:
• in the course of political denationalization, potentially defiant *transnational* social movements emerge and oppose the undermining of national decision-making authority as a result of the supranationalization and transnationalization of international institutions and executive multilateralism. These transnational social movements mostly have a leftist outlook and are mainly directed against

---

[43] As an example, normatively oriented economists like to point out that the constitutionalization of the free trade regime in particular – by which the strengthening of supranational components is also meant – has a legitimizing effect (cf. esp. E.-U. Petersmann, 'Human Rights and International Economic Law in the 21st Century: The Need to Clarify Their Interrelationships', *Journal of International Economic Law*, 4: 1 (2001), pp. 3–39, and R. Howse and K. Nicolaidis, 'Legitimacy and Global Governance: Why a Constitution for the WTO is a Step too Far?', in R. Porter, P. Sauve, A. Subramanian and A. Zampetti (eds), *Equity, Efficiency and Legitimacy: The Multilateral System at the Millennium*, Washington, DC, Brookings Institution, 2001, pp. 227–52, take a contrary stance, more in line with the argument developed here).

liberalizing international institutions such as the WTO, the World
Bank or the Multilateral Agreement on Investment (MAI);
• the growth of international institutions with supranational and
transnational components leads to national resistance which is, paradoxically, not based in the respective nation-states' 'obsession' with
sovereignty, but within the national *societies*. This national resistance
often has a rightist outlook and is directed against interventionist
international institutions such as the criminal courts, international
environmental agreements, etc.

On Transnational Resistance

At first sight, it may seem an over-exaggeration to interpret the
protests in Seattle in the autumn of 1999, Prague in autumn 2000,
Quebec City in spring 2001 and Genoa in summer 2001 – to name
but a few dramatic eruptions – as part of the process of reflexive
denationalization, since the protest groups explicitly oppose globalization, and thus ultimately the international institutions with which
it is associated. In this sense, the protests against the WTO, the World
Bank and the IMF must be interpreted as the anti-systemic resistance
of groups who are hardly likely to consider the reform of these international institutions for the purposes of legitimizing them as an
option.

This may be underrating the issue, however. While it can hardly
be denied that many of these groups see globalization as the root of
all evil, to classify the movement summarily as anti-globalist would be
to overlook its diversity and the constructive endeavours of many
parts of the movement.[44] Many groups, in fact, mainly focus on 'initiatives *for* a *just* world economy'. To a certain degree they accept
globalization as given and strive to exert their influence on its political control. After all, mere anti-globalization rhetoric alone would
be a contradiction in terms, as the anti-globalization movement itself
is an expression of political denationalization. Kaldor, for instance,
discusses the phenomenon of 'globalisation from below' and sees
Seattle as a victory for *political* globalization, or – to put it in the terms
of reflexive denationalization – an expression of the politicization of

---

[44] See R. Broad, *Global Backlash: Citizen Initiatives for a Just World Economy*, Lanham,
MD, Rowman & Littlefield, 2002.

globalization.[45] This second view interprets the disturbances above all as a consequence of the legitimacy deficit of executive multilateralism and the poor accountability of its political elites. The politicization of executive multilateralism thus brings legitimacy problems and issues of accountability to the fore. Moreover, the dual impetus of this movement against the *disembedding* of liberalism *and* for the democratization of global governance makes sense insofar as the executive locking-in of decision-making processes in order to accelerate liberalization means locking out national parliaments and the political alternatives put forward by the transnational movement.[46] In other words, there is just as much an elective affinity between executive multilateralism and excessively liberal policies as there is between the welfare state and democracy. It was only possible for social policy to become well-established in the nation-state when the democratization of political institutions was emphatically demanded and later pushed through. Moreover, there is also a distributive aspect to the debates over the legitimation of international institutions. In this respect, transnational nongovernmental organizations and protest groups quite rightly have a double agenda: campaigning for *new policies* in *new institutions*.

There are at least three developments which ought to be taken into consideration in empirical studies when interpreting transnational resistance in terms of reflexive political denationalization:
- *the justificatory strategies of the globalization critics.* In Europe, at least, legitimacy has meanwhile become a key issue for many transnational groups that are critical of globalization. In its manifesto of 2002, the Association for the Taxation of financial Transactions for the Aid of Citizens (ATTAC) – in its origins arguably one of the most outspokenly anti-globalization groups – identifies the legitimacy problem as its main focus: 'it is high time that we shed light on these institutions (EU, WTO, IMF, World Bank, OECD) and made those decision-makers accountable who ostensibly act in our name.'[47] Susan George,

---

[45] M. Kaldor, ' "Civilising" Globalisation? The Implications of the "Battle in Seattle"', *Millennium*, 29: 1, 2000, pp. 105–14; 105.

[46] S. Gill, 'Toward a Postmodern Prince? The Battle of Seattle as a Moment in the New Politics of Globalization', *Millennium*, 29: 1 (2000), pp. 131–40; 134; and Howse and Nicolaidis, 'Legitimacy and Global Governance', op. cit., p. 235.

[47] ATTAC Frankreich, 'Mit Attac die Zukunft zurück erobern. Manifest 2002', *Blätter für deutsche und internationale Politik*, 47: 3 (2002), pp. 347–62; 349; translation MZ.

vice-president of the French branch of ATTAC, even assumes that we are currently in an 'historic phase . . . in which we are striving for a kind of global democracy';[48]

• *the reform strategies of the international institutions.* Undoubtedly, among the most fiercely criticized international institutions are the WTO, the IMF and the World Bank. These institutions especially are under criticism from all sides and are a popular target for protest movements. All three international economic institutions are aware of the issue of acceptance, but put it down less to the content of their policies than to institutional deficits. Therefore, in the light of growing societal resistance, the three aforementioned institutions have taken measures to 1) increase control over the decision-makers through various evaluation procedures, 2) improve the scrutibility of the decision-making processes and 3) increase the share of power of transnational society. Ngaire Woods and Amrika Narlikar have examined these reform measures and ascertained that the predominant reaction to the growing criticism is a substantial improvement in the horizontal accountability of these institutions.[49] The self-interpretation of the legitimacy crisis by the relevant international institutions appears rather to correspond to the logic of reflexive political denationalization than an interpretation of the resistance as anti-globalist.

• *the 'new' conditions for successful international negotiations.* The results of international negotiations seem to depend increasingly on the consent and support of transnationalizing sectoral publics. Traditional international institution theory, according to which the success of international negotiations through international institutions depends on specific intergovernmental interest coalitions on the one hand and the support of strong national interest groups on the

[48] S. George, 'Was ist Attac – und was nicht?', *Blätter für deutsche und internationale Politik*, 47: 4 (2002), pp. 419–30; 430. For the intellectual background of these movements see C. Leggewie, *Die Globalisierung und ihre Gegner*, Munich, C. H. Beck, 2003, ch. 1.

[49] Woods and Narlikar, 'Governance and the Limits of Accountability', op. cit., p. 15. See also G. Marceau and P. N. Pedersen, 'Is the WTO Open and Transparent? A Discussion of the Relationship of the WTO with Non-governmental Organizations and Civil Society's Claim for more Transparency and Public Participation', *Journal of World Trade*, 37: 1, 1999, pp. 5–49, for a detailed account of the relationship of the WTO with NGOs.

other,[50] no longer seems to hold completely. A comparison, for example, of the successful negotiations on the Anti-Bribery Convention and the Ottawa Convention on Landmines with the failed round of WTO negotiations in Seattle (1999) and the aborted attempt to establish a new MAI, quickly reveals that one major difference between the two sets of negotiations lay in the campaign networks of transnational NGOs.[51] The international constellation of power and interests is certainly an inadequate explanation for the outcome of these negotiation processes.[52] In the reflexive phase of denationalization, it appears that negotiators have to justify the results of their negotiations both to the transnational sectoral publics and the national publics, which are increasingly interconnected. One can thus say that international politics are then no longer a matter for a few corporative agents – in particular states – which coordinate their

---

[50] Cf. A. Moravcsik, *The Choice for Europe. Social Purpose and State Power from Messina to Maastricht*, Ithaca, NY, Cornell University Press, 1998; B. Zangl, *Interessen auf zwei Ebenen. Internationale Regime in der Agrarhandels-, Währungs- und Walfangpolitik*, Baden-Baden, Nomos, 1999 and Zürn, *Interessen und Institutionen in der internationalen Politik*, op. cit.

[51] Cf. e.g., N. Bayne, 'Why Did Seattle Fail? Globalization and the Politics of Trade', *Government and Opposition*, 35: 2 (2000), pp. 131–51, and C. Warkentin and K. Mingst, 'International Institutions, the State, and Global Civil Society in the Age of the World Wide Web', *Global Governance*, 6: 2 (2000), pp. 237–57. In a project carried out at the Institute for Intercultural and International Studies (InIIS), Günter Metzges examines the significance of NGO networks by comparing two negotiation processes initiated by the OECD on international conventions – the Anti-Bribery Convention and the Multilateral Agreement on Investments (G. Metzges, *Advocacy Networks als Einflußfaktor in internationalen Regimebildungsprozessen. Das MAI und die 1997 Anti-Bribery Convention*, 2003). In these studies it is shown on the one hand that transnational protests were not the direct reason for the failure of the negotiations on the MAI and in Seattle. A careful comparison clearly reveals, however, that owing to the protests a context was developed for the negotiations which made intergovernmental compromise in the executive multilateralist tradition exceedingly difficult.

[52] Metzges, ibid., argues convincingly that it is very difficult to account for this difference in outcomes in terms of power (the US was dominant in both cases), intergovernmental interest constellations (initially more supportive in the MAI case), or domestic preferences (which were originally less diverse in the MAI case). It seems that the different role of transnational policy networks made the decisive difference. While these transnational policy networks and the most important transnational NGOs were involved and had a say in the negotiations to the Anti-Bribery Convention right from the beginning, they were excluded from the MAI negotiations.

interests *in camera* and arrive at common policies which then have to be implemented domestically. World politics are then less a form of 'executive multilateralism', but rather developing into a form of multilateralism borne by society and accountable to both national and transnational publics.

National Resistance

From the point of view of traditional state theories and theories of international politics, the delegation of decision-making authority to supranational institutions and non-state, transnational actors ought to lead to resistance on the part of national governments or the national executives, who one would expect to be reluctant to lose their sovereignty. In this context U. K. Preuß discusses the 'inner necessity – one could almost say instinct – to jealously and suspiciously guard the territorial integrity and exclusivity of the power exercised over it. The reason for this is that both these elements define the state.'[53] From the perspective of reflexive denationalization, however, the greatest potential for resistance to executive multilateralism and the institutional dynamic with which it is associated should be expected to emanate from the societal sphere. In actual fact, the supranational components of international institutions are often thwarted by intersocietal resistance. Consequently, the growth of international institutions with supranational components breeds less resistance from nation-states than from national societies. Two developments especially seem to support this hypothesis:

• *Resistance within societies to decisions made by international institutions.* A typical example here would seem to be the referendums in smaller states on entering the EU or on large-scale integrative measures such as the Maastricht Agreement. A positive decision in such cases implies the recognition that in some areas national subordination to supranational European procedures, for example at the European Court, are inevitable. Nevertheless, while the national political elites of Denmark, Norway and Ireland stood firmly behind their respective governments and supported their pro-European policy, the

[53] U. K. Preuß, *Krieg, Verbrechen, Blasphemie. Zum Wandel bewaffneter Gewalt*, Berlin, Wagenbach, 2002, p. 22.

referendums all failed in the first round. The resistance came from society – from 'below'. In general, the European public is less keen on shifting authority to the European level than the elites. Whereas on average 93 per cent of the political elites support European integration, this is true only for 53 per cent of the general public.[54] It might possibly be worthwhile examining whether such resistance to 'the new raison d'état'[55] can also be categorized as a phenomenon of reflexive political denationalization. After all, these are by no means isolated incidents. Compliance with institutionalized EU regulations also appears to be thwarted more often by the resistance of national societies than by national states, as witnessed during the BSE crisis.[56] After the EU lifted the export ban on British beef in 1999, Germany and France, both facing on-coming elections, threatened to implement unilateral consumer protection measures – which constituted an open challenge to European Law. The decisive reason for this lay in the compromise made at the height of the BSE crisis in March 1996 that led to the short-term export ban for British beef and an agreement on the conditions under which British beef could be traded freely again. The negotiations leading up to this compromise involved executive decision-makers, transnational scientific experts and the societal addressees of the regulation – mainly the food industry. The broad national publics were excluded. If, however, the national publics refuse to accept the central implications of a supranational regulation, then even transnational, legally internalized institutions reach the limit of their capacity to elicit compliance.[57] The national governments, especially in democratic states, must then yield to societal pressure.

[54] L. Hooghe, 'Europe Divided? Elite vs. Public Opinion on European Integration', *European Union Politics*, 4: 3 (2003).

[55] K. D. Wolf, *Die Neue Staatsräson – Zwischenstaatliche Kooperation als Demokratieproblem in der Weltgesellschaft*, Baden-Baden, Nomos, 2000.

[56] This seems to be especially true for European regulations that are perceived as undermining the welfare state, while the general public's support is stronger for regulations that stand for the resurrection of the welfare state on the European level (Hooghe, 'Europe Divided?', op. cit.).

[57] See the case study by J. Neyer, 'Domestic Limits of Supranational Law. Comparing Compliance with European and International Foodstuffs Regulations', in C. Joerges and M. Zürn (eds), *Governance and Law in Postnational Constellations. Compliance in Europe and Beyond*, Cambridge, Cambridge University Press, i.p., which was carried out in the context of a project on 'Compliance in Postnational Constellations'.

• *Populism – the Achilles heel of International Institutions.* Increasingly, the vulnerability of international institutions to pressure from broad national societal coalitions is not only restricted to exceptional cases. They also generally seem to be an easy target for right-wing populist polemics on the 'political elites'. All right-wing populist parties in OECD states use a strong anti-internationalist, pro-renationalization rhetoric. Be it Le Pen, Haider or the German Republicans, they all brand 'international bureaucracies' and 'international agreements' as the reason why the 'simple man in the street' no longer earns enough pay. Conversely, office-holders endeavour to keep international pledges and participation in international institutions out of the election campaigns, and if all else fails, they tend to make rhetorical concessions to those favouring renationalization. These processes could also be examined to establish whether they can be interpreted as an expression of reflexive political denationalization.

Generally, therefore, our proposition is that political denationalization has become a reflexive process. The intrusiveness and visibility of the new international institutions gives rise to a politicization of these institutions. It is no longer accepted that executives draw up international policies – to a great extent prejudicing national policies – behind closed doors, but still in the name of the people. Many societal actors who feel affected by these international decisions want to have a say in the decision-making. Executive multilateralism must be extended to include transnational policy networks, even if these networks are hardly representative of the national societies. On the other hand, when international institutions deal with contentious issues that also concern broad publics, then the mere extension of executive multilateralism to transnational policy networks will not suffice either. What is then required is a transnational societally-backed system of multilateralism, with full mass media coverage, and with procedures that provide all those affected by the decision with the information they need as well as a chance to participate.

FROM EXECUTIVE TO SOCIETALLY BACKED MULTILATERALISM

Despite unquestionable democratic deficits, international institutions are, from a normative perspective, at least in part a sensible response to the problems facing modern societies in the age of societal denationalization. International institutions help resolve the incongruence between social and political spaces so that they at least partially correspond. Theoretically, the 'emergence of denational-ized *governance* structures'[58] helps integrate everybody affected by a political decision into the decision-making process, thus even observ-ing the fundamental principle of democracy. Furthermore, interna-tional institutions give back to national policy-makers the capacity to deal effectively with denationalized economic structures. Seen thus, international institutions are not the problem, but part of the solution to the problems confronting democracy in the age of globalization.

At the same time, the societal acceptance of international institu-tions clearly seems to be in decline. The constantly growing intru-siveness of international institutions highlights the democratic deficits and generates resistance, which in turn undermines the effectiveness of these institutions. The anti-globalization movement is usually portrayed as a movement protesting against the *disembed-ding* of liberalism. There are, however, good reasons for the assump-tion that the real source of upheaval is executive multilateralism. The more intrusive these international institutions become, the more justified and intense the demands will be for their democratization. Without an improvement of the legitimacy of decision-making processes, i.e. the incorporation of affected societal actors into the decision-making process, there is a danger that the effectiveness of international institutions will weaken. In order to avoid an accept-ance crisis, and consequently an effectiveness crisis, it therefore appears that some kind of *societally backed multilateralism with full multi-media* coverage is necessary to save multilateralism by putting an end to executive exclusiveness.[59]

The major objection to the concept of societally backed multilat-eralism with multi-media coverage is that the democratic deficits of international institutions can only be remedied under the right sociocultural conditions, i.e., with some sense of political community and a common ground for communication – both of which are still

[58] C. Joerges, *The Emergence of Denationalized Governance Structures and the European Court of Justice*, ARENA Working Paper 16, Oslo, ARENA, 1996.

[59] Leggewie, *Die Globalisierung und ihre Gegner*, op. cit., p. 112, seems to be quite sceptical about making international politics public. For him, it is the medial visibil-ity of international meetings that has created the resistance. Making international pol-itics public then would be the cause of, not the cure for, the problem of lacking societal support.

lacking at all levels beyond the nation-state. That is an important objection, but it must not blind us to the potential of a gradual democratization of international institutions. The pressure to democratize them certainly increases as societal acceptance diminishes. It therefore appears most sensible to continue the search, backed by theoretical findings, for the potentials and limits of democratizing international institutions. Two strategies appear to be particularly promising here.[60] First, institutional mechanisms must be created which allow the highest degree of democratization under the given conditions. Secondly, international institutions must contribute to democratization by facilitating the emergence of transnational political communities and transnational communication channels, and thus in the medium term improve the institutional scope for direct democratization. One can see the development of a European Convention and debates over it, in spite of all its drawbacks, as an attempt to optimize on both of these counts. And indeed, since the late 1990s the general public's satisfaction with the EU has grown. In any case, without a strategy for increasing the democratic legitimacy of international institutions, internationalizing politics and multilateralism will be defeated by a lack of societal acceptance.

[60] Cf. Zürn, *Democratic Governance Beyond the Nation-State*, op. cit.

8
Global Governance and Communicative Action

Thomas Risse

THE DEBATE ABOUT GLOBAL GOVERNANCE AND ABOUT NEW MODES OF governance focuses almost exclusively on the question of whether the inclusion of new and mostly private actors can increase both the democratic quality and the problem-solving capacity of institutionalized cooperation in the international system.[1] At the same time, many international organizations and actors – from the United Nations to the European Commission – emphasize learning processes and policy diffusion as a means of overcoming the limitations of 'top down' hierarchical steering. Yet, if we conceive of learning and policy diffusion not just as cognitive processes 'inside the human brain', but as inherently social and intersubjective processes, communicative practices quickly become the micro-mechanisms by which ideas get diffused and new ways of thinking are learned. At this point, arguing and reason-giving assume centre-stage in the debate about new modes of governance.

This chapter discusses arguing and communicative action as significant tools for non-hierarchical steering modes in global governance. Arguing is based on a logic of action that differs significantly both from the rational choice-based 'logic of consequentialism' and from the 'logic of appropriateness' theorized by sociological institutionalism. Arguing constitutes a learning mechanism by which actors acquire new information, evaluate their interests in light of new empirical and moral knowledge, and – most importantly – can reflexively and collectively assess the validity claims of norms and standards of appropriate behaviour. As a result, arguing and persuasion constitute tools of 'soft steering' that might improve both the legitimacy problems of global governance by providing voice opportunities to

[1] I thank Mathias Koenig-Archibugi and David Held for their comments on the draft of this chapter.

various stakeholders and the problem-solving capacity of governance institutions through deliberation.

I proceed in the following steps. I begin by defining my understanding of 'global governance' and by locating arguing and communicative action within this concept. Some conceptual remarks on what arguing is all about and how to think about it follow. I then discuss how arguing and deliberative processes affect rule-setting and rule-implementation processes in global governance. The chapter concludes with some remarks about the relationship between arguing and the legitimacy problem in global governance.

'GLOBAL GOVERNANCE' AND THE NEW MODES OF GOVERNANCE DEBATE

There is quite some confusion in the debate over global governance that needs to be clarified before one can discuss how arguing and communicative action relate to it. The term 'governance' has become such a catchword in the social sciences that its content has been used to connote a variety of things. In the broadest possible definition, 'governance' relates to any form of creating or maintaining political order and providing common goods for a given political community on whatever level.[2] A more narrow view has been promoted by international relations scholars, such as James N. Rosenau and Ernst-Otto Czempiel.[3] Accordingly, 'governance without government' refers to political arrangements which rely primarily on non-hierarchical forms of steering. In other words, governance is confined to creating political order in the absence of a state with a legitimate monopoly over the use of force and the capacity to authoritatively enforce the law and other rules. Of course, there is no state

---

[2] Cf. Oliver E. Williamson, *Markets and Hierarchies: Analysis and Anti-Trust*, New York, Free Press, 1975; see also the Commission on Global Governance's rather broad conceptualization in *Our Global Neighbourhood*, Oxford, Oxford University Press, 1995.

[3] See Ernst-Otto Czempiel and James Rosenau (eds), *Governance Without Government: Order and Change in World Politics*, Cambridge, Cambridge University Press, 1992. See also the excellent reviews in Renate Mayntz, *New Challenges to Governance Theory*, Jean Monnet Papers, Florence, European University Institute, 1998; Renate Mayntz, 'Common Goods and Governance,' in Adrienne Heritier (ed.), *Common Goods. Reinventing European and International Governance*, Lanham, MD, Rowman & Littlefield, 2002, pp. 15–27.

or world government in the global realm, even though the United Nations Security Council has limited authority to impose world order and peace. As a result, to the extent that the international system contains rule structures and institutional settings, this constitutes 'governance without government' almost by definition.

But why do we need to use the language of 'governance', if we can talk about international institutions, such as international organizations (IOs) or international regimes?[4] While IOs are inter-state institutions 'with a street address', international regimes are defined as international institutions based on explicit principles, norms and rules, that is, international legal arrangements agreed upon by national governments. The nuclear non-proliferation regime, the world trade order, the regime to prevent global climate change, or the various human rights treaties all constitute international regimes, i.e., form part of global 'governance without government'. These regimes have in common that they are based on voluntary agreements by states and that there is no supreme authority in the international system capable of enforcing these rules. Hence the elaborate schemes to monitor and verify compliance with the rules and regulations of international regimes!

There is one emerging realm of international institutions which is not covered by the language of international inter-state regimes or organizations as commonly used in the international relations literature. The Internet Corporation for Assigned Names and Numbers (ICANN) regulates the internet, but is a nongovernmental institution. Private rating agencies claim authoritative, consensual and therefore legitimate knowledge about the credit worthiness of companies and even states and, thus, play an enormous role in international financial markets. The UN Global Compact consists of firms voluntarily agreeing to comply with international human rights and environmental norms. Thus, we observe the emergence of governance structures in international life which are based on private authority, private regimes, or some mix of public and private actors.[5]

---

[4] On these concepts see, e.g., Robert O. Keohane, *International Institutions and State Power*, Boulder, CO, Westview, 1989.

[5] For a discussion see Rodney Bruce Hall and Thomas J. Biersteker (eds), *The Emergence of Private Authority in Global Governance*, Cambridge, Cambridge University Press, 2002; Claire A. Cutler et al. (eds), *Private Authority and International Affairs*, Albany, NY, State University of New York Press, 1999; Virginia Haufler, 'Crossing the Boundary between Public and Private: International Regimes and Non-State Actors', in Volker

In particular, there seems to be an increasing number of 'public private partnerships' (PPPs) in international life, some of which are concerned with international rule-setting, such as the World Commission on Dams. Other PPPs – the Global Compact and other global public policy arrangements, for example – focus on rule implementation or service provision.[6]

In the following, I am not concerned with governance in the general sense of steering and creating political order, but with these 'new modes of governance' which are 'distinct from the hierarchical control model characterizing the interventionist state. Governance is the type of regulation typical of the cooperative state, where state and non-state actors participate in mixed public/private policy networks.'[7] As a result, 'new modes of global governance' would refer to those institutional arrangements beyond the nation-state that are characterized by two features (see Figure 1):
• the inclusion of non-state actors, such as firms, private interest groups, or nongovernmental organizations (NGOs) in governance arrangements (actor dimension);
• an emphasis on non-hierarchical modes of steering (steering modes).
While most of the literature on 'new modes of governance' is concerned with the actor dimension and, thus, with the inclusion of private actors in global governance, I concentrate on the steering modes. Modes of political steering concern both rule-setting and rule-implementation processes including ensuring compliance with international norms. In Figure 1, hierarchical steering refers to classic statehood in the Weberian or Eastonian sense (politics as the 'authoritative allocation of values for a given society') and connotes

Rittberger (ed.), *Regime Theory and International Relations*, Oxford, Clarendon Press, 1993, pp. 94–111; Wolfgang H. Reinicke, *Global Public Policy. Governing without Government?*, Washington, DC, Brookings Institution, 1998; Wolfgang H. Reinicke and Francis Deng, *Critical Choices. The United Nations, Networks, and the Future of Global Governance*, Ottawa, International Development Research Centre, 2000.

[6] On PPPs see Pauline Vaillancourt Rosenau (ed.), *Public-Private Policy Partnerships*, Cambridge, MA, MIT Press, 2000; Tanja A. Börzel and Thomas Risse, 'Public-Private Partnerships: Effective and Legitimate Tools of International Governance?,' in Edgar Grande and Louis W. Pauly (eds), *Reconstituting Political Authority: Complex Sovereignty and the Foundations of Global Governance*, forthcoming.

[7] Mayntz, 'Common Goods and Governance', op. cit., p. 21.

Figure 1
The Realm of New Modes of Global Governance

Actors involved steering modes	Public actors only	Public and private actors	Private actors only
Hierarchical: Top-down; (threat of) sanctions	• traditional nation-state; • supranational institutions (EU, partly WTO)[8]	• Contracting out and out-sourcing of public functions to private actors	• corporate hierarchies
Non-hierarchical: Positive incentives; bargaining; non-manipulative persuasion (learning, arguing etc.)	• international regimes • international organizations	• corporatism • public–private networks and partnerships • bench-marking	• private interest government/private regimes • private–private partnerships (NGOs–companies)

(Shaded area = new modes of governance)

Source: Börzel and Risse, 'Public-Private Partnerships: Effective and Legitimate Tools of International Governance?', op. cit.

the ability of states to enforce the law through sanctions and the threat of force, if need be. In the international system, modes of hierarchical steering are notably absent except, for example, in supranational organizations such as the European Union (EU) where European law constitutes the 'law of the land' and, thus, some elements of hierarchy are always present.

However, no modern state can rely solely on coercion and hierarchy to enforce the law. The main difference between modern states and global governance is not that non-hierarchical modes of steering do not exist in the former. The main difference is that global governance has to rely *solely* on non-hierarchical modes of steering in the absence of a world government with a legitimate monopoly over the use of force. As to these non-hierarchical modes of steering, we can further distinguish between two forms which rely on different modes of social action and social control:
1. Non-hierarchical steering can use positive incentives and negative sanctions to entice actors into compliance with norms and rules. The

[8] This is not to suggest that non-hierarchical steering does not occur inside nation-states or inside the EU. However, the new modes of governance take place under the 'shadow of hierarchy' in those institutional contexts.

point is to use incentives and sanctions to manipulate the cost-benefit calculations of actors so as to convince them that rule compliance is in their best interest. As to rule-setting, 'bargaining' during which self-interested actors try to hammer out agreements of give-and-take based on fixed identities and interests has to be mentioned here, too. This mode of steering essentially follows a logic of instrumental rationality as theorized by 'rational choice'. Actors are seen as egoistic utility-maximizers or optimizers who agree to rules, because they are in their own interests. Voluntary compliance follows from self-interested behaviour in this case.

2. A second type of non-hierarchical steering focuses on increasing the moral legitimacy of the rules and norms in question.[9] The idea is that, the more they are convinced of the legitimacy of the rule, the more will actors comply voluntarily with norms and rules. The legitimacy of a rule can result from beliefs in the moral validity of the norm itself, but it can also result from beliefs in the validity of the procedure by which the rule had been worked out. Voluntary rule compliance is based on the acceptance of a particular logic of appropriateness.[10] But how do actors come to accept a new logic of appropriateness? They acquire the social knowledge to function appropriately in a given society or they start believing in the moral validity of the norms and rules in question. In either case, the micro-mechanism underlying this type of social steering concerns learning and persuasion.

This second mode of non-hierarchical steering provides the link between theories of communicative action, deliberative democracy and new forms of global governance. Arguing and persuasion pertain to a logic of social action and interaction which differs substantially from those theorized by rational choice. Let me, therefore, continue with some conceptual clarifications, before I get back to the question of how global governance and communicative action are related.

---

[9] On this point see also Ian Hurd, 'Legitimacy and Authority in International Politics,' *International Organization*, 53: 2 (1999), pp. 379–408.

[10] On the 'logic of appropriateness' versus the 'logic of consequentialism' see James G. March and Johan P. Olsen, *Rediscovering Institutions*, New York, Free Press, 1989; James G. March and Johan P. Olsen, 'The Institutional Dynamics of International Political Orders', *International Organization*, 52: 4 (1998), pp. 943–69.

ARGUING AND DELIBERATION: CONCEPTUAL CLARIFICATIONS[11]

When actors deliberate in settings such as the ones found in multi-lateral negotiations, they try to figure out in a collective communicative process

• whether their assumptions about the world and about cause-effect relationships in the world are correct (the realm of theoretical discourses), or

• whether norms of appropriate behaviour can be justified and which norms apply under given circumstances (the realm of practical or moral discourses).

Arguing implies that actors try to challenge the validity claims inherent in any causal or normative statement and to seek a communicative consensus about their understanding of a situation as well as justifications for the principles and norms guiding their action. Argumentative rationality also means that the participants in a discourse are open to be persuaded by the better argument and that relationships of power and social hierarchies recede in the background.[12] Argumentative and deliberative behaviour is as goal-oriented as strategic interactions, but the goal is not to attain one's fixed preferences, but to seek a reasoned consensus. Actors' interests, preferences and the perceptions of the situation are no longer fixed, but subject to discursive challenges. Where argumentative rationality prevails, actors do not seek to maximize or to satisfy their given interests and preferences, but to challenge and to justify the validity claims inherent in them – *and* are prepared to change their views of the world or even their interests in light of the better argument. In other words, argumentative and discursive processes

[11] For the following see Thomas Risse, ' "Let's Argue!" Communicative Action in International Relations', *International Organization*, 54: 1 (2000), pp. 1–39; Cornelia Ulbert and Thomas Risse, 'Arguing and Persuasion in Multilateral Negotiations: Theoretical Approach and Research Design', paper presented at the Fourth Pan European International Relations Conference, University of Kent, Canterbury, 7–10 September 2001.

[12] Jürgen Habermas calls this 'communicative action', Jürgen Habermas, *Theorie des kommunikativen Handelns*, 2 vols, Frankfurt am Main, Suhrkamp, 1981. Since communications are all-pervasive in social action and interaction – including strategic behaviour (see below), I prefer the term 'argumentative' rationality, since the goal of such communicative behaviour is to reach argumentative consensus on validity claims of norms or assertions about the world.

challenge the truth of claims which are inherent in identities, interests and norms.

Habermas introduces behaviour oriented towards reaching a common understanding (*verständigungsorientiertes Handeln*) as follows: 'I speak of *communicative* actions when the action orientations of the participating actors are not coordinated via egocentric calculations of success, but through acts of understanding. Participants are not primarily oriented toward their own success in communicative action; they pursue their individual goals under the condition that they can co-ordinate their action plans on the basis of shared definitions of the situation.'[13] The goal of such communicative action is to seek a reasoned consensus (*Verständigung*). In arguing mode, actors try to convince each other to change their causal or principled beliefs in order to reach a reasoned consensus about validity claims. As Müller put it,

once collective actors – states – reach the limits of purely strategic behavior, they know intuitively and by experience that the repertoire for action of all actors – their own and that of their opponents – contains the alternative of action oriented toward common understanding (*Verständigungshandeln*). This is the decisive difference to the utilitarian paradigm which does not entail this alternative. ... (Actors) also have indicators at their disposal – intuitively and by experience – by which to judge if and when the partner is willing and able to switch from one mode of action to the other. Communicative discourse allows for the test of these criteria.[14]

Argumentative rationality in the Habermasian sense is based on several pre-conditions. First, argumentative consensus-seeking requires the ability to empathize, i.e., to see things with the eyes of

---

[13] Ibid., vol. 1, p. 385 (my translation). For the following, see Volker von Prittwitz (ed.), *Verhandeln und Argumentieren. Dialog, Interessen und Macht in der Umweltpolitik*, Opladen, Westdeutscher Verlag, 1996; Thomas Saretzki, 'Wie unterscheiden sich Argumentieren und Verhandeln?', in von Prittwitz, *Verhandeln und Argumentieren*, op. cit., pp. 19–39; Lars G. Lose, 'Communicative Action and the Social Construction of Diplomatic Societies: Communication and Behavior in the Real World', paper presented at the Femmoller Workshop, 24–8 June 1998; Erik Oddvar Eriksen and Jarle Weigard, 'Conceptualizing Politics: Strategic or Communicative Action?', *Scandinavian Political Studies*, 20: 3 (1997), pp. 219–41.

[14] Harald Müller, 'Internationale Beziehungen als kommunikatives Handeln. Zur Kritik der utilitaristischen Handlungstheorien', *Zeitschrift für Internationale Beziehungen*, 1: 1 (1994), pp. 15–44; 28 (my translation). See also Neta C. Crawford, *Argument and Change in World Politics. Ethics, Decolonization, and Humanitarian Intervention*, Cambridge, Cambridge University Press, 2002.

the interaction partner. Second, actors need to share a 'common lifeworld' (*gemeinsame Lebenswelt*), a supply of collective interpretations of the world and of themselves. The common lifeworld consists of a shared culture, a common system of norms and rules perceived as legitimate, and the social identity of actors being able to communicate and to act.[15] The common lifeworld provides arguing actors with a repertoire of collective understandings to which they can refer when making truth claims. At the same time, communicative action and its daily practices reproduce the common lifeworld.

Finally, actors need to recognize each other as equals and need to have equal access to the discourse which must also be open to other participants and public in nature. In this sense then, relationships of power, force, and coercion are assumed absent when argumentative consensus is sought. This implies respect for two principles: universal respect as the recognition of all interested parties as participants in the argumentative discourse, and the recognition of equal rights for all participants concerning making an argument or challenging a validity claim.[16] The point is not that power asymmetries do not exist when argumentative consensus is sought. There is no 'ideal speech situation' in real life. Yet, such an ideal speech situation assumes the status of a counterfactual presupposition when actors engage in argumentative discourse. If we try to understand each other, if we start deliberating in this sense, we cannot do so without assuming that relationships of power and other asymmetries recede to the background for the time being.

In sum and following Saretzki, ideal typical arguing as reason-giving can be distinguished analytically from 'bargaining' in modal, structural and procedural terms, and in terms of possible observable outcomes.[17] In Figure 2, arguing and bargaining are defined as ideal types representing the end points of a continuum. Thus, arguing is a mode of communication in which the mutual assessment of the validity of an argument geared towards reaching a reasoned consensus rather than instructions, rules, votes, force, manipulation,

[15] Habermas, *Theorie des kommunikativen Handelns*, op. cit., vol. 1, p. 209.

[16] Lose, 'Communicative Action and the Social Construction of Diplomatic Societies', op. cit. p. 9.

[17] Cf. Saretzki, 'Wie unterscheiden sich Argumentieren und Verhandeln?', op. cit., pp. 32–6. See also Jon Elster, *Arguing and Bargaining in Two Constituent Assemblies*, The Storr Lectures, New Haven, Yale Law School, 1991, p. 5.

Figure 2
Arguing and Bargaining as Modes of Communication

Mode of communication /characteristics	ARGUING	BARGAINING
Modal	Empirical and normative assertions with validity claims (assessment criteria: empirical proof and consistency or in the case of normative assertions consistency and impartiality); based on: 'argumentative power' in the sense of good reasoning	Pragmatic demands with credibility claims (assessment criteria: credibility of speaker); based on: 'bargaining power' in the sense of material and ideational resources and exit options
Procedural	Reflexive	Sequential
Possible observable outcome	Reasoned consensus, actors submitting to the better argument and changing interests/preferences accordingly	Compromise without change in preferences/interests
Structural	Triadic (speaker and listener have to refer to some external authority to make validity claims)	Dyadic (only mutual assessment counts)

tradition etc. is crucial for decision-making.[18] Moreover, arguing is a reflexive process that does not take place in distinct sequences. The process of arguing is rather characterized by an exchange of arguments that is based on a common frame of reference that is adjusted in the course of communication.

As to structural features, arguing can be distinguished from bargaining through its triadic nature (see Figure 3). Bargaining actors assess the moves in negotiations based solely on their own utility functions including private information, while validity claims such as the truthfulness of speakers, the truth of empirical assertions, or the rightness of normative claims, recede in the background and are irrelevant for the bargaining situation. This is the dyadic nature of bargaining. Third parties might be present in bargaining situations as mediators or as enforcers of commitments. But pure bargaining does not involve references to common values or to shared knowledge. Bargainers have to assess whether their counterparts can

---

[18] Eriksen and Weigard, 'Conceptualizing Politics: Strategic or Communicative Action?', op. cit., p. 227.

Figure 3
The Triadic Structure of the Process of Arguing

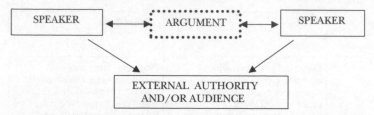

deliver on their promises or can issue credible threats, but the normative validity of the bargaining moves are irrelevant in this context.

In contrast, arguing always involves references to a mutually accepted external authority to validate empirical or normative assertions. In international negotiations, such sources of authority (*Berufungsgrundlagen*) can be previously negotiated and agreed-upon treaties, universally held norms, scientific evidence, and other forms of consensual knowledge. In each case, there are different sources of external authority to which speakers can refer in order to validate their claims. A special case of this kind of triadic situation occurs when speakers argue in front of an audience which serves as an adjudicator of the 'better argument'. In such cases, they do not only refer to some external authority, but the audience itself might become that external authority as part of the reflexive process.

While, analytically speaking, arguing and reason-giving as modes of communication have to be strictly separated from 'bargaining' (see Figure 2 above), empirical research demonstrates that arguing and bargaining usually go together in reality.[19] Pure arguing in terms

---

[19] For the following see Ulbert and Risse, 'Arguing and Persuasion in Multilateral Negotiations: Theoretical Approach and Research Design', op. cit.; Katharina Holzinger, 'Verhandeln statt Argumentieren oder Verhandeln durch Argumentieren? Eine empirische Analyse auf der Basis der Sprechakttheorie', *Politische Vierteljahresschrift*, 42: 3 (2001), pp. 414–46; Katharina Holzinger, 'Kommunikationsmodi und Handlungstypen in den Internationalen Beziehungen', *Zeitschrift für Internationale Beziehungen*, 8: 2 (2001), pp. 243–86; Frank Schimmelfennig, 'Liberal Norms, Rhetorical Action, and the Enlargement of the EU', *International Organization*, 55: 1 (2001), pp. 47–80.

of deliberative and truth-seeking behaviour occurs as rarely as pure bargaining in terms of the exchange of demands, threats, promises and the like. Rather, pure arguing and pure bargaining represent opposite ends of a continuum whereby most of the actual communicative processes take place somewhere in between. Bargaining actors tend to constantly justify their demands in terms of generally accepted norms as well as consensual knowledge. Arguing actors tend routinely to use reasons in order to persuade *others* of the validity and the justifiability of their claims. But the ubiquity of arguing in negotiation systems should not be confused with the assertion that, therefore, reason-giving always matters and always influences results. Rather, it leads to shift the focus slightly: Instead of analysing whether arguing or bargaining modes dominate in various phases of the negotiations, we need to identify the conditions under which arguing leads to changes in actors' persuasions and, thus, influences the process and outcomes of negotiations. Instead of stipulating *whether* actors use arguments and reason to justify their actions and their interests, we need to focus on the conditions under which arguing and reason-giving actually matter.

A second finding concerns the interaction orientations and motivations of actors involved in arguing and bargaining situations. Some theoretical claims imply that actors engaged in arguing must be motivated towards truth-seeking in order to be able to exchange and challenge validity claims mutually. Such claims stem from a specific interpretation of the Habermasian theory of communicative action, including a peculiar understanding of the ideal speech situation. However, it is empirically impossible to ascertain with certainty the interaction orientations of actors engaged in arguing and bargaining. At the same time, it is not necessary to make heroic assumptions about truth-seeking actors to find them engaged in argumentative exchanges and reason-giving. In particular circumstances, even instrumentally rational and strategically motivated actors need to engage in serious dialogue and in reason-giving with their counterparts in order to be able to influence the course and outcome of negotiations. Ritualistic rhetoric that repeats the same arguments over and over again tends to be rather self-defeating behaviour (actors retain some veto power, but are unlikely to influence the course of the talks positively). Even actors with initially strategic motivations must engage in the give and take of arguing in order to affect negotiations. They must demonstrate their truthfulness and their open-mindedness to the 'better argument'. I have suggested calling this process 'argumentative entrapment' for lack of a better term.[20] One can explain this finding on the basis of the above-mentioned triadic structure of arguing as compared to the dyadic structure of bargaining. As a consequence, it is no longer necessary to determine the interaction orientations of negotiators in order to claim that arguing influences the course of negotiations. Rather, one should focus on the social and institutional context in which arguing takes place. The question then becomes what type of contextual conditions are required to enable the triadic structure of arguing to become effective. Take a court room situation, for example: we can safely assume that both state attorneys and defence lawyers are instrumentally motivated in a court room. However, they need to persuade an audience (the judges and/or the jury) by reference to generally acknowledged legal principles and norms. Judges and jury are required by law to be open to persuasion. As a result, speakers in a court room must submit to the logic of arguing in order to be able to make their case. Thus, the institutional context and setting of a court guarantees that the triadic nature of arguing can operate.

COMMUNICATIVE ACTION AND GLOBAL GOVERNANCE

Having clarified what constitutes communicative action and arguing, I now turn back to the question of what a focus on processes of arguing and persuasion adds to the literature on global governance. I see three connections to the discussion surrounding new modes of (global) governance as defined above:
• as to rule-setting processes, arguing and persuasion represent modes of social action by which actors' preferences and even identities can be challenged and changed *during* social interaction;
• as to rule implementation and compliance, communicative action so defined is crucial for social learning as an important mechanism for socializing actors into new (international) norms and rules;
• last, but not least, arguing and persuasion are directly linked to the issue of legitimacy and accountability in global governance, as the

[20] Thomas Risse, 'International Norms and Domestic Change: Arguing and Communicative Behavior in the Human Rights Area', *Politics & Society*, 27: 4 (1999), pp. 526–56.

literature on deliberative democracy demonstrates. I comment on this point in the conclusions below.

Arguing and Rule-setting

As suggested above, there are two ideal typical ways in which actors can reach voluntary agreements about new norms and rules.[21] Bargaining compromises refers to cooperative agreements through the give and take of negotiations based on fixed interests and preferences. Reasoned consensus refers to the voluntary agreement about norms and rules reached through arguing and persuasion. How do we know a reasoned consensus when we see one? In contrast to a bargaining compromise, actors have to give similar reasons and justifications for why they agreed to the consensus. Otherwise, they would not have been persuaded.[22] In reality, though, bargaining sequences and arguing processes usually go together (see above). Most actors justify their preferences on the basis of general principles and norms assuming that these norms are shared by the participants. Thus, they use arguments for instrumental purposes thereby engaging in rhetorical action.[23] Yet, even rhetoric is subject to the triadic structure of arguing. Rhetorical reasons can be challenged by other speakers as purely instrumental as a result of which rhetorical actors need to demonstrate their sincerity in an arguing process. This constitutes what I have called 'argumentative entrapment'.[24]

But how do we know that arguing actually mattered in a negotiation process? How do we know that the 'power of the better

[21] A third and fourth way would be voting and coercion which are neglected here. Very few international bodies use voting procedures in negotiation systems. As to coercion, it is ultimately based on the threat to use force and is inconsistent with voluntary agreement.

[22] See Jens Steffek, 'The Legitimation of International Governance: A Discourse Approach', *European Journal of International Relations*, 9: 2 (2003), 249–75; 264, on this point.

[23] See Schimmelfennig, 'Liberal Norms, Rhetorical Action, and the Enlargement of the EU', op. cit.; Frank Schimmelfennig, *Rules and Rhetoric. The Eastern Enlargement of NATO and the European Union*, Cambridge, Cambridge University Press, forthcoming.

[24] See Risse, 'International Norms and Domestic Change: Arguing and Communicative Behavior in the Human Rights Area', op. cit.

argument' prevailed? The first test concerns whether we can actually read the negotiation outcome from the interests of the actors at the beginning of the process. If we found 'surprises' and some unexpected outcomes, or agreements beyond the lowest common denominator, then something must have happened *during* the negotiations. At this point, we need to take a closer look at the negotiation process itself. One could map the process by identifying bargaining and arguing speech acts.[25] The second test would then consist of figuring out whether progress in negotiations resulted from typical bargaining tools such as issue linkage, package deals, promises, threats, and the like, and/or whether we can identify elements of reasoned consensus on principles and norms. In sum, careful process-tracing is required to find out whether processes of persuasion actually mattered leading to changes in policy preferences or even in actors' interests over outcomes.

Empirical research demonstrates that arguing and persuasion matters particularly during specific phases of negotiations.[26] First, processes of persuasion are particularly relevant during agenda-setting and pre-negotiations. How do new issues enter the agenda of global governance? Policy and norm entrepreneurs of all kinds usually engage in framing.[27] Frames are persuasive, because they shed new light on old questions, because they resonate with people's previous beliefs, or because they identify a new problem of international governance. Second, arguing becomes relevant again when crises in the bargain setting have to be overcome. Many negotiation processes break down or reach impasses because actors stick to their fixed preferences, leaving no room for compromise. Turning into arguing mode offers a way out of these bargaining blockages because it allows actors to reflect anew about their interests and preferences, to see information in a new light, etc.

[25] For such a procedure see Holzinger, 'Verhandeln statt Argumentieren oder Verhandeln durch Argumentieren?', op. cit; Holzinger, 'Kommunikationsmodi und Handlungstypen in den Internationalen Beziehungen', op. cit.

[26] For the following see Cornelia Ulbert et al., *Arguing and Persuasion in Multilateral Negotiations*, Berlin and Frankfurt am Main, Freie Universität Berlin and Hessische Stiftung Friedens- und Konfliktforschung, forthcoming.

[27] See Rodger A. Payne, 'Persuasion, Frames, and Norm Construction', *European Journal of International Relations*, 7: 1 (2001), pp. 37–61; William A. Gamson, *Talking Politics*, Cambridge, Cambridge University Press, 1992.

The more arguing matters in negotiation processes, the more we should also observe that actors with lesser material resources get empowered through the process. While genuine truth-seeking and ideal speech situations are usually absent during international negotiations, institutional settings that allow or even force actors to shift towards reasoning and deliberation should level the playing field between the materially powerful and the powerless. Assuming that the materially more powerful do not necessarily control the 'better arguments', we should expect materially weaker actors to improve their negotiating position the more arguing matters in such institutional settings.

Take, for example, trisectoral public policy networks such as the World Commission on Dams or the UN Global Compact in which states, international organizations, private firms, and international nongovernmental organizations (INGOs) cooperate to seek common solutions for various collective action problems.[28] If material bargaining power is all that counts in such settings, we would expect states, IOs and private firms to prevail in such networks, because they usually command vastly superior material resources over INGOs, knowledge-based epistemic communities, or transnational advocacy networks.[29] The more these trisectoral networks and 'public private partnerships' privilege learning processes and the mutual exchange of ideas and knowledge to enhance the problem-solving capacity of global governance, the more arguing and reason-giving should matter. As a result, ideational resources such as the knowledge power of expert communities or the moral authority of INGOs are expected to become increasingly relevant in such trisectoral networks. The Global Compact, for example, is explicitly designed to operate as a learning network that works through processes of arguing and persuasion, naming and shaming. Firms commit themselves to comply with international human rights and

[28] On trisectoral networks in general see Reinicke, *Global Public Policy. Governing without Government?*, op. cit.; Reinicke and Deng, *Critical Choices. The United Nations, Networks, and the Future of Global Governance*, op. cit. See also Hall and Biersteker (eds), *The Emergence of Private Authority in Global Governance*, op. cit.

[29] On the latter groups see Peter M. Haas (ed.), 'Knowledge, Power and International Policy Coordination', *International Organization*, 46 (special issue, 1992); Margret Keck and Kathryn Sikkink, *Activists Beyond Borders. Transnational Advocacy Networks in International Politics*, Ithaca, NY, Cornell University Press, 1998.

environmental norms, but there is no enforcement mechanism and rather limited monitoring capacity. The idea behind it is that compliance is ultimately achieved through peer pressure and persuasion. Whether or not the Global Compact and other global partnerships achieve their goals through learning and arguing alone, remains to be seen. The empirical record so far seems to be mixed at best. We know very little about the particular scope conditions under which learning networks are successful in either rule-setting or rule-implementation. We also know little about the particular mix of material incentives, on the one hand, and learning opportunities based on arguing mode, on the other, which would achieve the desired outcomes.

As to the World Commission on Dams, another trisectoral body designed to develop rules for the construction of large dams, it was also set up institutionally so as to maximize arguing and learning. It did produce a policy report, but there is little agreement in the literature and the policy world alike whether it actually achieved its goal of reaching a reasoned consensus that would allow the World Bank to construct a sustainable policy toward large dams without antagonizing any of the various stakeholders.[30]

In sum, emphasis on arguing, learning and persuasion holds quite some promise in improving the quality of international negotiation outcomes and with regard to transnational trisectoral public policy networks. Concepts of learning and persuasion have also entered the official language of international organizations and other bodies, such as the United Nations, the World Bank and even the European Commission.[31] Yet, we need to know more empirically about the institutional environments conducive to learning and persuasion.[32]

[30] See, e.g., Sanjeev Khagram, 'Toward Democratic Governance for Sustainable Development: Transnational Civil Society Organizing Around Big Dams', in Ann M. Florini (ed.), *The Third Force. The Rise of Transnational Civil Society*, Tokyo and Washington, DC, Japan Centre for International Exchange and Carnegie Endowment for International Peace, 2000, pp. 83–114; Klaus Dingwerth, 'Globale Politiknetzwerke und ihre demokratische Legitimation', *Zeitschrift für Internationale Beziehungen*, 10: 1 (2003), pp. 69–111.

[31] On the latter see, e.g., European Commission, *European Governance: A White Paper*, Luxembourg, Office for Official Publications of the European Communities, 2001.

[32] For some propositions see also Jeffrey T. Checkel, 'Why Comply? Social Learning and European Identity Change', *International Organization*, 55: 3 (2001), pp. 553–88.

Arguing and Compliance

Learning and persuasion not only play a role in multilateral negotiations including private actors for international rule-setting. They also provide a micro mechanism for socializing actors in new rules. One of the main problems of contemporary global governance is to decrease the growing gap between international norm acceptance and recognition, on the one hand, and rule compliance, on the other.[33] The problem of international governance seems no longer to be a lack of international rules and norms regulating ever more aspects of international life. We live in a strongly regulated and legalized international system[34] that no longer resembles the anarchic system or a pre-social state of nature, as (neo-)realist thinking wants us to believe. Take international human rights, for example. There is no state in the international system which has not signed and ratified at least one of the international legal human rights instruments and conventions. One simply has to recognize international human rights norms in order to become a 'good international citizen' and a recognized member of the international community 'in good standing'. Yet, even a brief look at the annual reports of Amnesty International or Human Rights Watch reveals that compliance with international human rights norms has not increased simultaneously.[35] Similar findings seem to hold true for international environmental norms. While we can see norm cascades in both issue

[33] On compliance problems in general see Kal Raustiala and Anne-Marie Slaughter, 'International Law, International Relations, and Compliance', in Walter Carlsnaes et al. (eds), *Handbook of International Relations*, London, Sage, 2002, pp. 538–58; Tanja A. Börzel and Thomas Risse, 'Die Wirkung internationaler Institutionen: Von der Normanerkennung zur Normeinhaltung', in Markus Jachtenfuchs and Michele Knodt (eds), *Regieren in internationalen Institutionen. Festschrift für Beate Kohler-Koch*, Opladen, Leske & Budrich, 2002, pp. 141–81; Checkel, 'Why Comply? Social Learning and European Identity Change', op. cit.

[34] On legalization see Judith L. Goldstein et al. (eds), 'Legalization and World Politics', *International Organization*, 54: 3 (special issue, 2000).

[35] See also Linda Camp Keith, 'The United Nations International Covenant on Civil and Political Rights: Does It Make a Difference in Human Rights Behavior?', *Journal of Peace Research*, 36: 1 (1999), pp. 95–118; Andrea Liese, 'Staaten am Pranger. Zur Wirkung internationaler Regime auf die innerstaatliche Menschenrechtspolitik', unpublished PhD dissertation, Universität Bremen, 2001.

areas,[36] there seems to be a growing gap between international norm recognition and rule compliance.

The question then is how actors can be socialized into sustained compliance with international norms. To put it differently: under what conditions do actors internalize the logic of appropriateness of international norms as a result of which they acquire a 'taken for granted' nature and are complied with habitually?[37] Of course, material incentives as well as the threat of sanctions matter in inducing compliance with international norms. Yet, socializing actors into new norms requires more than simply manipulating cost-benefit calculations. Assuming instrumental rationality, one would expect actors to violate costly rules once again if the material incentives and/or the threat of sanctions are removed. Thus, sustained compliance cannot be achieved without some degree of rule internalization.

This is where arguing and persuasion become relevant for socialization processes. Voluntary defection from international rules cannot be avoided through sanctions and manipulating incentive structures alone. Rather, one can engage actors – governments and private actors alike – in an arguing process to persuade them of the normative appropriateness of international rules and of the need to accept them as behavioural standards. Voluntary rule compliance would become a matter of persuasion. Our own research on compliance with international human rights norms indicates that arguing and persuasion matter particularly at the latter stages of a

[36] On the concept of 'norm cascades' see Martha Finnemore and Kathryn Sikkink, 'International Norm Dynamics and Political Change', *International Organization*, 52: 4 (1998), pp. 887–917.

[37] On the logic of appropriateness see March and Olsen, 'The Institutional Dynamics of International Political Orders', op. cit. It must be noted here, however, that internalization of norms does not necessarily require that actors are personally convinced of the moral validity of a norm. It is sufficient that they know about what (international) society expects of them. See on this point Ronald L. Jepperson, 'The Development and Application of Sociological Institutionalism', in Joseph Berger and Zelditch Morris Jr. (eds), *New Directions in Sociological Theory: The Growth of Contemporary Theories*, Lanham, MD, Rowman & Littlefield, 2000, pp. 229–66.

socialization process.[38] During the early stages, rule-violating governments are usually forced to make concessions on human rights issues through a mix of international social pressure, incentives to comply (e.g., the EU's conditionality criteria), and the threat of sanctions. Later on and once governments have signed on to international treaties, naming and shaming and, thus, the use of communicative action, becomes more important. Moreover, arguing and persuasion matter increasingly.[39]

We have observed time and again that governments accused of human rights violations were forced to engage in a dialogue with transnational advocacy groups on the precise applicability of international norms in a given context. Norm-violating governments accepted the norms rhetorically in order to decrease the international and domestic pressures against them. Argumentative concessions were part of a larger picture of tactical concessions. There was no dialogue between norm-violating governments and their critics, but their arguments were directed at various audiences, both in domestic society and abroad. Both sides attempted to win over their audiences, to increase international pressures on norm-violating governments, for example, or to rally one's domestic society around a nationalist discourse. Nevertheless, this process increasingly entrapped norm-violating governments into the triadic structure of arguing developed above.

If norm-violating governments found it necessary to make rhetorical concessions and to cease denying the validity of the human rights norms, this provided a discursive opening for their critics to challenge them further: If you say that you accept human rights, why do you violate them systematically? The usual response was that such violations either did not occur or were marginal developments. The discourse then shifted towards the issue of whether norm violations constituted isolated incidents or were systematic in character. It was no longer a discourse on the validity of the norm, but on the

---

[38] See Thomas Risse et al. (eds), *The Power of Human Rights: International Norms and Domestic Change*, Cambridge, Cambridge University Press, 1999, Thomas Risse et al., *Die Macht der Menschenrechte. Internationale Normen, kommunikatives Handeln und politischer Wandel in den Ländern des Südens, Weltpolitik im 21. Jahrhundert*, Baden-Baden, Nomos, 2002. On socialization in general see also Jeffrey Checkel (ed.), *International Institutions and Socialization in Europe*, forthcoming.

[39] For the following see Risse, 'International Norms and Domestic Change: Arguing and Communicative Behavior in the Human Rights Area', op. cit.

situation on the ground and the interpretation of the law of the land. At the same time, the two sides gradually accepted each other as valid interlocutors. At this point, the public discourse increasingly fulfilled the conditions of an argumentative dialogue as outlined above. First, both sides treated each other as equal participants in the discourse. Second, they started sharing a common lifeworld in terms of a mutual acceptance of the underlying norm of human rights. Third, the argumentative consistency of actors, irrespective of the audience, increased dramatically.

Our evidence showed a process of argumentative 'self-entrapment' which starts as rhetorical action and strategic adaptation to external pressures, but ends with argumentative behaviour. How can one explain this process? It certainly does not constitute an 'ideal speech situation' in the Habermasian sense, since governments rarely enter the process of arguing voluntarily, but are forced into a dialogue by the pressure of fully mobilized domestic and transnational networks. They might also face economic or political sanctions by the international community. Over time, however, the dialogue no longer resembles rhetorical exchanges by which both sides use arguments to justify their given interests and behaviour. Even these 'forced dialogues' start having all the characteristics of true argumentative exchanges. Both sides accept each other as valid interlocutors, try to establish some common definition of the human rights situation, and to agree on the norms guiding the situation. Moreover, the actors do not simply repeat their arguments in the public discourses, but respond in increasing detail to the points made by their communication partners. What then looks like 'argumentative concessions' tends to have real consequences in a public debate and in behaviour on the ground. In sum, actors behave as if they were engaged in a true moral discourse. What starts as rhetoric develops its own dynamics and argumentative rationality increasingly takes over. This is precisely what Jürgen Habermas calls communicative rationality in the sense of a counterfactual presupposition of the ideal speech situation and what Jon Elster means when he talks about the 'civilizing effects' of public deliberation.[40]

[40] See Habermas, *Theorie des kommunikativen Handelns*, op. cit., Jürgen Habermas, *Faktizität und Geltung. Beiträge zur Diskurstheorie des Rechts und des demokratischen Rechtsstaats*, Frankfurt am Main, Suhrkamp, 1992; Jon Elster, 'Introduction', in Jon Elster (ed.), *Deliberative Democracy*, Cambridge, Cambridge University Press, 1998, pp. 1–18; 12.

The evidence from the international human rights area suggests that arguing and persuasion are crucial for socialization processes to ensure the compliance of actors – whether public or private – with international norms. It is interesting to note in this context that international organizations increasingly use these mechanisms in trisectoral networks to induce, for example, firms to obey international human rights and environmental rules. Many multinational corporations are particularly vulnerable to processes of naming and shaming which can quickly result in consumer boycotts. As a result, they start accepting corporate social responsibilities by committing themselves to comply with various international norms (cf. once again, the Global Compact, and other mechanisms). Yet, while this might initially be a tactical move, the process does not stop here. Advocacy networks and INGOs start monitoring firms' behaviour and reminding them of their commitments. The arguing and persuasion process gets underway pretty much following the same logic and mechanisms as in the case of human rights networks and norm-violating governments reported above.

The significance of arguing and learning to improve rule compliance has one more implication for global governance. Compliance is not an objectively measurable correspondence between a rule and actual behaviour, but constitutes an interpretive process.[41] As lawyers keep reminding us, compliance involves negotiating over meanings of norms and their applicability in a given social context. Arguing over such legal interpretations provides a means by which actors can reach a reasoned consensus on how to apply an international rule in a domestic setting. The more actors are persuaded about the applicability of the rule in a given context, the more they will comply voluntarily. At this point, the discussion about arguing as a mode of global governance is directly linked to the debate about international legitimacy.

[41] See Friedrich Kratochwil, *Rules, Norms, and Decisions*, Cambridge, Cambridge University Press, 1989; Abram Chayes and Antonia Handler Chayes, 'On Compliance', *International Organization*, 47: 2 (1993), pp. 175–205.

ARGUING, PERSUASION, AND THE LEGITIMACY OF GLOBAL GOVERNANCE

I have suggested in this chapter that the debate about 'new modes of global governance' does not only concern the inclusion of new (non-state) actors in rule-setting and rule-implementation, but also the moving away from hierarchical and 'command and control' modes of steering. Arguing and persuasion constitute such a non-hierarchical steering mode enabling actors to change voluntarily their perceptions of the situation and even their preferences through reasoned consensus. The article then tried to explicate the triadic nature of arguing and applied this concept to problems of global governance in terms of both rule-setting processes and ensuring compliance with international rules.

Yet, arguing and persuasion are directly related to the debate about the legitimacy of global governance. Proponents of deliberative democracy claim that deliberation constitutes a significant means of increasing the democratic legitimacy of governance mechanisms, particularly in situations in which democratic representation and/or voting mechanisms are not available options.[42] The general idea of this literature is that democracy is ultimately about involving the stake-holders, i.e., those concerned by a particular social rule, in a deliberative process of mutual persuasion about the normative validity of a particular rule. Once actors reach a reasoned consensus, this should greatly enhance the legitimacy of the rule, thus ensuring a high degree of voluntary compliance in the absence of sanctions. As Ian Hurd put it, '(w)hen an actor believes a rule is legitimate, compliance is no longer motivated by the simple fear of retribution, or by a calculation of self-interest, but instead by an internal sense of moral obligation . . .'.[43] Such an internal sense of moral obligation,

---

[42] On deliberative democracy and global governance see particularly David Held, *Democracy and the Global Order. From the Modern State to Cosmopolitan Governance*, Cambridge, Cambridge University Press, 1995; Klaus Dieter Wolf, *Die Neue Staatsräson – Zwischenstaatliche Kooperation als Demokratieproblem in der Weltgesellschaft*, Baden-Baden, Nomos, 2000; James Bohman and William Regh, *Deliberative Democracy. Essays on Reason and Politics*, Cambridge, MA, MIT Press, 1997; Elster, *Deliberative Democracy*, op. cit., Christian Joerges and Jürgen Neyer, 'Transforming Strategic Interaction into Deliberative Problem-Solving: European Comitology in the Foodstuffs Sector', *Journal of European Public Policy*, 4 (1997), pp. 609–25.

[43] Hurd, 'Legitimacy and Authority in International Politics', op. cit., p. 387.

which accepts the logic of appropriateness behind a given norm, requires some measure of moral persuasion. Advocates of deliberative democracy argue, therefore, that deliberation and arguing not only tackle the participatory deficit of global governance ('input legitimacy' in Fritz Scharpf's terms), but also increase voluntary compliance with inconvenient rules by closing the legitimacy gap.

However, institutional solutions in global governance to increase the deliberative quality of decision-making face major obstacles that need to be addressed. First, involving stakeholders in rule-setting processes is easier said than done. It is often unclear who the stakeholders are, whom they actually represent, and to whom they are accountable. Take trisectoral public policy networks, for example: (democratic) states are accountable to their citizens and IOs to their principals, i.e., states, while firms are accountable to their shareholders and INGOs to their members. But are these lines of accountability all equally legitimate? And, once again, who decides?

Second, decisions about selection of members in deliberative bodies with some policy-making power are still about inclusion and exclusion. Whom to include, whom to exclude and who actually decides about inclusion and exclusion represent, therefore, most contentious processes in the establishment of trisectoral public policy networks of global governance. This problem is exacerbated by the fact that specific stakeholder interests can usually be organized and represented much easier than diffuse stakeholder interests.

Third, once the stakeholders have been selected, how can deliberation and arguing be ensured to improve the quality of the negotiations? Specific institutional settings are required that enable actors to engage in the reflexive process of arguing. These settings must provide incentives for actors to evaluate critically their own interests and preferences, if the arguing process is supposed to go beyond simply mutual information and explicating one's preferences to others. At this point, a trade-off between transparency and argumentative effectiveness in deliberative settings has to be considered. Many negotiation systems show that arguing and persuasion work particularly well behind closed doors, i.e., outside the public sphere.[44] A reasoned consensus might be achievable more easily if secrecy of the deliberations prevails and actors are not required to

---

[44] See Checkel, 'Why Comply? Social Learning and European Identity Change', op. cit.

justify their change of position and the like in front of critical audiences. Behind closed doors, negotiators can freely exchange ideas and thoughts more easily than in the public sphere where they have to stick to their guns. Yet, transparency is usually regarded as a necessary ingredient for increasing the democratic legitimacy of global governance. If we can only improve the deliberative quality of global governance by decreasing the transparency of the process even further, the overall gain for democratic legitimacy and accountability might not be worth the effort.

This leads to a final point, namely potential tensions between accountability and deliberation. Negotiators – be it diplomats or private actors in trisectoral networks – usually have a mandate from their principals to represent the interests of their organizations and are accountable to whoever sent them to the negotiating body. As a result, there are limits in the extent to which they are allowed to engage in freewheeling deliberation. What if negotiators change sides in the course of negotiations because they have been persuaded by the better argument?[45] Of course, it makes no sense to consider negotiators as nothing but transmission belts of their principals' preferences with no leeway at all. But it does raise issues of accountability, if negotiators are so persuaded by the arguments of their counterparts that they change sides. At least, one would have to require that they engage in a process of 'two level arguing', i.e. of trying to persuade their principals that they should change their preferences, too.[46] It is not enough to institutionalize deliberative processes in multilateral negotiations including trisectoral public policy networks. There needs to be a communicative feedback loop into the domestic and other environments to which negotiating agents are accountable. Otherwise, one would sacrifice accountability and legitimacy for efficiency. Two level arguing might also be necessary to overcome the tension between the effectiveness of delib-

---

[45] Take the World Commission on Dams: a construction industry representative actually changed his position during the negotiations as a result of which the sending body did not accept the Commission's final report, thereby seriously hampering the implementation of the deal.

[46] 'Two level arguing' is analogous to Putnam's 'two level games,' see Robert Putnam, 'Diplomacy and Domestic Politics. The Logic of Two-Level Games', *International Organization*, 42: 2 (1988), pp. 427–60. I thank Mathias Koenig-Archibugi and David Held for alerting me to this point.

eration in secrecy, on the one hand, and ensuring the transparency of the process, on the other.

There are various institutional solutions to tackle these problems. I have suggested in this chapter that it is mainly the social and institutional context rather than actors' individual motivations which determine whether arguing and communicative action can exert influence on negotiation systems. Thus, it becomes a question of designing appropriate global governance institutions and of transforming existing institutions into discourse arenas that ultimately decide whether the legitimacy of global governance can be increased through deliberation.

9
Global Governance, Participation and the Public Sphere

Patrizia Nanz[1] and *Jens Steffek*

AMONG THE MOST COMMON CRITIQUES OF GLOBALIZATION IS THAT this process sacrificed democratic politics to the demand for functional international cooperation and economic liberalization. Since the Second Word War, a considerable number of international legal regimes have developed which institutionalize some kind of centralized legislation or executive with more or less influence on domestic law and its every day practice.[2] A most striking example is the World Trade Organization (WTO) whose rules increasingly determine the environmental, agricultural, health and food safety rules of democratic communities, and, thus, affect the fundamental welfare of their citizens. The increasing capacity of international governance regimes to generate law and regulations binding all citizens has come to conflict with this problem of democratic legitimacy. The idea of democratic legitimacy is that the citizens decide for themselves the content of the laws that organize and regulate their political association. Separating the process of rule-making from politically accountable institutions, global governance is argued to suffer a massive 'democratic deficit'.[3]

[1] Patrizia Nanz's research has been supported by a Marie Curie Fellowship of the European Union (contract number MCFI-2001-01348). We would like to thank Daniele Archibugi, Mathias Koenig-Archibugi and Michael Zürn for helpful comments.

[2] Armin von Bogdandy, 'Law and Politics in the WTO: Strategies to Cope with a Deficient Relationship', *Max Planck Yearbook of United Nations Law*, 5 (2001), pp. 609–74.

[3] While the decisions of international institutions have an effect on the citizens, the only form of legitimation available today is a highly indirect one derived from the (democratically elected) national governments (and their representatives in international organizations), rather than from the collectivity of world citizens.

In this chapter, we explore the possibility of democratic and legitimate decision-making at the global level – in both its normative and its analytical dimensions – from the perspective of a deliberative theory of politics. This theory claims that democratic legitimation[4] can be generated by means of deliberation between a variety of social actors (e.g. government officials from different national communities, scientific experts, NGOs, etc.).[5] Political decisions are reached through a deliberative process where participants scrutinize heterogeneous interests and justify their positions in view of the common good of a given constituency. In our view, any bestowal of democratic legitimacy on global governance must ultimately depend on the creation of an appropriate public sphere, i.e., an institutionalized arena for (deliberative) political participation beyond the limits of national boundaries.

Moreover, we argue that actors from organized civil society play an important role in the creation of a public sphere. They have the potential to act as a discursive interface between international organizations and a global citizenry. Their role is to monitor policy-making in these institutions, to bring citizens' concerns into their deliberations and to empower marginalized groups so that they too may participate effectively in global politics. Given the functionally differentiated and often highly technical nature of global governance, we do not envisage the transnational public sphere as a distinct or overarching realm of broad public deliberation at the global level. Rather, our vision of the public sphere corresponds to the model of functional decision-making and functional participation in the deliberative forums of governance arrangements.[6]

---

[4] Legitimacy can be understood as a general compliance of the people with decisions of a political order that goes beyond coercion or the contingent representation of interests. Normatively, democratic legitimacy results from a rational agreement among free and equal citizens.

[5] Robert Howse is one of several authors who argue that the provisions of the WTO and their interpretation by the dispute settlement body can be understood not as usurping legitimate democratic choices for stricter regulations, but as enhancing the quality of deliberation among citizens about risk and control, although only at the level of membership (R. Howse, 'Democracy, Science, and Free Trade: Risk Regulation on Trial at the World Trade Organization', *Michigan Law Review*, 98: 7 (2000), pp. 2329–57).

[6] Stijn Smismans, 'The European Economic and Social Committee: towards Deliberative Democracy via a Functional Assembly', *European Integration Online Papers*, 4: 12 (2002).

Deliberative participatory publics at the global level stimulate a criss-cross of broader public deliberation in which policy choices (reported and discussed, e.g. within national media) are exposed to public scrutiny. Such a conception of a transnational public sphere and its specific relation to decision-making processes within international organizations is lacking from the current global governance debate.

This chapter is organized as follows: The next section briefly reviews different approaches to democratic legitimacy of international governance and locates our own theoretical standpoint in the deliberative tradition. In the following part we develop an argument about the central role of the public sphere in democratizing global governance. We highlight the close normative connection between processes of political decision-making, citizen participation and public deliberation. Moreover, we specify the central role that civil society can play in establishing such a global public sphere. The final section then illustrates our claims about the democratizing potential of civil society involvement and critical public discourse with some empirical examples from the WTO.

DEMOCRATIZING GLOBAL GOVERNANCE: THE DELIBERATIVE APPROACH

a) *Democracy without Representation and without a* Demos?

Democracy is a political ideal that applies principally to the arrangements for making binding collective decisions. Such arrangements are democratic if they ensure that the authorization to exercise public power arises from collective decisions by the citizens over whom that power is exercised. There are a variety of institutional forms of modern government that resolve this principle of democratic will-formation in slightly different ways. Most western countries have developed some form of electoral democracy. It formally secures the inclusion of citizens, their interests and concerns into government by means of aggregation of individual interests through political parties, corporations and parliaments. For the majority of citizens, participation in this system is reduced to voting in more or less frequent political elections.[7] In addition, there are indirect and voluntary forms of participation in the political process, as, for example, through active involvement in political parties, interest groups, social movements and civil society associations. By addressing problems through public discussion, democracy not only assumes access to information but also exposure to a range of alternative solutions to practical problems.

International governance is remote from citizens, its procedures are opaque, and it is dominated by diplomats, bureaucrats and functional specialists. Although the foundational legal acts of international governance are often subject to national ratification processes, its everyday norms and standards are negotiated by non-elected experts and government officials. They come together behind closed doors, free from the usual intrusion of mandated public representatives and interest groups in their decision-making processes. International organizations do not ensure adequate information to the (ordinary) interested citizen nor is there sufficient public debate about their policy choices. Critics who see international organizations as the triumph of global technocracy see them enshrining professional expertise at the expense of popular sovereignty. Along these lines, it has been forcefully argued that international organizations cannot be democratic because, first and foremost, international policy elites are not (elected) representatives of the people and, second, there is no shared collective identity (a *demos*) and no common political culture supportive of international institutions.[8]

Yet, if global governance will be democratic, it will certainly not be a national democracy writ large.[9] How can we devise an

---

[7] The prevalent design of a western parliamentary mass democracy has been criticized extensively for being remote from citizens, for not reflecting their true concerns, and for fostering an empirical trend away from the active *citoyen* towards the passive and disinterested *bourgeois*. In the view of participatory democrats, interest aggregation dominates over the value-oriented discussion seeking political consensus and novel solutions to problems through a cooperative and creative process of dialogical exchange; see Carol Pateman, *Participation and Democratic Theory*, Cambridge, Cambridge University Press, 1970; Benjamin Barber, *Strong Democracy: Participatory Politics for a New Age*, Berkeley, University of California Press, 1984.

[8] Robert A. Dahl, 'Can International Organizations Be Democratic? A Skeptic's View', in I. Shapiro and C. Hacker-Cordon (eds), *Democracy's Edges*, Cambridge, Cambridge University Press, 1999, pp. 19–36.

[9] Eric Stein, 'International Integration and Democracy: No Love at First Sight', *American Journal of International Law*, 95: 3 (2001), pp. 489–534.

alternative model of democratic will-formation that corresponds to the emerging system of global governance? This contribution argues that a deliberative understanding of democratic collective decision-making is particularly suited for global governance where there is a lack of competitive elections[10] and, as yet, a condition of scarce transnational public sphere. Here, democracy is understood as a framework of social and institutional conditions that facilitate the expression of citizens' concerns and ensures the responsiveness of political power. Democracy is regarded as intrinsically enhancing the legitimacy of government or governance because it ensures the (procedural) conditions for a high quality of the decision-making process, with respect to both regulatory choices and equality of access of affected citizens (or their representatives) in this process. Deliberation, understood as reasoning that is aimed at best addressing practical problems, focuses political debates on the common good: interests, preferences and aims that comprise the common good are those that 'survive' deliberation.

b) Deliberation without Participation?

In the context of international relations, the model of deliberative decision-making has taken on a vision *sui generis*. Since a parliamentarization of politics above the nation-state is not in sight,[11] enhanced political deliberation has been regarded as an alternative avenue for global governance. Well-informed and consensus-seeking discussion in expert committees that are embedded in international decision-making procedures has been suggested as an effective remedy to the legitimation problems of international governance. In this perspective, political deliberation is viewed primarily in a functional fashion as a prerequisite for a high level of efficiency, efficacy and quality in political regulation. This approach to deliberation is inspired by thinking from public policy and international relations

[10] Given the huge differences in the size of the populations of different countries, no system of representation could give equal weight to the vote of each citizen and prevent small countries from being outvoted by larger countries.

[11] Only few believe that international institutions not only should, but actually can be, democratized in this sense, e.g., Richard Falk and Andrew Strauss, 'Toward Global Parliament', *Foreign Affairs*, 80: 1 (2001), pp. 212–20.

theory that have highlighted the importance of scientific expertise and consensus-seeking within epistemic communities of experts.[12] Global governance regimes are said to draw their legitimacy from the deliberative quality of their decision-making process: it is not designed to aggregate self-interests, but rather to foster mutual learning, and to eventually transform preferences while converging on a policy choice oriented towards the public interest.[13] Deliberation among experts becomes a key device of 'good governance' by a responsive administration.

The legitimizing capacity of expert deliberation has also been grounded in empirical arguments. It has been claimed that well-informed rules are effective because they can command assent and compliance by citizens, and thus enhance the (social) legitimacy of political authority. However, some important empirical arguments have been made against this alleged automatism. Thompson and Rayner,[14] for example, present evidence from environmental policy and risk regulation, which indicates that citizens assent to rules only if they have the impression that their own concerns have been treated fairly in the process of rule-making. Consequently, the authors argue for more inclusive institutional designs that accommodate the views of non-experts in deliberative decision-making. In the case of risk regulation, this implies consulting with consumer organizations, environmentalists and, when locating hazardous sites, the local population.

At the international level, the emergence of a transnational social movement against technocratic global governance is evidence of the fact that the 'permissive consensus' for secretive forms of rule-making among experts is vanishing. The legitimacy crisis of global governance manifests itself in transnational public discourse on these

[12] Peter M. Haas, 'Introduction: Epistemic Communities and International Policy Coordination', *International Organization*, 46: 1 (1992), pp. 1–35.

[13] However, it cannot be regarded as democratic: Even if we trust experts and scientists – for example in 'comitology' within the EU (see Christian Joerges and Jürgen Neyer, 'Transforming Strategic Interaction into Deliberative Problem-solving: European Comitology in the Foodstuffs Sector' *Journal of European Public Policy*, 4: 4 (1997), pp. 609–25) – to advocate norms that, in their view, serve the common good of a polity and not some particular interest, *their* assessment and *their* view of the good still prevails.

[14] Michael Thompson and Steve Rayner, 'Risk and Governance Part I: The Discourses of Climate Change', *Government and Opposition*, 33: 2 (1998), pp. 139–66.

international organizations and their policies.[15] The popular movement against the WTO and against the IMF does not only target capitalist principles of neo-liberal globalization. It also critiques their institutional arrangements – an expression of distrust regarding the role of experts and diplomats as protagonists of international governance. In the eyes of many stakeholders and affected citizens, elite expertise and bureaucratic deliberation alone do not suffice to make international organizations legitimate.

More importantly in the context of this paper, the desirability of 'good governance' by elites is also questionable from a normative perspective on democratic legitimacy. Deliberative government is not intrinsically democratic because 'it can be conducted within cloistered bodies that make fateful choices, but are inattentive to the views or the interests of large numbers of affected parties'.[16] Deliberative democracy must ensure that citizens' concerns feed into the policy-making process and are taken into account when it comes to a decision on binding rules. Hence, deliberative democracy relies on certain *participatory* conditions for rule-making. From such a standpoint, it is crucial that the process of (political) deliberation within international organizations is opened to both public scrutiny and to the input of stakeholders.

CITIZEN PARTICIPATION AND THE PUBLIC SPHERE

a) Democratic Legitimacy and the Public Sphere

The desirability of expert deliberation can be contrasted with the idea of *public* deliberation as a source of democratic legitimacy for governing (at the nation-state and global level). In Habermas's proceduralist theory, for example, the public sphere plays a key role: it is conceived as a dispersed, all-encompassing, discursive network within which citizens, connected by the means of mass communication, form currents of opinion in seeking how best to resolve

---

[15] Jens Steffek, 'The Legitimation of International Governance: a Discourse Approach', *European Journal of International Relations*, 9: 2 (2003), pp. 249–75.

[16] Joshua Cohen and Charles F. Sabel, 'Sovereignty and Solidarity: EU and US', in J. Zeitlin and D. Trubek (eds), *Governing Work and Welfare in a New Economy. European and American Experiments*, London, Oxford University Press, 2003, pp. 249–75.

common problems.[17] A public understood as a collectivity of persons connected by processes of communication over particular aspects of social and political life, can, in principle, extend beyond national borders. What is important to the notion of public deliberation is not so much that everyone participates but more that there is a warranted presumption that public opinion is formed on the basis of adequate information and relevant reasons, and that those whose interests are involved have an equal and effective opportunity to make their own interests (and their reasons for them) known. This 'public use of reason' depends on civil society as 'a network of associations that institutionalizes problem-solving discourses on questions of general interest inside the framework of organized public spheres'.[18]

Habermas's theory distinguishes between political institutions (or decision-making bodies) and the broader, decentred public sphere. Our conception departs from this view insofar as it focuses on sites of public deliberation between policy-makers and stakeholders. We emphasize the role of organized civil society participating *within* governance regimes as an intermediary agent between the political institutions and the wider public. We argue that, at the international level, the public sphere – conceived as a pluralistic social realm of a variety of sometimes overlapping or contending (often sectoral) publics engaged in transnational dialogue[19] – can provide an adequate political realm with actors and deliberative processes that help to democratize global governance practice. Deliberative participatory publics within governance regimes stimulate an exchange of arguments in which policy choices are exposed to public scrutiny.

At the national, regional and local level there are many forms of deliberative participation as a means of holding power accountable. It occurs in forums in which citizens (or representatives of organized civil society) discuss with one another and with power-holders their evaluation of policy choices. These participatory forums have different degrees of institutionalization and impact on the political system.

---

[17] Jürgen Habermas, *Between Facts and Norms*, Cambridge, MA, MIT Press, 1996, p. 360.

[18] Ibid., p. 367.

[19] Patrizia Nanz, 'Legitimation of Transnational Governance Regimes: Foodstuff regulation at the WTO', in C. Joerges, I. Sand and G. Teubner (eds), *Constitutionalism and Transnational Governance*, Oxford, Hart Publishing, forthcoming 2004.

They come in the form of civic review boards, implementation studies and periodic official participatory hearings that follow the policy-making process or consultation of civil society. Wider public spheres can further democratic legitimacy by means of questioning, praise, criticism and judgement.

What institutional mechanisms can be envisioned at the global level to serve as an institutional focus for a broader, decentred public sphere? We think of deliberative forums in which groups of social actors (e.g., national officials, scientific experts, NGOs, etc.) co-operatively address a certain global problem, and the ensemble of which could serve for enhancing broader transnational public debates. Such participatory arenas reserve themselves the prerogatives to scrutinize and monitor policy choices of international organizations. They introduce a deliberative element to the public level, while protecting the autonomy and internal complexity of the administrative realm (e.g., outreach meetings could be understood as such publics). If we conceptualize the public sphere as a communicative network where different (national and sectoral) publics partially overlap, the emerging features of global governance regimes can also be seen as offering the chance for the creation of new transnational communities of political action.[20] From such a perspective, global governance regimes – when understood as sites of public deliberation and cooperative inquiry – may yield unprecedented forms of trust and solidarity amongst a variety of social actors (government officials, experts, NGOs, stakeholders, etc.) with diverse (national/sectoral) perspectives on a certain issue. By fostering extended deliberation among those actors over the nature of problems and the best way to solve them, participatory arenas produce a pool of (transnationally) shared arguments which contribute to the emergence of a global public sphere.

b) The Role of Civil Society in Creating a Global Public Sphere

Global governance places new and more demanding epistemic requirements and normative constraints on participation in the

---

[20] Patrizia Nanz, 'Europolis. Constitutional Patriotism beyond the Nation State', PhD dissertation, European University Institute, Florence, 2001.

public sphere. Such entry requirements consist not only in cultural knowledge in general, but also in how to communicate across boundaries that differentiate the audience of modern societies, and, most importantly, in how to interact with and employ international institutions and global media of communication. We argue that organized civil society has a high potential to act as a 'transmission belt' between deliberative processes within international organizations and emerging transnational public spheres. Such a discursive interface operates in two directions: First, civil society organizations can give voice to citizens' concerns and channel them into the deliberative process of international organizations. Second, they can make the internal decision-making processes of international organizations more transparent to the wider public and formulate technical issues in accessible terms. From a normative point of view, these civil society actors must ensure that citizens' concerns are reflected in the decision-making process of international organizations.

This can function only under certain preconditions. First, international public organizations must provide appropriate access to documents and meetings to members of civil society. They must also incorporate all relevant concerns of civil society into their own agenda. Second, in order to contribute to the democratization of global governance, civil society organizations themselves must remain open to citizen input and take on board newly-emerging issues, including those of marginalized groups. Their own agenda must not be 'hijacked' by an elite group of professional activists or special interest groups. Only then can civil society organizations become 'legitimate' participants in global politics.

Transnational civil society is capable of bringing together people with shared (often highly specific) concerns, but very different identities, and considerable uncertainty as to how to address their aims. Deliberative processes among stakeholders thus can create the basis of solidarity beyond national boundaries: through a cooperative search for the best policy practice, engaging in (functional) political participation and sharing expertise. However, the emergence of a substantive (wider) transnational public sphere is not dependent on institutional arrangements. Moreover, enhancing transparency and generating public debate on global governance is only a necessary but not a sufficient precondition for its democratization. Whether (or not) a reformed world trade regime can become more democratic will crucially depend on its ability to develop institutional mechanisms to make trade debates substantially more inclusive, for example through 'participatory publics' which monitor policy choices. Here disadvantaged groups of stakeholders should be able to participate actively either directly or indirectly through civil society organizations which systematically take on board their concerns.

How?

By now, transnational civil society interacts with virtually all international organizations. There are, however, various degrees of institutionalization and formalization of this interaction.[21] The fact that it interacts with international public organizations does not mean that it is necessarily influential in determining policy outcomes. Yet, as the case study below will illustrate, civil society can expose these organizations to public scrutiny and can force them to engage with certain issues they would have otherwise ignored. This is precisely what we claim about civil society's role in democratization: it helps to create a transnational public sphere in which the policies of international institutions are scrutinized and through which citizen concerns can be brought to bear in decision-making within these institutions.

TOWARDS A PUBLIC SPHERE OF GLOBAL GOVERNANCE:
THE CASE OF THE WTO

a) The Deficits of the Status Quo

In the theoretical part of this chapter we have outlined a deliberative approach to the democratization of global governance and highlighted the crucial importance of a transnational public sphere for this project. In this second section we will illustrate our theoretical argument with some empirical evidence from one core institution of global governance, the WTO. There is wide consensus that the WTO is not among the most open or transparent international organizations, and that its democratic legitimacy is questionable. Yet what would it take, in practice, to promote a deliberative

---

[21] Steve Charnovitz, 'Two Centuries of Participation: NGOs and International Governance', *Michigan Journal of International Law*, 18: 1 (1997), pp. 183–286.

democratization of the WTO and the emergence of a public sphere in the functional realm of world trade policy? In the following sections we discuss some key problems, assess the status quo and propose a list of measures to promote the emergence of a public sphere of world trade.

Before we sketch possible remedies to the legitimacy deficit of the WTO, a brief outline of this deficit is in order. The WTO is a member-driven organization where the international bureaucracy plays a subordinate role in policy-making. Important decisions are taken by member states at the biannual Ministerial Conference or at the level of ambassadors in the permanent General Council in Geneva. Moreover, the WTO has adopted and formalized the practice of consensus voting from the GATT. In the GATT, virtually all decisions were taken by consensus. In practice, this meant that a text was negotiated until no party would object to it any more. The WTO charter includes the possibility of majority voting if no consensus can be reached. Yet a vast majority of three-quarters of the members is required in these instances, so that this possibility plays a minor role in practice and consensus-seeking still prevails. Therefore, one could be tempted to conclude that there is an efficient protection of national sovereignty and equality in the WTO.[22]

In reality, however, the procedures at the WTO are much more problematic, and in order to explain the difference between paper form and actual practice a historical perspective should be adopted.[23] Although the WTO is formally an organization with almost universal membership and equal voting rights, it retains important characteristics of the 'club model' of international cooperation that characterized its predecessor, the GATT.[24] The club design aims at crafting 'coalitions of the willing and able' among the powerful players. That this prevails in the WTO is historically rooted in the fact that the GATT had not been designed as an international political forum, but

[22] John H. Jackson, *The World Trade Organization*, London, Pinter, 1998, p. 47.

[23] Rorden Wilkinson, 'The WTO in Crisis. Exploring the Dimensions of Institutional Inertia', *Journal of World Trade*, 35: 3 (2001), pp. 397–419.

[24] Robert O. Keohane and Joseph S. Nye, 'The Club Model of Multilateral Cooperation and the World Trade Organization: Problems of Democratic Legitimacy', in R. Porter et al. (eds), *Efficiency, Equity and Legitimacy: the Multilateral Trading System at the Millennium*, Washington, DC, Brookings Institution, 2001, pp. 264–93.

as a rudimentary institutional framework for tariff bargaining. This task is facilitated by keeping marginal political players, domestic interest groups and the critical public out of the organization's business.

Due to this club tradition, which many WTO officials and delegates still hold dear, the decisive political debates over many world trade issues still take place in informal meetings between the big trading nations. The infamous 'green room' consultations at the Ministerial Conferences have become a synonym for obscure and secretive ways of international decision-making.[25] No records are kept of these meetings, thus preventing even ex-post reconstruction of the political debate. The heavily criticized green room style of decision-making is by no means a practice of the past. In November 2002 the Australian government invited representatives of 25 selected WTO members for a 'mini-ministerial' to clear some obstacles on the road to the Cancún Ministerial Conference in 2003. This procedure triggered a sharp response from several governments but also the concerted protest of some 150 NGOs.

Since key deliberations are informal and by invitation only, the WTO has a problem with internal as well as with external transparency. Its policy-making process not only excludes the public, but also the majority of WTO member states. To exclude state representatives from decisive deliberations is of course a manifest breach of democratic principles. As a consequence, the club system tends to privilege the concerns and interests of the key trading nations at the expense of marginalized stakeholders. Yet even if all member states were represented in all decisive meetings, the problem of accountability towards the ultimate stakeholders of governance, i.e. the world's citizens, would still remain. Due to its secretive style of policy-making, the WTO inhibits informed public debate and critical reflection. For deliberative democratization of world trade governance additional steps are required, which can be subsumed under the following headings:

- transparency of the rule-making process;
- inclusion of stakeholder concerns;
- empowerment of marginalized groups of stakeholders.

---

[25] Green room consultations normally involve 10 to 25 out of more than 140 members.

b) Transparency

The enduring lack of transparency prevents the emergence of a public sphere on world trade policy. At present the WTO is in the middle of a process of institutional reform that aims officially at enhancing external transparency, access to documents and NGO participation. This process was initiated by reform pressure from the outside, and the organization, in fact, responded to it. In 1996 the WTO General Council took a first step towards an opening up of the organization by adopting official guidelines for the consultation of non-state actors.[26] In recent years the WTO has adopted a derestriction policy with the aim of facilitating public access to its policy documents.[27] By now, the WTO's presentation of documents on the internet is regarded to be among the best of all public international organizations in terms of content and user guidance.[28] These changes would definitely not have come about without a sustained campaign by civil society, in particular by activist NGOs, to open up the black box of world trade governance.[29] However, these reforms aimed at transparency and participation of non-state actors have gone only half way and the public sphere of world trade governance must be still regarded as in its infant phase.[30] Why is this so?

One major problem remaining is that of access to political deliberation within the WTO. Neither political meetings of the General Council and the committees, nor the norm review process of the dispute settlement panel are accessible to observers, let alone to the

[26] Gabrielle Marceau and Peter N. Pedersen, 'Is the WTO Open and Transparent?', *Journal of World Trade*, 33: 1 (1999), pp. 5–49; see also WTO document WT/L/162 (23 July 1996).

[27] The decision on speeding up the derestriction procedure was taken in May 2002, see WTO document WT/L/452.

[28] See One World Trust (ed.), *Global Accountability Report*, London, One World Trust, 2003, p. 15.

[29] Diana Tussie and Maria P. Riggirozzi, 'Pressing Ahead with New Procedures for Old Machinery: Global Governance and Civil Society', in V. Rittberger (ed.), *Global Governance and the United Nations System*, Tokyo, United Nations University Press, 2001, pp. 158–80.

[30] Peter Willetts, 'Civil Society Networks in Global Governance: Remedying the World Trade Organisation's Deviance from Global Norms', presentation for the Colloquium on International Governance, Palais des Nations, Geneva, 20 September 2002.

general public. In this respect the WTO is not much different from many other international organizations. However, there are in fact, regimes of multilateral international cooperation that are much more open to the scrutiny of registered observers. In the political process of the United Nations Framework Convention on Climate Change, for example, registered observers have access to a broad variety of political and expert meetings.[31] If, in deliberation within, and deliberation about, the world trade system is to be inclusive the WTO must change its restrictive policy on observer access; the international public must have a chance to learn what is going on in its political meetings.

External transparency is a precondition for informed political debate and consequently also for the formulation of stakeholder concerns. It is obvious that stakeholders of governance can only formulate their concerns and interests if they have adequate information and capacity of critical judgement. Stakeholders need a good grasp of the social, legal and political problems involved in trade policy in order to be able to make (critical) use of information and participate effectively in the political process. They need to be able to anticipate the consequences of WTO decisions in fields such as intellectual property. However, even if actors have access to minutes of countless WTO meetings and records of complex decision processes, they are not automatically able to process this information. It threatens to create overload more than it facilitates oversight. Deliberatively democratizing WTO governance, therefore, implies that the citizens of the world should be able to receive comprehensive (and comprehensible) information about what is at stake in the WTO. This is, of course, a difficult task, as many world trade topics are extremely technical in nature and the consequences of decisions are not easy for non-experts to assess.

Complexity is a challenge experienced not only by ordinary citizens and stakeholders but also by some bureaucrats and state representatives within the trade regime. In fact, political officials in charge of negotiating at the WTO in many cases lack the expertise to envisage fully the whole range of consequences of their decisions. This is particularly problematic for representatives from developing countries, who often cannot rely upon the same expertise of supporting

---

[31] Sebastian Oberthür et al., *Participation of Non-Governmental Organisations in International Environmental Co-operation*, Berlin, Erich Schmidt Verlag, 2002, pp. 117–41.

staff in Geneva or at their home base, which most northern delega-tions enjoy.[32] Massive communication problems also occur between national delegations to the WTO and the elected members of par-liament at home. With the notable exception of the US Congress, there is very little interaction between national trade negotiators and their parliamentary constituency. It has been observed that legisla-tors' scrutiny in the ratification process of the Uruguay round results was perfunctory.[33] Again, this problem affects developing countries to a higher degree than industrialized WTO members.

With regard to the mass media, there still is a lack of substantial coverage on trade issues that would otherwise work to facilitate the understanding of a wider audience. Journalists, not unlike some national members of parliament, might sometimes underestimate the political implications of WTO decisions. Nevertheless it is quite clear that many WTO topics are of limited interest to the mass media and general public. Yet we do not require the global public sphere to be all-encompassing and permanently to include all members of world society. What matters is *access* to comprehensible information for all those who seek it. In this respect, organized civil society can make an important contribution by processing and dissemi-nating information on world trade, with an emphasis on critical perspectives.[34]

c) Inclusion of Stakeholder Concerns

As in the case of information, the activities of civil society seem equally indispensable with regard to the representation of stakeholder con-cerns in deliberative processes at the WTO. Yet the possibility of non-state actors in bringing topics onto the official, inter-

[32] Elisabeth Türk, 'The Role of NGOs in International Governance. NGOs and Developing Country WTO Members: Is there Potential for Alliance?', in S. Griller (ed.), *International Economic Governance and Non-Economic Concerns: New Challenges for the International Legal Order*, Vienna and New York, Springer, 2003, pp. 162–211.

[33] Christoph Bellmann and Richard Gerster, 'Accountability in the World Trade Organization', *Journal of World Trade*, 30: 6 (1996), pp. 31–74.

[34] A prominent example for respected and widely used independent information on trade is the newsletter 'Bridges', published by the International Center for Trade and Sustainable Development (ICTSD), see http://www.ictsd.org. See also the newsletter 'Harmonization Alert' published by the organization Public Citizen.

governmental, agenda is still limited in practice. At the moment, the WTO invites submissions of NGO papers and grants a limited possibility of presenting issues at Ministerial Conferences. In its everyday business, however, the concerns of nongovernmental and even other intergovernmental organizations are invisible.[35] A recently invented instrument to tackle this deficit is symposia on trade-related issues that bring a wide variety of civil society actors into contact with WTO officials.[36] Those symposia are not likely to be sufficient, however, because they do not include state representatives as the real decision-makers in the WTO. In the dispute settlement procedure there is the possibility for non-state actors to present unsolicited statements as so-called 'amicus curiae briefs'. However, whether these will be considered or not still lies at the discretion of the panel.[37]

Hence there is yet a need for improving and institutionalizing stakeholder input at the WTO. With regard to policy-making we should consider a procedure that forces decision-makers to respond to stakeholders and to publicly justify their actions, similar to parliamentary question times.[38] How could such a public confrontation be institutionalized? For the WTO we propose a public assembly that could, for example, precede every Ministerial Conference. This assembly should comprise the heads of national delegations on the one hand, and representatives of civil society on the other, with the mass media as observers. To make this procedure feasible, one would

[35] For example, not even the representatives of international *governmental* organizations such as the United Nations Environment Programme are admitted as observers to the meetings of the WTO Committee on Trade and Environment.

[36] A symposium on the 'Doha Development Agenda' took place from 29 April to 1 May 2002 in Geneva, see also http://www.wto.org/english/tratop_e/dda_e/symp_devagenda_prog_02_e.htm.

[37] See the Appelate Body's report on amicus curiae briefs of 8 November 2000, and WTO document WT/DS135/9 on the procedure of amicus brief submission; see also Petros C. Mavroidis, 'Amicus Curiae Briefs before the WTO: Much Ado About Nothing', in A. v. Bogdandy, P. C. Mavroidis and Y. Mény (eds), *European Integration and International Coordination: Studies in Transnational Economic Law in Honour of Claus-Dieter Ehlermann*, Den Haag, Kluwer Law International, pp. 317–29.

[38] Jens Steffek, 'Free Trade as a Moral Choice: How Conflicts of Principle Have Troubled Transatlantic Economic Relations in the Past, and How a "Council on Trade and Ethics" Could Help Prevent them in the Future', in European University Institute (ed.), *Preventing Transatlantic Trade Disputes: Four Prize-winning Essays*, Florence, European University Institute, 2001, pp. 45–55.

probably need to have civil society actors agree in advance on a limited number of statements on the WTO political programme or on a single decision. The decisive advantage of having such an assembly would be a direct, public give-and-take of reasons, rather than, as it is now, the WTO publishing its decisions and the reasons for them in press releases, while NGOs present critical counter-arguments in their own briefings and own websites. As an institutional focal point, such an assembly could foster the public visibility of trade policy. In addition, media coverage on the WTO and world trade issues is highest at the time of ministerial conferences. With regard to deliberative democracy, the function of such a consultative assembly would be two-fold: First, it demands enhanced public justification of political choices by decision-makers. Second, it secures stakeholders' access to bring their concerns directly to the attention of policy-makers.

d) Empowerment of Marginalized Groups

A central problem in having more inclusive deliberation on world trade is a manifest 'unequal opportunity' amongst actors. Representatives and stakeholders coming from developing countries, for example, experience major disadvantages that prevent them from participating effectively in debates on world trade. There is, first of all, an inequality in the capacity to gather and assess relevant information. This leads to further inequalities in the capacity to identify and formulate one's own interests and concerns. Even if political interests are well-defined, obstacles remain with regard to participation simply because developing country governments and their civil society organizations have far fewer resources to bring their concerns to bear in Geneva.

In order to enhance participation in rule-making and to make deliberation on world trade more inclusive, the WTO will have to actively support developing countries. To overcome the representation problem, some additional financial means would have to be provided for countries without representation in Geneva. A developing country fund, which might also sponsor the representation of extremely disempowered groups such as indigenous peoples, would be a step into the right direction. Yet, inviting officials to Geneva is not enough to guarantee the plurality of opinions and arguments;

critical voices of civil society actors have to be included in the political process.[39]

With regard to civil society actors from the south, their problems resemble those of their official delegates – namely limited capacities to gather and process relevant information and insufficient representation at the sites of political meetings. Thus far, the majority of civil society organizations participating in the world trade debate are based in the north. Many of them claim to fight for issues that mainly concern developing countries, such as trade and development. As many critics have remarked, the danger of 'benevolent patronizing' is imminent whenever northern-based organizations speak on behalf of the developing world.[40] Not only but not least for this reason, official representatives of developing countries have been sceptical about strengthening the role of nongovernmental organizations in world trade governance.

It will be a major challenge for nongovernmental actors to gain the trust of developing country representatives in their ability to assist them in improving know-how and in the formulation of political positions without imposing their own agenda. The participation of civil society actors from the south should be promoted as well. Using public money to organize southern civil society is problematic with regard to their capacity to adopt alternative views and to criticize the official line of their governments. Therefore, assistance is to come from within self-organized transnational civil society in the form of partnerships between northern and southern actors. Beyond the transfer of material resources and technical know-how, this kind of transnational cooperation holds the promise of fostering mutual learning and perspective-taking. As it is likely to produce political arguments that are shared across boundaries, it can also contribute to the emergence of a more encompassing and more truly global trade governance.

[39] There are already some efforts at training developing country delegations, and in particular those without permanent representation in Geneva. Since 1998 the Geneva-based Agency for International Trade Information and Cooperation (AITIC) provides technical assistance to developing country delegates. The WTO itself holds training sessions for member governments without permanent representation, the so-called 'Geneva weeks'. In 2001, the Advisory Centre on WTO Law was established as a law office specializing in international economic law, providing legal services and training exclusively to developing countries and economies-in-transition.

[40] See Miles Kahler's contribution to this issue.

The table on p. 211 summarizes the proposed measures that should be taken to promote public deliberation on world trade issues and, thus, foster the emergence of a global public sphere. It lists the type of actions that can be taken by the WTO itself, or also by some member governments, and by international civil society.

CONCLUSION

We argued in this essay that the democratization of international governance will ultimately depend upon the creation of an appropriate transnational public sphere. The public sphere is a communicative space where arguments on the merits and defects of international governance are generated and negotiated. It reaches from within international organizations to national decision-makers to citizens, and it uses many different channels of communication (from informal conversations to media to institutionalized meetings of voluntary associations). Reporting by mass media is but one element of a public sphere, although an important one, given the number of addressees it can potentially reach. Certainly, the internet plays a central role for connecting people interested in the governance of global issues. Even more important, we have argued, is organized civil society.

A global public sphere will hardly be as all-encompassing and unitary as national ones, but rather the ensemble of overlapping (national/sectoral) public communication about the same (sometimes very specific) issue or problem. Making global governance public presupposes that relevant political information is made available to interested stakeholders. Since modern politics in general, and international governance in particular, are highly complex and functionally fragmented, we cannot assume that citizens will be routinely interested. We assume that interested citizens will actively search for ways of receiving information on international governance and of bringing their own concerns in. International public (sic) organizations have the duty to inform their stakeholders about their policies. Only civil society, however, can add critical, alternative perspectives. The task of transnational civil society is to enable stakeholders of global governance to make informed judgements and choices. Civil society can (and should) give voice to citizens affected by regulations made at the global level. A particularly important form of empowerment is to assist those marginalized groups of stakeholders that face the greatest obstacles to political participation.

Our normative approach to the legitimation and democratization of global governance can be summed up as follows: By fostering extended deliberation among stakeholders over the nature of problems and the best way to solve them, participatory arenas produce a pool of (transnationally) shared arguments which – often disseminated by civil society organizations – contribute to the emergence of a wider public sphere, in which the decisions of international organizations are exposed to 'transnational' public scrutiny. Global governance arrangements should ideally become sites of public deliberation between social actors (e.g., representatives of international organizations, scientific expertise, NGOs, etc.) that generate democratic legitimation in a heterogeneous global polity.

Table 1

Elements for Promoting Public Deliberation about World Trade Policy

Issue	WTO/governmental action	Civil society action
Exposing world trade governance to public scrutiny	Dissemination of official information. Providing documents, internet access, press releases	Dissemination of critical information. Informing press, national parliaments, grass-roots groups
Bringing stakeholder concerns into the WTO	Organization of outreach meetings; granting speaking time to NGOs; obliging state representatives to justify decisions taken	Participation in meetings with officials and state representatives. Debating political proposals among civil society groups
Empowering disadvantaged stakeholders	Technical training of developing country representatives; financial assistance to underrepresented countries/groups	Providing critical expertise to state representatives and non-state actors. Cooperation with NGOs from developing countries

10
Is there a 'Democratic Deficit' in World Politics? A Framework for Analysis

Andrew Moravcsik

IS GLOBAL GOVERNANCE – THE STRUCTURE OF INTERNATIONAL institutions – democratically legitimate, or does it suffer from a 'democratic deficit'? This is emerging as one of the central questions – perhaps *the* central question – in contemporary world politics. Whatever their underlying motivations, critics these days ranging from the extreme right to the extreme left, and at almost every point in between, couch criticisms of globalization in democratic rhetoric.

There is a consensus answer to this question, among scholars and among commentators, politicians and the general public, namely that international organizations are normatively suspect. Those who invoke democratic ideals to assess international organizations consistently conclude that they suffer from a severe 'democratic deficit'. One is hard-pressed to think of a single application of democratic standards to an international organization – whether the European Union, the International Monetary Fund (IMF), the World Trade Organization (WTO), or even the United Nations – that does not conclude with a serious criticism of the organization. Most such judgements are so unequivocal that authors devote most of their time to proposals for solutions.[1]

The reasons seem obvious. International organizations encompass large geographical domains. Robert Dahl maintains that international organizations are therefore inherently unable to support direct democratic deliberation and decision.[2] They characteristically

---

[1] For exceptions, see F.W. Scharpf, *Governing in Europe: Effective and Democratic?*, Oxford, Oxford University Press, 1999; Giandomenico Majone, *Regulating Europe*, London, Routledge, 1996; and Giandomenico Majone, 'Europe's Democratic Deficit', *European Law Journal*, 4: 1 (1998), pp. 237–56.

[2] Robert Dahl, 'Can International Organizations Be Democratic? A Skeptic's View', in Ian Shapiro and Casiano Hacker-Cordon (eds), *Democracy's Edges*, Cambridge, Cambridge University Press, 1999, pp. 19–36.

lack what fully developed institutions for direct electoral or interest group accountability as national political systems provide. Thus, as David Held argues, 'Systematizing the provision of global public goods requires not just building on existing forms of multilateral institutions, but also on extending and developing them in order to address questions of transparency, accountability and democracy.'[3]

My central contention in this article is that an assessment of the democratic legitimacy of a real-world international institution is as much social scientific as philosophical. If such an assessment is not to be an exercise in utopian thinking, then international institutions should not be compared to ideal democratic systems. Instead we must ask whether they approximate the 'real world' democracy generally achieved by existing advanced democracies, which face constraints of limited public information and interest, regulatory capture, the credibility of commitments, and bounded consensus. Any democratic metric derived from ideal theory must therefore be 'calibrated' in order to assess whether the current arrangements are the best that are feasible under 'real-world' circumstances. One essential standard for evaluating how a modern constitutional system should deal with these imperfections is a comparative empirical analysis of the general practice of modern advanced industrial democracies and the specific conditions prevailing in this case. Where international organizations perform about as well as the existing, generally legitimate, national systems they (partially) supplant, they should receive the benefit of the doubt. If we adopt these reasonable normative and empirical criteria for evaluating democracy, moreover, it is unclear that international institutions lack democratic legitimacy, as most analysts assume. *Some* international organizations may suffer from a 'democratic deficit', but it is by no means obvious that many do – and to demonstrate the contrary requires more and different empirical analysis than has heretofore been conducted.

By way of illustration, I consider the case of the world's most ambitious system of pooling sovereignty under an international institution, namely the European Union. It is widely considered to suffer from a 'democratic deficit', the redressing of which was the primary purpose for calling the ongoing constitutional convention and negotiation. I consider four philosophical conceptions of democracy on which such a critique of the EU has been grounded – respectively,

---

[3] See the chapter by David Held in this volume.

libertarian, pluralist, social democratic and deliberative democracy – and present empirical evidence to suggest that in each case the EU's democratic credentials are well within the norm of advanced industrial democracies. Though centralized electoral control and collective deliberation remain relatively weak and diffuse, constitutional and material restrictions on the EU's mandate, inter-institutional checks and balances, indirect democratic control via national governments, and the modest but increasing powers of the European Parliament are more than sufficient to assure that in most of what it does, EU policy-making is generally clean, transparent, effective and politically responsive to the demands of Europeans. The near consensual criticism of European integration as democratically illegitimate is thus unwarranted. I conclude by generalizing the theoretical framework in future work, but cautioning against the overhasty generalization of its optimistic empirical conclusion in the case of Europe.

ASSESSING TRANSNATIONAL DEMOCRATIC LEGITIMACY: A GENERAL FRAMEWORK

Any assessment of the democratic legitimacy of real existing institutions, and thus any proposal to improve that legitimacy, must meet two criteria, one philosophical and one pragmatic. It must be *philosophically coherent* and *pragmatically viable*. Let us consider each in turn.

Philosophical Coherence

Any criticism of real-world democratic legitimacy, or proposal for its enhancement, must be *philosophically coherent*. This means that it must be based on a fundamental normative conception of democracy that is both coherent and generally applicable. A philosophically coherent conception of democracy contributes to the justification of a particular real-world democratic form of government by recommending a mix of fundamental values – liberty, equality, solidarity – that the system is justified in promoting. Most contributions to ongoing discussions of the democratic legitimacy of international organizations draw on one or more of four traditions: libertarian, pluralist, social democratic and deliberative.

The *libertarian* conception of constitutional democracy views a democratic political order primarily as a means to protect individual liberties against the potentially arbitrary, corrupt and tyrannical power of the modern state. This is the classical liberal justification for democratic rights, dating back to John Locke and others in early modern Europe, as a means to assure 'limited government'. Of course most democratic political theorists are libertarians to the extent they accept that a ban against certain actions – such as torture, genocide, deprivation of liberty without due process, the basic laws of war, for example – ought to be enforced, even when such actions are favoured by a legitimate democratic majority and would not endanger the future stability of the political system.[4] Agreement that majorities cannot violate basic rights is widely viewed as part of a pre-commitment prior to the launching of democratic politics, which should be enforced even against the perceived interests of a transient majority. More extreme libertarian conceptions of democracy more emphatically privilege liberty over equality. Such theorists maintain that certain individual rights, such as the 'negative' rights to property and security, should be enforced strictly, even against majoritarian demands for redistribution or claims for the recognition of a broader set of 'positive' rights like a minimum standard of welfare.[5] They tend to distrust the motives of government officials, whom they view as arbitrary and meddlesome at best and self-interested or corrupt at worst. To judge by popular rhetoric, one or another form of this critique forms the basis for widespread complaint against international institutions and their officials, who are often portrayed as excessively, albeit technocratically, self-serving. Others criticize international institutions as insufficiently attentive to existing individual or local interests and values. The purest form of this critique is found among Anglo-American conservatives, who portray international institutions as the start of liberal and socialist regulation of the economy.[6]

---

[4] Though even so persistent questions arise as to how rigidly human rights should be maintained in the face of overwhelming widely-acknowledged threats.

[5] For a critique that these cannot be so strictly separated, see Cass Sunstein and Stephen Holmes, *The Cost of Rights: Why Liberty Depends on Taxes*, New York, Norton, 2000.

[6] Jeremy Rabkin, *Why Sovereignty Matters*, Washington, DC, AEI Press, 1998. For a critique, see Andrew Moravcsik, 'Conservative Idealism and International Institutions', *Chicago Journal of International Law*, (2000), pp. 291–314.

The *pluralist* conception of democracy equates it with the direct formal accountability of decision-makers to electoral incentives and sanctions. Systems are democratically legitimate to the extent that they afford active individuals a meaningful and equal opportunity to influence policy outcomes. On this ground Robert Dahl expresses pessimism about international organizations, which he views as inherently unable to support democratic politics by virtue of their large scale and distance from the electorate. Existing institutions for direct electoral or interest group accountability, in his view, are absent from international organizations.[7] Dahl writes:

> My argument is simple and straightforward. In democratic countries . . . it is notoriously difficult for citizens to exercise direct control over many key decisions on foreign affairs. What grounds do we have for thinking, then, that citizens in different countries engaged in international systems can ever attain the degree of influence and control over decisions that they now exercise within their own countries?[8]

Dahl is similarly critical of large-scale domestic systems, such as the US system of quasi-majoritarian checks and balances, particularly in regard to federalism, the electoral college, and the Supreme Court, which tend to act in a counter-majoritarian fashion.[9]

In recent years a number of conservative scholars, often called 'sovereigntists', have justified American non-adherence and non-compliance with regard to international law on the ground that each democratic government ought to be able to defend its own sovereignty and independence. This, it is argued, because a single government can be and generally is more attentive to 'democratic values' and 'popular sovereignty' than are international organizations. Such views have been voiced primarily by scholars associated with think tanks like the American Enterprise Institute, such as Jeremy Rabkin and John Bolton.[10] Recently Jed Rubenfeld, a more liberal constitutional lawyer at Yale, has gone one better than the 'sovereigntists', arguing that the US is entitled to engage in 'exceptional' behaviour in this regard because of what he portrays as a more political and populist conception of constitutional law, as compared

---

[7] Dahl, 'Can International Organization be Democratic?', op. cit.

[8] Ibid., p. 23.

[9] Ibid.

[10] For the conservative variant of 'sovereigntism' associated with AEI, see Rabkin, *Why Sovereignty Matters*, op. cit., and the special issue of *Chicago Journal of International Law* (Autumn 2000).

to more rigidly legalist and authoritarian models prevalent in Europe.[11] Some Europeans – with considerably more evidence on their side – might argue that European systems, with their coalition governments and broader range of social democratic options, consistently generate outcomes that are more broadly acceptable, in the sense of being closer to the median opinion in most advanced industrial societies.[12] This brings us to the next critique.

The *social democratic* conception of democracy views political institutions as a means to offset the natural power of concentrated wealth that accrues in capitalist economies.[13] While libertarians prize liberty over equality, social democrats espouse the opposite. Following Karl Polanyi and other social democratic theorists, for example, Fritz Scharpf argues that the most important element in a democratic polity is to maintain the balance between market liberalization and social protection. In this view, international institutions lack democratic legitimacy to the extent that they bias policy-making in a neo-liberal direction and fail to promote the necessary social protection to offset the expansion of markets and the concentration of wealth.[14] International institutions tend to incorporate this bias, so the argument goes, in two ways. One is simply by giving rich countries more voting power than poorer countries, as has been charged with respect to international financial institutions.[15] The other is by restricting the agenda. While many domestic systems provide equal opportunities to legislate market-promoting policies and redistributive policies, international institutions (singly and collectively) do not. The strongest and most established among international institutions, in this view, tend to be focused on trade liberalization (WTO, NAFTA,

---

[11] For a liberal echo, see Jed Rubenfeld, 'The Two World Orders', *Wilson Quarterly*, 27 (2003), pp. 22–36. The notion that the US is, overall, a more 'democratic' country than most European, in the sense of being more committed to strict 'popular sovereignty' is a curious one. For a critique, see Andrew Moravcsik, 'The Paradox of US Unilateralism in Human Rights', in Michael Ignatieff (ed.), *American Exceptionalism and Human Rights*, Princeton, Princeton University Press, forthcoming.

[12] Dahl, 'Can International Organization be Democratic?', op. cit.

[13] Charles E. Lindblom, *Politics and Markets: The World's Political-Economic Systems*, New York, Basic Books, 1977.

[14] Yet they need not be so. Many libertarians believe that policy in the EU, as well as in Europe as a whole, is biased in a social democratic direction. For example, see Rabkin, *Why Sovereignty Matters*, op. cit.

[15] See the paper by David Held in this volume.

EU), creditor rights (IMF), and pro-business regulation (EU). Social welfare provision is relegated to national governments. This division of labour undermines domestic redistribution and regulatory protection, so it is argued, because it triggers a 'race to the bottom', in which the competitive market pressures of external liberalization undermine uncoordinated domestic policies. While libertarians criticize the international organizations for doing too much, social democrats criticize them for doing too little.

The *deliberative* conception of democracy views political institutions as a means not just to assure equal opportunities for participation and representation or to offset existing biases, but as a means to improve the political capacity of the citizenry. The argument here is that political institutions must not only provide opportunities for participation, but must be designed to encourage and promote meaningful and effective participation. They must help to create active, informed, tolerant, and engaged citizens – or, at least, shape such participation among the political representatives.[16] For this purpose, it is essential that a democratic system has not only representative institutions, but political parties, interest groups, plentiful information and a common discourse. These things give politics meaning, engage citizens in political education, and permit the discussion and resolution of disputes not just over conflicting interests but over morality.[17] Deliberative democrats tend to reject the entire trend toward insulated decision-making, whether domestic or international. In this view, however, international institutions are particularly suspect. No matter how formally democratic and inclusive they may be, political institutions with a politically passive citizenry can generate little meaningful public deliberation and thus little democratic legitimacy. The distance and lack of intermediating social and cultural institutions render international institutions arid; they encourage the trend toward technocratic decision making and a passive and perhaps disgruntled population.[18]

---

[16] Amitai Etzioni, *Political Unification Revisited. On Building Supranational Communities*, Lanham, MD, Rowman & Littlefield, 2001.

[17] Amy Gutmann and Dennis Thompson, *Democracy and Disagreement: Why Moral Conflict Cannot Be Avoided in Politics, and What Should Be Done about It*, Cambridge, MA, Harvard University Press, 1996.

[18] Larry Siedentop, *Democracy in Europe*, London, Allen Lane, Penguin Press, 2000; Philippe Schmitter, *How to Democratize the European Union . . . And Why Bother?*, Lanham, MD, Rowman & Littlefield, 2000.

Pragmatic Viability

Most existing analyses of deliberative democracy draw on one or more of these conceptions of democracy. It is not my purpose in this chapter – nor am I qualified – to criticize them in detail. My concern is instead with their application to real world situations. If they are not to be utopian, I argue in this section, such concrete applications necessarily rest on a series of largely *empirical* judgements. These empirical judgements require detailed social scientific analysis, which must be placed in a comparative perspective in order to calibrate the realistic expectations of how directly democratic a system could reasonably be expected to be.

There are two related senses in which an applied evaluation of the democratic legitimacy of an international institution rests on empirical judgements. First, each of the four ideal theories discussed above rests on explicit empirical judgements about politics and society. Libertarians stress the tendency for regulators to act for narrow and arbitrary rather than for publicly justifiable reasons, the unbounded power of international institutions, and the socialist bias of policy-making. Pluralists stress the lack of democratic constraints on policy-making in international organizations. Social democrats stress the neo-liberal bias in international policy-making and the existence of pressures triggering a 'race to the bottom'. Deliberative democrats argue that international institutions help create a passive, unsatisfied public. Each of these empirical claims can and should be subjected to rigorous testing before we accept the normative conclusions that follow.

Second, each of the four ideal theories above remains a normative ideal of democracy. Each invites a comparison between international institutions and an ideal form of perfectly participatory, egalitarian, deliberative politics. Such ideals are frankly utopian. They are not realized anywhere today, and not even in the ancient or Westminster-style systems sometimes held up as exemplars. It is thus a trivial matter to deploy this metric to demonstrate that the EU, or any other international organization, is 'illegitimate'. This type of ideal, isolated, and essentially utopian analysis is not very helpful for the sort of real-world constitutional construction in which the EU and other international organizations are currently engaged.

One particular difference between ideal and applied theory is particularly relevant here. Ideal democratic theories tend systematically to ignore the transaction costs of political participation. That is, they overlook limitations on the ability and willingness of individuals to involve themselves extensively in politics, to develop expertise, to manage credible commitment problems and to overcome existing differentials in social resources. In the real world, individual citizens suffer from a limited and unequal ability to devote time and energy to learning about and engaging in politics. In the real world, citizens remain 'rationally ignorant' or non-participatory with regard to most issues, most of the time. Applied democratic theory must work with individuals as they truly are – inattentive, inexpert, uncertain about the future and unequal – not as one might wish them to be.[19]

One way constitutional systems cope with such imperfections is by insulating policy-makers and delegating to political authorities. Such delegation often reflects a 'second-best' solution to representing and realizing widespread interests in a system where individuals cannot be assumed to pursue consistently their own interests effectively. Three structural circumstances in which this often occurs are of particular relevance to an assessment of international organizations: social complexity, political uncertainty and differentials in social power.

• *Social complexity and the role of expertise.* Citizens delegate to assemble more efficient decision-making in areas where expertise is required. Involvement in the full range of government policies would impose costs beyond the willingness of any modern citizen to bear. Whether the area is environmental policy, medical drug authorization, or criminal law, we do not expect complex medical, legal, or technical decisions to be made by direct popular vote.

• *Political uncertainty and the role of rights.* Citizens of democratic societies generally favour policies that reduce the risk to any given individual of catastrophic loss of life or liberty in an uncertain future. Philosophically, this might be viewed as a concession to

[19] Russell Hardin distinguishes the claims based on the 'street-level epistemology . . . of an ordinary person' and those claims that meet 'standard epistemological criteria for justification'. Democracy must, he argues, be understood, at least in part, from the street level. As such, it is unlikely to impose more than a crude, largely negative constraint on policy-makers. Participation in majoritarian decision-making, therefore, takes place 'on the margin', rather than being the necessary characteristic of all democratic decisions. See Russell Hardin, 'Democratic Epistemology and Accountability', *Social Philosophy and Policy*, 17 (2000), pp. 110–26.

fundamental human dignity or as a reflection of a basic human preference for the reduction of catastrophic risk.[20] Yet it is difficult for majorities credibly to commit future majorities not to tyrannize minorities. To this end, democratic systems commonly constrain majority decision-making through established individual and group rights that protect individual liberty, welfare and culture against not only the arbitrary power of the state, but the potential demands of the majority. Such rules enforce a basic minimum level of equality in the name of justice.[21] Often insulated authorities, such as constitutional courts, are called upon to enforce individual or minority prerogatives against majority opinion. In constitutional orders, there thus customarily arises a tension between rights and participation.[22] This tendency has spread in recent years as increasing numbers of governmental functions have been recognized as basic or human rights that are judicially or administratively enforced, often at the international level, against political authorities. For precisely this

[20] There are many reasons why such a notion might be philosophically defensible. Some simply postulate that individuals are to be accorded minimal natural or human rights as recognition of basic 'human dignity' – as do most post-Second World War international human rights documents. (See, for example, Louis Henkin, Gerald L. Neuman, Diane F. Orentlicher and David W. Leebron, *Human Rights*, New York, Foundation Press, 1999.) One might postulate a near consensual preference in favour of a reduction in the individual risk of absolute deprivation, which would then be reflected in any institutional pre-commitments into the future that individuals must necessarily make under uncertainty. (This formulation appears to be empirically more accurate, as a description of human psychology, than the assumption that individuals generally favour a narrowing of inequality.) One might think of either restriction as a reflection of the varying 'intensity' of preferences, with individual preferences that can safely be assumed to be intense (e.g., against being tortured) counting for more than preferences that can be assumed to be less so (e.g., feeling or being marginally 'safer' from crime or terrorism).

[21] If a given decision is of vital importance to the long-term well-being of those involved, then it is questionable whether they have a necessary obligation to obey government dictates, even if the democratic decision-making procedures by which the dictates were generated were clear and fair. See Brian Barry, 'Is Democracy Special?', in Brian Barry (ed.), *Essays in Political Theory*, Cambridge, Cambridge University Press, 1999, pp. 54–72.

[22] Stephen Holmes, *Benjamin Constant and the Making of Modern Liberalism*, New Haven, Yale University Press, 1984; Fareed Zakaria, *The Future of Freedom: Illiberal Democracy at Home and Abroad*, New York, W. W. Norton, 2003. Not an absolute tension, however. Cf. John Ely, *Democracy and Distrust: A Theory of Judicial Review*, Cambridge, MA, Harvard University Press, 1981.

reason, many Europeans view with abhorrence the tendency, common in the US, to elect state and local judges.

• *Underlying differentials in social power and the role of linkage.* Delegating and insulating political power can help redress biases in national democratic representation that arise because diffuse majorities are consistently under-represented. The most common distortion is the capture of government policy by narrow but powerful interest groups opposed to the interests of majorities with diffuse, longer-term, less self-conscious concerns. Consider free trade: even Adam Smith and Richard Cobden realized that the broadly liberal interests of diffuse consumers and firms would often be trumped by pressure from concentrated groups of protectionist producers. Many of the same Europeans who criticize the democratic deficit also call for the US to retain 'fast track' authority to pass trade liberalization – nothing less than empowering the US executive to act with minimal legislative constraints. In this and other areas, the WTO and NAFTA might be thought of as institutional complements to 'fast track' – and, in the case of the EU, perhaps a substitute for it – in that they empower national executives to override powerful particularistic interests in the name of the national (or median) interest.

Institutional pre-commitment is a policy with limits. It works insofar as social groups lack alternatives that are, on balance, more attractive than withdrawal from the organization. In the real world, democratic politics cannot be pushed beyond the point where powerful, potentially self-sufficient groups prefer withdrawal from collective action.[23] This latter constraint is particularly important in international politics, where the pre-existence of competent national governments, in most cases far larger and more powerful than any international organization, renders unilateralism a more viable option than it is for an individual in domestic politics. If democratic decision-making is pushed too far, the result can be the collapse of democracy, if not violent conflict.

These three structural circumstances – social complexity, political uncertainty, and underlying differentials in social power – give rise to widespread, consistent, normatively justified exceptions to direct democratic participation in decision-making. In each of these cases, under many circumstances *more insulated and delegated authority of*

---

[23] Hardin, 'Democratic Epistemology and Accountability', op. cit.

global governance structures might be thought of as more 'representative' of citizen concerns precisely because they are less directly 'democratic'.

The ubiquity of these non-ideal circumstances in political life, and the tendency to employ insulated or delegated power to manage their consequences, has important implications. Any assessment of the democratic legitimacy of an international organization must be based not only on a coherent philosophical analysis using ideal democratic theory, but on an empirical evaluation of the extent to which ideal democratic participation can best be approximated under the constraints imposed by the 'second-best' world of the specific case in question. This latter, empirical judgement, which translates from the ideal to the real, is essentially social scientific in nature.

This empirical translation from the ideal to real is likely to be complex and non-linear, such that the ideal policy in a 'best' world of perfect citizens (e.g. participation) often runs directly counter to the 'good' policy in a second-best world of concrete politics (e.g. delegation). While, for example, we can say with considerable confidence that an *entirely* undemocratic system – that is, a system that offers no meaningful participation in decision-making at any level – is democratically illegitimate, the same proposition does not hold *on the margin*. In other words, there is no reason to believe that a marginal increase in direct participation by the average citizen in majoritarian or consensus decision-making, as opposed to delegation and insulation of policy-makers, promotes outcomes that can be more easily justified in terms of normative and positive democratic theory.

One way to calibrate the standards used to assess real-world democratic systems is to employ comparative social scientific analysis. In order to assess the extent to which a given insulation or delegation of power in an international organization is democratically legitimate, we may ask whether a similar institutional adaptation is widely accepted in existing democratic systems. Such national systems, at least among the advanced industrial democracies, can be presumed to be democratically legitimate in a broad sense, and thus the practices widely employed among such countries provide a meaningful baseline for assessing the democratic legitimacy of international organizations. For example, if domestic political systems often grant constitutional courts and central banks a certain measure of political independence, this is one reason to believe that a similar grant is legitimate. The analyst can then ask whether the essential circumstances set forth in theories of judicial or central bank independence are met. This is an essential, yet often neglected, element in any applied evaluation of democratic legitimacy – and offers a measure of protection against utopian condemnation of existing political institutions. We turn now to an example of this sort of analysis.

APPLYING THE FRAMEWORK: THE CASE OF THE EUROPEAN UNION

Is the European Union democratically legitimate?[24] It is an appropriate moment to pose this question. The last decade has witnessed the emergence of a stable constitutional order in Europe after a decade of nearly continuous debate over the proper constitutional structure for Europe. In a widely praised book, Oxford don Larry Siedentop asks, 'Where are the Madisons for Europe?'[25] Yet the more appropriate question for those who have followed European thinking is: 'Why are there so many Madisons?'[26] Hundreds, perhaps even thousands, of scholars, commentators, lawyers and politicians have analysed the problem of European constitutionalism.

These debates have focused, perhaps above all, on the question of whether the EU is democratically legitimate. Most politicians, scholarly commentators and members of the European public appear to agree that the EU suffers from a severe 'democratic deficit'. Only one branch of the EU is directly elected: the European Parliament (EP). Though stronger than it once was, the EP remains only one of three major actors in the EU legislative process. Its elections are decentralized, apathetic affairs, in which a relatively small number of voters select among national parties on the basis of national issues. Little discussion of European issues, let alone an ideal transnational deliberation, takes place. For its part, the European Commission, which enjoys a powerful role as an agenda-setter and regulatory coordinator, is widely perceived as a technocracy. The European Court of

---

[24] This section draws Andrew Moravcsik, 'Despotism in Brussels? Misreading the European Union', *Foreign Affairs*, (May/June 2001), pp. 603–24; and Andrew Moravcsik, 'Federalism in the European Union: Rhetoric and Reality', in Robert Howse and Kalypso Nicolaïdis (eds), *The Federal Vision: Legitimacy and Levels of Governance in the US and the EU*, Oxford, Oxford University Press, (2002), pp. 163–87.

[25] Siedentop, *Democracy in Europe.*, op. cit.

[26] Moravcsik, 'Despotism in Brussels?', op. cit.

Justice, comprised of fifteen appointed judges, is unusually power-ful. Most powerful of all, the Council of Ministers brings together national ministers, diplomatic representatives, and administrative officials from member states, who often deliberate in secret. While indirectly accountable to voters, the link is too tenuous and the mode of interaction too diplomatic or technocratic to satisfy many observers. These procedural qualms might be tolerable were it not for the perceived bias in the outputs of European policy-making. Many view the EU as a throw-back to the nineteenth century – a fis-cally weak, neo-liberal state. For these reasons, many believe it is self-evident that the EU is not democratically legitimate.

My central contention here is that if we adopt reasonable criteria for judging democratic governance, the widespread criticism of the EU as democratically illegitimate is unsupported by the existing empirical evidence – much of it provided by critics of the 'democratic deficit'. At the very least, their critique must be heavily qualified. *Con-stitutional checks and balances, indirect democratic control via national gov-ernments and the increasing powers of the European Parliament are sufficient to assure that the EU policy-making is, in nearly all cases, clean, transpar-ent, effective, and politically responsive to the demands of European citizens.*

In successive sections below, I analyse the constraints inherent in the European Constitutional Settlement that guarantee that the EU will not become a despotic 'superstate', the democratic pro-cedures that prevent the EU from becoming an arbitrary and unaccountable technocracy within its domain, the legitimate reasons for shielding certain EU decision-makers from direct democratic contestation, the underlying social reasons why political participation in the EU cannot be radically expanded and the extent to which EU policy-making suffers from an excessive neo-liberal bias. Final sections consider whether these assessments are likely to change with the enlargement of the EU, and how the analysis might be generalized.

THE LIBERTARIAN CRITIQUE: IS THE EU AN ARBITRARY 'SUPERSTATE'?

The classical libertarian justification for democracy, we have seen, is to check and channel the arbitrary and potentially corrupt power of the state. Arbitrary rule by supranational technocrats – 'bureaucratic despotism' by a 'super-state' in Brussels, as one widely heralded formulation has it – is a widespread concern in regard to contemporary EU politics.[27] This is the stuff of British tabloid articles, often fuelled by ignorance of what the EU actually does, but it underlies much legitimate concern, particular by those on the libertarian right of the political spectrum. This concern appears to gain plausibility from the overtly technocratic nature of much EU regulation, the open role played by non-elected officials in Brussels, and the geographical and cultural distance between those regulators and the average European 'person in the street'.

Yet the threat of a European superstate is a myth. To a first approximation, the EU does not tax, spend, implement, or coerce, and in many areas, it does not hold a legal monopoly of public authority. The EU's constitutional order imposes tight substantive, fiscal, administrative, legal and procedural constraints on EU policymaking that are embedded in treaty and legislative provisions, which have the force of constitutional law – to which we now turn. This is not simply a 'snapshot' judgement about the present, overlooking the future trajectory of integration, but an assessment of the EU's underlying institutional capacity to act in new areas and new ways.

• *Substantive constraints.* The EU's current activities are restricted by treaty and practice to a modest subset of the substantive activities pursued by modern states. The core of EU activity and its strongest constitutional prerogatives still lie almost exclusively in the area of trade in goods and services, the movement of factors of production, the production of and trade in agricultural commodities, exchange rates and monetary policy, foreign aid and trade-related environmental, consumer and competition policy. Much is thereby excluded: taxation and the setting of fiscal priorities, social welfare provision, defence and police powers, education policy, cultural policy, non-economic civil litigation, direct cultural promotion and regulation, the funding of civilian infrastructure, and most other regulatory policies unrelated to cross-border economic activity. Certainly, the EU has made modest inroads into many of these areas, but largely

---

[27] Siedentop, *Democracy in Europe*, op. cit.; cf. Moravcsik, 'Despotism in Brussels?', op. cit.

in limited areas directly related to cross-border flows.[28] The result is that the EU has been, overall, strongly liberal in its impact on European policy-making, which makes the virulent opposition by some right-wing libertarians somewhat puzzling.[29]

- *Fiscal constraints.* It is not coincidental that the policies absent from the EU's policy portfolio – notably social welfare provision, defence, education, culture and infrastructure – require high government expenditure. The ability to tax and spend is what most strikingly distinguishes the modern European state from its predecessors, yet the EU's ability to tax is capped at about 2–3 per cent of national and local government spending (1.3 per cent of GDP) and is unlikely to change soon. Fiscal constraints have decisive consequences. There is little money for discretionary funding by Brussels technocrats, which limits their arbitrary power as well as the prospect of corruption. The EU is destined to remain what Giandomenico Majone has termed a 'regulatory polity'.[30]

- *Administrative constraints.* Analysts often observe that the essential politics of regulation lie in implementation, yet the EU implements very few of its own regulations. How could it be otherwise, given the extraordinarily small size of the Brussels bureaucracy? The EU employs fewer people than a modest European city. They total about one-fortieth of the number of comparable civilian federal employees even in the United States, a jurisdiction of comparable size but noted in cross-national perspective for the small size of its national government workforce. Except in a few areas the task of legally or administratively implementing EU regulations falls instead to national parliaments and administrations. The EU has no police, military force, or significant investigatory capacity – and no realistic prospect of obtaining any of these.

[28] The scholarly literature on European integration seems to pay disproportionate attention to exceptional cases of 'spillover' in cases such as gender discrimination, the initial experience with environmental policy and structural funding, the jurisprudence of supremacy and direct effect, the Commission's use of Article 90, and the possible, but as yet undocumented, effects of the Open Method of Coordination. These are important trends, but atypical of the EU as a whole.

[29] One suspects a measure of ideology or opportunism. See Andrew Moravcsik, 'A Tory Referendum', *Prospect*, (July 2003) pp. 16–17.

[30] Majone, *Regulating Europe*, op. cit.; and Majone, 'Europe's Democratic Deficit', op. cit.

• *Procedural constraints.* Its lack of constitutional mandate, fiscal discretion and administrative clout would be of less consequence if the EU technocracy could act unhampered by procedural constraints. Yet EU policy-making is constrained by institutional checks and balances, notably the separation of powers, a multi-level structure of decision-making, and a plural executive.[31] The most fundamental constraint lies in the requirement of unanimity for amendment of the Treaty of Rome, followed by electoral, parliamentary, or administrative ratification – a high standard for any fundamental act of substantive redirection or institutional delegation. Even 'everyday' EU directives must be promulgated under rules that require the concurrent support of between 70 and 100 per cent of the weighted votes of territorial representatives in the Council of Ministers – a level of support higher than that required for legislation in any existing national polity or, indeed, to amend nearly any national constitution. Add to this that the Commission must propose, the Parliament must consent, if challenged, the Court must approve, national parliaments or officials must transpose into national law, and national bureaucracies must implement. EU decision-making is consensus decision-making.

These myriad institutional constraints not only not only render arbitrary and capricious action almost impossible, but assure that legislation out of Brussels is likely to represent an exceptionally broad consensus among different groups at many levels of governance. This should give us reason for confidence that it legislates in the broad public interest. And because the limitations on substantive activities are grounded in the very constitutional structure of the EU, none of this is likely to change soon.

THE PLURALIST CRITIQUE: IS THE EU AN UNACCOUNTABLE TECHNOCRACY?

The *pluralist* conception of democracy stresses the direct accountability of governing officials to public preferences, as expressed

---

[31] Such institutional procedures are the conventional tool for protecting the interests of vital minorities – a design feature generally thought to be most appropriate to polities, like the EU, designed to accommodate heterogeneous cultural and substantive interests. See Arend Lijphart, *Democracies: Patterns of Majoritarian and Consensus Government in 22 Countries*, New Haven, Yale University Press, 1990.

through elections. Dahl has criticized the EU as being an elite-driven project that does not deserve to be called 'democratic'. He notes: 'To ensure public debate, it would be necessary to create an international equivalent to national political competition by parties and individuals seeking office'.[32] This is impossible in the EU because of its large scope, as well as varied and diffuse national interests.

Yet the insulation of the EU from mechanisms to assure democratic accountability is easily exaggerated, particularly by those who tend to overlook the multi-level constraints embedded in the European constitutional order, arising from democratic control over national governments, as well as the powers of the EP. Where neither sort of constraint is directly imposed – as where power is delegated to a European-level constitutional court, central bank or other semi-autonomous authorities – the structure of the EU is entirely consistent with the late twentieth-century practice of most advanced industrial democracies.

Direct Democratic Accountability

For over a decade, the EP has been progressively usurping the role of the Commission as the primary agenda-setter vis-à-vis the Council in the EU legislative process. It is now the EP that, late in the legislative process, accepts, rejects or amends legislation in a manner more difficult for the Council to reject than to accept – a prerogative traditionally accorded to the Commission. The EP is directly elected, generally by proportional representation within nation-states, and often acts independently of ruling national parties. Whereas one might criticize the desultory participation and the absence of clear programmatic discourse in European elections, the EP nonetheless has an effective system of party cooperation, with votes most often splitting along party lines and in which recognizable ideological cleavages shape voting patterns. Among the most relevant difference between the European Parliament and national parliaments appears to be the tendency of the EP to reach decisions by large majorities. Yet this tendency underscores the tendency of the EU to reach decisions by consensus – unsurprising given the high level of support required in the Council of Ministers – and should

---

[32] Dahl, 'Can International Organization be Democratic?', op. cit.

give us reason for confidence that it is legislating in the 'European' interest.[33]

Indirect Democratic Accountability

If European elections were the only form of democratic accountability to which the EU were subject, scepticism might be warranted. Yet a more important channel lies in the democratically elected governments of the member states, whose direct diplomatic representatives dominate the still largely territorial and intergovernmental structure of the EU. In the European Council, which is consolidating its position as the EU's dominant institution, elected heads of state and government wield power directly.[34] In the Council of Ministers, which more often than not imposes the binding constraint on everyday EU legislation, permanent representatives, ministerial officials and the ministers themselves from each country act under constant instruction from national executives, just as they would at home. The bonds of accountability are tight: National representatives can be recalled or re-instructed at will, often more easily than parliamentarians in national systems. In addition, national parliaments consider and comment on many EU policies, though their de facto ability to influence policy fluctuates greatly by country.

The multi-stage legislative process, whereby legislation must traverse the Commission, Council, Parliament and domestic implementing authorities, encourages highly transparent policy-making. In contrast to the widespread vision of a cadre of secretive gnomes burrowing away in Brussels, supranational officials in fact work under intense public scrutiny. The legislative process works slowly, without any equivalent to ruling by executive decree or pushing legislation swiftly through a friendly parliament, and information appears as plentiful about the EU political and regulatory process, at least at the Brussels level, than about similar processes in nearly all of its member states. With 20 commissioners and their staffs, fifteen national

[33] Simon Hix, Abdul Noury and Gerard Roland, ' "Normal" Parliament? Party Cohesion and Competition in the European Parliament, 1979–2001', paper presented at the Public Choice Society conference, San Diego, 21–3 March 2002.

[34] Peter Ludlow, *The Laeken Council*, Brussels, Intercommunity, 2002.

delegations, over 600 parliamentarians, hundreds of national ministers and thousands of national officials, *ex ante* parliamentary scrutiny in some countries and *ex post* parliamentary scrutiny in nearly all, combined with the subsequent need for domestic administrative implementation, there can be no such thing as a monopoly of information in the EU. Whereas it is true that certain aspects of the system, such as early discussions in the lower levels of COREPER, tend to take place in relative secret, the same might be said of the *de facto* preparation of legislation in national systems. Recent research seems to reveal that the EU regulatory processes are as open to input from civil society, and as constrained by the need to give reasons, as the (relatively open) systems of Switzerland and the US. Discussions within the *comitologie* appear to take due account of public interest considerations, though the precise reasons for this – socialization, insulated expert discussion, external pressure of member states, structured deliberation, anticipated non-compliance – remain unclear.[35]

The Legitimacy of Semi-Autonomous Judges and Technocrats

It might be objected that, as compared to national systems, a greater proportion of EU decisions are made by autonomous technocrats in the Commission, constitutional court judges, or central bankers. These appointed officials resolve essentially political questions involving the apportionment of costs, benefits and risks. Yet little is in fact distinctive about the pattern of delegation we observe in the EU. The late twentieth century was a period of the 'decline of parliaments' and the rise of courts, public administrations and the 'core executive'. Accountability is imposed, increasingly not through direct participation in majoritarian decision-making but instead through complex systems of indirect representation, selection of

---

[35] Christian Joerges and E. Vos (eds), *EU Committees: Social Regulation, Law and Politics*, Oxford, Hart Publishing, 1999; Majone, 'Europe's Democratic Deficit', op. cit.; Thomas D. Zweifel, 'Democratic Deficits in Comparison: Best (and Worst) Practices in European, US and Swiss Merger Regulation', *Journal of Common Market Studies*, 41 (2003), pp. 541–66. Also see Pierpaolo Settembri, 'Transparency of the EU Legislator', unpublished paper, University of Florence, 2003.

representatives, professional socialization, *ex post* review, and balances between branches of government.[36]

The critical point for the study of the EU is this: within the multi-level governance system prevailing in Europe, EU officials (or insulated national representatives) enjoy the greatest autonomy in precisely those areas – central banking, constitutional adjudication, criminal and civil prosecution, technical administration and economic diplomacy – in which many advanced industrial democracies, including most member states of the EU, insulate from direct political contestation. *The apparently 'undemocratic' nature of the EU as a whole is largely a function of this selection effect.* As we have seen, insulation is not simply an empirical observation; it has normative weight. Given such justifications, the burden of proof rests on critics of the EU. We may debate whether the EU's central bank, constitutional court, or competition authorities are properly constructed, but any such criticism must first concede the legitimacy and general acceptability of a greater measure of insulation and autonomy in precisely these areas than elsewhere in political life.

THE SOCIAL DEMOCRATIC CRITIQUE: DOES THE EU IMPOSE A NEO-LIBERAL BIAS?

The *social democratic* conception of democracy stresses the role of political institutions in offsetting social inequality. Fritz Scharpf has argued that most Europeans favour maintaining current levels of welfare spending, as demonstrated by the decentralized tendency of member states to spend increasing percentages of GNP on welfare as per capita income increases.[37] Yet the status quo cannot be maintained today because of the tendency of decentralized market competition to generate an interstate 'race to the bottom' in regulatory protection. Trade, immigration and especially foreign investment and capital flows create strong incentives for countries to reduce

[36] Majone, *Regulating Europe*, op. cit.

[37] Scharpf, *Governing in Europe*, op. cit. For a more detailed discussion of Scharpf, from both positive and normative perspectives, see Andrew Moravcsik and Andrea Sangiovanni, *On Democracy and Public Interest in the Europe Union*, Center for European Studies Working Paper Series, Cambridge, MA, Harvard University, forthcoming.

welfare expenditures. The EU cannot respond effectively to this tendency, despite overwhelming support for the maintenance of welfare systems, because of a neo-liberal bias in the constitutional structure of the EU, and the rhetoric that surrounds it, which favours market liberalization ('negative integration') over social protection ('positive integration').

In this view, the EU lacks democratic legitimacy not so much because it stifles political participation, but because its policies are biased against particular interests that are consensually recognized as legitimate. Such accounts tend to be social democratic, that is, they tend to argue that the EU systematically biases policy-making in a neo-liberal direction.[38] It does this, so the argument goes, by excluding particular issues, in particular social welfare and some public interest regulation, from the agenda, while facilitating common liberalization of trade and factor flows. The entire arrangement is locked in by the European legal order. Opposition does not form, because it is kept off the agenda by the European constitutional compromise, which leaves social welfare provision to the national governments, and by the ignorance of less fortunate individuals and groups about their own interests. Scharpf's argument is without a doubt the most empirically and theoretically nuanced social democratic criticism of the EU 'democratic deficit' that currently exists. Yet there is good reason to qualify his formulation of the argument, above all since these qualifications are acknowledged in Scharpf's own empirical analysis.

There is in fact little evidence of a race to the bottom. Scharpf himself concludes ultimately that there can be such a race in only a few areas, there is relatively little evidence that it has yet occurred, and the effects have been limited. The level of social welfare provision in Europe remains relatively stable. National welfare systems are no longer moving strongly in the direction of greater redistribution, but they are not imploding either. Recent OECD analyses report that fiscal consolidation over the past 20 years has almost always led to increases in government revenues as a percentage of GNP, and in most cases the burden of consolidation is placed primarily on revenue increases.

[38] Yet they need not be so. Many libertarians believe that policy in the EU, as well as in Europe as a whole, is biased in a social democratic direction. For example, see Rabkin, *Why Sovereignty Matters*, op. cit.

Much recent research, moreover, suggests that the adverse impact of globalization on the major areas of social spending in Europe (pénsions, medical care and labour market policy) is easily exaggerated. The most important factors behind increasing social spending are instead domestic: the shift to a post-industrial economy, lower productivity growth, shifting demand for less skilled workers, rising costs of health care, pensions and employment, exacerbated by increasingly unfavourable demographic trends. These factors fuel welfare deficits and fiscal strains, yet any reform is opposed by entrenched constituencies (the elderly, medical-care consumers, and the full-time unemployed) well-placed to resist it. *No* responsible analyst believes that current individual social welfare entitlements can be maintained in the face of these structural shifts, regardless of how they are structured and how they interact with the global economy. In this context, the neo-liberal bias of the EU, if it exists, may well be partially justified by the social welfarist bias of current national policies, and marginal pressure towards consolidation of national welfare systems should be considered a benefit not a threat.

Certainly there is little evidence that the EU is driving social protection downwards. By contrast, the EU has often permitted high standards and supportive institutional reform, and thus has tended to re-regulate at a high level.[39] Anecdotal evidence suggests that the EU is responsive to public and interest group concerns in a way quite similar to national polities.[40] For reasons set out by Scharpf, there is far less reason for a social democrat to fear the piecemeal evolution of European law than might have been the case five years ago.[41] Whatever consequences there may be lie largely in the future. The major difference between apparently intractable issues of EU discussion such as social and tax harmonization, and similar issues where European regulation is effective, such as worker health and safety, appears not to lie in constitutional structure but in the precise nature

[39] David Vogel, *Trading Up*, Cambridge, MA, Harvard University Press, 1995; Joerges and Vos, *EU Committees*, op. cit.

[40] The life-cycle of an issue like Mad Cow Disease is just as it would be in any western democracy: some bureaucracies are captured; a crisis emerges; and reforms are put in place that lay greater emphasis on the broader public interest. Joerges and Vos, *EU Committees*, op. cit.

[41] Also Scharpf, *Governing in Europe*, op. cit.

of conflicts of interest among national governments. In the case of taxation, some governments remain deeply opposed to the harmonization of taxation and social welfare, whereas there are few die-hard defenders of unilateralism in matters of worker health and safety or pollution abatement. In this sense, the EU reflects patterns of consensus and contestation within European publics.[42]

THE DELIBERATIVE DEMOCRATIC CRITIQUE: DOES THE EU ENCOURAGE PUBLIC PASSIVITY?

Radical democrats might nonetheless be tempted to reject the entire trend toward insulated decision-making, domestic and international, because the cost in terms of political participation and civic virtue is perceived as too high.[43] Such critics might observe that the European Constitutional Settlement has failed to promote the transnational political parties, identities and discourses that might help render European political participation meaningful and effective for citizens. A number of analysts propose to employ European institutions to induce social cooperation in pursuit of common interests – political parties, interest groups, a common discourse, and so on. This in turn, they expect, will generate legitimacy.

Unless entirely grounded in an ideal preference for participation, however, these criticisms rest on the questionable premise that greater participation in European political institutions will generate a deeper sense of political community in Europe or, at the very least, greater popular support for the EU. Yet there are at least three reasons to doubt that this is the case.

First, insulated institutions – constitutional courts and administrative bureaucracies, for example – are often more popular with the

---

[42] From the perspective of democratic theory, finally, it is important to note that Scharpf's proposals are concerned primarily to maintain social protection in richer member states. They are quite conservative in that they favour domestic redistribution over transnational redistribution; the defence of German welfare standards takes precedence over schemes for transnational redistribution. Scharpf's justification lies in the subjective perceptions of identity of national citizens in countries like Germany, which do not support a heavy commitment to redistribution.

[43] For discussions of this argument, see Weiler, *The Constitution of Europe*, op. cit.; Schmitter, *How to Democratize the European Union*, op. cit.; Seidentop, *Democracy in Europe*, op. cit.

public than legislatures. Internationally, institutions like the European Court of Human Rights (ECHR) in Strasbourg command great legitimacy despite their near total lack of direct democratic legitimacy. The EU's position in the institutional division of labour involves such political functions, as we have just seen, and it is unclear whether more participation in such functions would legitimate them. Whereas a greater sense of common identity might indeed increase support for the EU, this does not bear on the case for democratic reform but on the question of how extensive European integration should be.[44]

Second, EU legislative and regulatory activity is inversely correlated with the salience of issues in the minds of European voters, so any effort to expand participation is unlikely to overcome apathy. Among the most significant consequences of the limitation of the substantive scope of the EU, discussed above, is that the issues handled by the EU, and even more so second-order institutional choices about how to manage them, lack salience in the minds of European voters. Of the five most salient issues in most West European democracies – health-care provision, education, law and order, pension and social security policy, and taxation – none is primarily an EU competence. Among the next ten, only a few (managing the economy, the environment, alongside the anomalous issue of Europe itself) could be considered major EU concerns, none exclusively so.[45] By contrast, the issues in which the EU specializes – trade liberalization, monetary policy, the removal of non-tariff barriers, technical regulation in the environmental and other areas, foreign aid and general foreign policy coordination – which tend to be low-salience issues in most European polities.

Lack of salience, not lack of opportunity, may be the critical constraint on European political participation. This would explain why European citizens fail to exploit even the limited opportunities they have to participate. It follows that referendums, parliamentary elections, or constitutional conventions based on such issues encourage informationally impoverished and institutionally unstructured deliberation, which in turn encourages unstable plebiscitary politics

[44] James Gibson and Gregory A. Caldcira, 'Legitimacy, Judicial Power and Emerging Transnational Insitutions: The Court of Justice in the European Community', mimeograph, University of Houston, 1993.

[45] I am indebted to Bonnie Meguid for access to her systematic data on issue salience in European countries.

in which individuals have no incentive to reconcile their concrete interests with their immediate choices. The typical result is a debacle like the recent Irish referendum on the Nice Treaty. Not only does this demonstrate the existence of significant substantive constraints on EU policy-making, but it implies – as we shall see below – that even if a common European 'identity' and the full panoply of democratic procedures existed, it would be very difficult to induce meaningful citizen participation.

Of course this could change in the future. But the proposals to construct greater citizen involvement in EU politics that are most plausible in theory are patently implausible in practice. In order to give individuals a reason to care about EU politics, it is necessary to give them a stake in it – a fact that many discussions of a *demos*, 'we-feeling', 'community', and 'constitutional patriotism' elide.[46] The most compelling schemes for doing so rest not on the creation of new political opportunities, but the emergence of entirely new political cleavages based on interest. Philippe Schmitter argues that agricultural supports and structural funds should be replaced with a guaranteed minimum income for the poorest one-third of Europeans, national welfare systems should be rebalanced so as not to favour the elderly, and immigrants and aliens should be granted full rights.[47] With the EU acting as a massive engine of redistribution, individuals and groups would reorient their political behaviour on whether they benefit or lose from the system.

This is a coherent scheme targeted at precisely those groups most dissatisfied with European integration today – broadly speaking, the poorer, less well-educated, female, and public sector populations – but it is utterly impractical. It would run up against one of the fundamental 'real-world' constraints on democracy, namely the willingness of some groups to continue to participate in the project of European integration. In search of legitimacy, Schmitter breaks entirely with existing EU practices, divorcing the EU entirely from its ostensible purpose of regulating cross-border social behaviour, and would thereby undermine the legitimacy of almost everyone currently involved with it. The result would almost certainly be a higher level of political conflict, domestic and interstate, than Europe has seen in several generations – and perhaps the collapse of the organization.

[46] For an exception, see Weiler, *The Constitution of Europe*, op. cit.
[47] Schmitter, *How to Democratize the European Union*, op. cit.

IMPLICATIONS FOR GLOBAL GOVERNANCE

Any assessment of the democratic legitimacy of regional and global governance must not just be philosophical, but empirical and social scientific as well. Rather than comparing international organizations to idealized ancient, Westminster-style, or imaginary political systems, the baseline should be the real-world practices of existing governments acting imperfectly under complex constraints. Above I presented a simple framework for conducting such an analysis and applied it to the EU. In that case, a failure to view democracy realistically, as well as the failure to take into account the empirical idiosyncrasies of the European case – notably its limited mandate and the continuing strong role of national governments – has given critics the *impression* that the EU is undemocratic. In fact it is merely specializing in those aspects of modern democratic governance that typically involve less direct political participation. The apparently 'counter-majoritarian' tendency of EU political institutions insulated from direct democratic contestation arises out of factors that themselves have normative integrity, notably efforts to compensate for the ignorance and non-participation of citizens, to make credible commitments to rights enforcement, and to offset the power of special interests. These institutional adaptations are normal in the 'second best' world of advanced industrial democracies. This is not to say that there is no cause for concern. There are a few areas where the EU departs modestly from existing national practices without a compelling substantive justification. The most important is the structure of European Central Bank, which is more independent of political pressure than any known national example.[48] Yet, overall, when judged by the practices of existing nation-states and in the context of a multi-level system, there is little evidence that the EU suffers from a fundamental democratic deficit. We might of course nonetheless choose to criticize the broader trend toward professional administration, judicial enforcement of rights, and strong executive leadership, but it is unrealistic to expect the EU to bear the brunt of such a critique.

---

[48] Matthias J. Herdegen, 'Price Stability and Budgetary Restraints in the Economic and Monetary Union: the Law as Guardian of Economic Wisdom', *Common Market Law Review*, 35 (1998), pp. 9–32.

The framework for analysis I have presented is general, but can the relatively optimistic conclusion be generalized? I am sceptical. The favourable assessment of the EU rests on a number of assumptions that may not be universally true of international organizations. Above all, the democratic legitimacy of the EU rests on the fact that national-states remain influential, democratic and technically competent. These conditions cannot be assumed to be true of all national governments, particularly in the developing world.[49] Nonetheless, the EU establishes one endpoint in the current empirical continuum of international organizations – an endpoint that can serve as a starting point for future comparative research.

---

[49] See the chapter by David Held in this volume.

11
Democratic Accountability and Political Effectiveness from a Cosmopolitan Perspective

David Held

FROM THE DESTRUCTION OF THE TWIN TOWERS ON 11 SEPTEMBER 2001 to the failure of trade discussions at Cancún in September 2003, issues are raised which not only concern large swathes of the world's population, but can only be adequately resolved by increased coordination and cooperation across borders. How such coordination and cooperation can be achieved, and how and to whom there should be accountability, are the themes of this article. The chapter is in six parts. The first part sketches the contemporary nature of global politics; the second examines problems and dilemmas of global public policy-making; the third explores how global governance can be strengthened; the fourth sets out the framework of a cosmopolitan polity which would place democratic accountability at its centre; the fifth unfolds a related concept of multilayered citizenship; and the final part explores the underlying cosmopolitan principles of the argument. The modern polity was built on the idea of the modern state and a system of state-based accountability. While this represented a hugely important paradigm shift, it is no longer sufficient to help understand the proper form of democratic accountability in a global age.

GLOBAL POLITICS

A distinctive aspect of the contemporary world order is the emergence of 'global politics'.[1] Political events in one part of the world can rapidly acquire world-wide ramifications. Sites of political action

---

[1] See A. McGrew, 'Conceptualizing Global Politics', in A. McGrew et al., *Global Politics*, Cambridge, Polity Press, 1992.

can become embedded in extensive networks of political interaction involving states and nonstate actors. As a result, developments at the local level – whether economic, social or environmental – can acquire almost instantaneous global consequences, and vice versa.[2]

Nations, peoples and social movements are linked by many new forms of communication. Over the last few decades a wave of new technological innovations, along with the transformation of older technologies, has generated global communication and transportation infrastructures. These have opened up a massive series of communication channels that cross national borders, increasing the range and type of communications to and from all the world's regions. In addition, contemporary patterns of communication have created a far greater intensity of concepts, symbols and images, moving with far greater extensity and at a far greater velocity than in earlier periods. This process is compounded by the fact that new global communication systems are used for business and commercial purposes. While there remain significant differences in information density and velocity in different parts of the globe, it is becoming increasingly difficult for people to live in any place isolated from the wider world.

These developments have engendered fundamental changes in the organization of political life. The intimate connection between 'physical setting', 'social situation' and politics, which distinguished most political associations from pre-modern to modern times, has been ruptured; the new communication systems create new experiences, new modes of understanding and new frames of political reference independent of direct contact with particular peoples, issues or events. The speed with which the events of 11 September 2001 ramified across the world and made mass terrorism a global issue is one poignant example.

The idea of global politics calls into question the traditional demarcations between the domestic and the foreign, and between the territorial and the non-territorial, found in modern conceptions of 'the political'.[3] These categories not only shaped modern political thought but also institution-building, as a clear division was

[2] See A. Giddens, *The Consequences of Modernity*, Cambridge, Polity Press, 1990, ch. 2.

[3] See D. Held, A. McGrew, J. Perraton and D. Goldblatt, *Global Transformations*, Cambridge, Polity Press, 1999, chs 1, 2 and 8.

established between great ministries of state founded to focus on
domestic matters and those created to pursue geopolitical questions.
Global problems highlight the richness and complexity of the inter-
connections which now transcend states and societies in the global
order. Moreover, global politics is anchored today not just in traditional geopolitical concerns – trade, power, security – but in a large
diversity of social and ecological questions. Pollution, water supply,
genetically engineered food and drugs are amongst an increasing
number of policy issues that cut across territorial jurisdictions and
existing political alignments, and which require international cooperation for their satisfactory resolution. In many parts of the world
the notion of global politics corresponds much more closely to the
character of politics than do obsolete images of politics as simply state
and interstate relations.[4] There are now multiple spheres of politics
and authority.

In mapping political globalization, it is important to explore the
way in which the sovereign state now lies at the crossroads of a vast
array of networks and organizations that have been established to
regulate and manage diverse areas of international and transnational
activity – trade, communications, crime and so on. The rapid growth
of transnational issues and challenges has generated a multicentric
system of governance both within and across political borders.[5] It has
been marked by the transformation of aspects of territorially based
political decision-making, the development of regional and global
organizations and, in many places, the increased importance of
regional and international law. There is nothing inevitable, it should
be stressed, about these developments. While they form highly significant trends, they are contingent upon many factors, and could be
halted or reversed by protracted global conflicts or cataclysmic
events.

At the core of these developments is the reconfiguration of
political power. While many states retain the ultimate legal claim to
effective supremacy over what occurs within their own territories,
this should be juxtaposed with, and understood in relation to,
the expanding jurisdiction of institutions of global and regional

    [4] R. O. Keohane and J. S. Nye, 'Globalization: What's New? What's Not (and So
What?)', *Foreign Policy*, 118 (2000), pp. 104–19.
    [5] J. Rosenau, 'Governance in a New Global Order', in D. Held and A. McGrew
(eds), *Governing Globalization*, Cambridge, Polity Press, 2002.

governance and the constraints of, as well as the obligations derived from, new and changing forms of international regulation. This is especially evident in the European Union, where sovereign power is divided between international, national and local authorities, but it is also evident in the operation of international governmental organizations (IGOs) such as the WTO.[6] However, even where sovereignty still appears intact, states do not retain sole command of what transpires within their own territorial boundaries. Complex global systems, from the financial to the ecological, connect the fate of communities in one locale to the fate of communities in distant regions of the world. Globalization, in other words, is associated with a transformation or an 'unbundling' of the relationship between sovereignty, territoriality and political power.[7]

This unbundling involves a plurality of actors, a variety of political processes, and diverse levels of coordination and operation. Specifically, it includes:
• different forms of intergovernmental arrangements embodying various levels of legalization, types of instruments utilized and responsiveness to stakeholders;
• an increasing number of public agencies – e.g. central bankers – maintaining links with similar agencies in other countries and thus forming transgovernmental networks for the management of various global issues;
• diverse business actors – i.e. firms, their associations and organizations such as international chambers of commerce – establishing their own transnational regulatory mechanisms to manage issues of common concern;
• nongovernmental organizations (NGOs) and transnational advocacy networks – i.e. leading actors in global civil society – playing a role in various domains of global governance and at various stages of the global public policy-making process;
• public bodies, business actors and NGOs collaborating in many issue areas in order to provide novel approaches to social problems through multi-stakeholder networks.

---

[6] M. Moore, *A World Without Walls*, Cambridge, Cambridge University Press, 2003.
[7] See J. Ruggie, 'Territoriality and Beyond', *International Organization*, 47: 1 (1993), pp. 139–74.

While many people – politicians, political activists and academics – link contemporary globalization with new constraints on politics, it is more accurately associated with the expansion of the terms of political activity. Not only has contemporary globalization triggered or reinforced the significant politicization of a growing array of issue areas, but it has been accompanied by an extraordinary growth of institutionalized arenas and networks of political mobilization, decision-making and regulatory activity which transcend national political jurisdictions. This has expanded the capacity for, and scope of, political activity and the exercise of political authority. Yet, this is not to overlook the many challenges posed by economic and political globalization to the public policy process at diverse levels. The focus here is on the global.

PROBLEMS AND DILEMMAS OF GLOBAL PUBLIC POLICY-MAKING

Problem-solving at the global level is marked by a number of difficulties. In the first instance, there is no clear division of labour among the myriad of international governmental agencies; functions often overlap, mandates frequently conflict, and aims and objectives too often get blurred. There are a number of competing and overlapping organizations and institutions, all of which have some stake in shaping global public policy. As one observer has noted in relation to global social policy, the fragmentation and competition that takes place is between:

- the World Bank, IMF, WTO and the UN system;
- the UN Secretariat and UN social agencies;
- the G7, G20, G16 and G77 and other groupings of countries;
- and a host of national social initiatives.[8]

The World Bank's health and social policies are not the same as those of the WHO, UNESCO or the International Labour Organization (ILO), to name but some agencies. The United Nations General Secretary's initiatives, such as those involving the Millennium Project, are not necessarily the same as, and are in some tension with, the social policies of the UN's Department of Economic and Social

---

[8] See B. Deacon, 'Global Social Governance Reform', in B. Deacon et al. (eds), *Global Social Governance*, Helsinki, Hakapaino Oy, 2003.

Affairs and the aims of the United Nations Development Programme (UNDP) and WHO. While the G7 often has a set of reasonably clear global policy objectives, these are typically in conflict with the G20 and G77, the latter often seeking to form an opposition grouping to the agenda of the G7.

Reflecting on the difficulties of interagency cooperation during his time as head of the WTO, Mike Moore has written that 'greater coherence amongst the numerous agencies that receive billions of taxpayers' dollars would be a good start . . . this lack of coherence damages their collective credibility, frustrates their donors and owners and gives rise to public cynicism . . . the array of institutions is bewildering . . . our interdependent world has yet to find the mechanism to integrate its common needs'.[9]

A second set of difficulties relates to the inertia found in the system of international agencies, or the inability of these agencies to mount collective problem-solving solutions when faced with disagreement over objectives, means, costs and so on. This often leads to the situation where the cost of inaction is greater than the cost of taking action. For the reform of the world trade regime and the treatment of serious diseases which threaten many countries, it has been estimated that the costs of inaction are about one hundred times greater than the costs of corrective action.[10] The failure to act decisively in the face of urgent global problems can not only compound the costs of dealing with these problems in the long run, but can also reinforce a widespread perception that these agencies are not just ineffective but unaccountable.

The perceived accountability deficit is linked to two interrelated difficulties: the power imbalances among states as well as those between state and non-state actors in the shaping and making of global public policy. Multilateral bodies need to be fully representative of the states involved in them, and they are rarely so. In addition, there must be arrangements in place to engage in dialogue and consultation between state and non-state actors, and these conditions are only partially met in multilateral decision-making bodies. Investigating this problem, Inge Kaul and her associates at the UNDP have made the telling point that 'the imbalances among states as well as

---

[9] Moore, *A World without Walls*, op. cit., pp. 220, 223.

[10] See P. Conceição, 'Assessing the Provision Status of Global Public Goods', in I. Kaul et al. (eds), *Providing Global Public Goods*, Oxford, Oxford University Press, 2003.

those between state and non-state actors are not always easy to detect, because in many cases the problem is not merely a quantitative issue – whether all parties have a seat at the negotiating table. The main problem is often qualitative – how well various stakeholders are represented.'[11] Having a seat at the negotiating table in a major IGO or at a major conference does not ensure effective representation. For, even if there is parity of formal representation, it is often the case that developed countries have large delegations equipped with extensive negotiating and technical expertise, while poorer developing countries often depend on one person delegations, or have even to rely on the sharing of a delegate. Moreover,

a one person delegation today does not necessarily have the same negotiating strengths as a one person delegation several years ago. The negotiating load has increased: the international policy agenda is lengthening, issues are becoming more complex, organizations are multiplying, conference venues are being shifted from continent to continent, meetings are being held in parallel sessions, and 'informal informals' are becoming a common negotiating tool.[12]

All of these issues stretch the capacities of small negotiating delegations to the limit. The difficulties that occur range from the significant under-representation of developing countries in agencies such as the IMF – where 24 industrial countries hold ten to eleven seats on the executive board while 42 African countries hold only two – to problems that result from an inability to develop substantial enough negotiating and technical expertise even with one person one country decision-making procedures.[13] Accordingly, many people are stakeholders in global political problems that affect them, but remain excluded from the political institutions and strategies needed to address these problems.[14]

An additional problem emerges as a result of issues which span the distinction between the domestic and the foreign. A growing

[11] See I. Kaul et al., 'How to Improve the Provision of Global Public Goods', in ibid., p. 30.

[12] Ibid., p. 31.

[13] See A. Buira, 'The Governance of the International Monetary Fund'; P. Chasek and L. Rajamani, 'Steps towards Enhanced Party Parity'; and R. V. Mendoza, 'The Multilateral Trade Regime' – all in ibid.

[14] There were interesting signs at the September 2003 trade discussion at Cancún that leading developing countries are beginning to learn from these problems and combine expertise and negotiating resources.

number of issues can be characterized as intermestic – that is, issues which cross the *inter*national and do*mestic*.[15] These are often insufficiently understood, comprehended or acted upon. For there is a fundamental lack of ownership of global public problems at the global level.[16] It is far from clear which global issues are the responsibility of which international agencies, and which issues ought to be addressed by which particular agencies. The institutional fragmentation and competition leads not just to the problem of overlapping jurisdictions among agencies, but also to the problem of issues falling between agencies. This latter problem is also manifest between the global level and national governments. The time has come – to say the very least – to examine these matters again.

Underlying these institutional difficulties is the breakdown of symmetry and congruence between decision-makers and decision-takers.[17] The point has been well articulated recently by Kaul and her associates in their work on global public goods. They speak about the forgotten *equivalence* principle.[18] This principle suggests that the span of a good's benefits and costs should be matched with the span of the jurisdiction in which decisions are taken on that good. At its simplest, the principle suggests that those who are significantly affected by a global good or bad should have a say in its provision. Yet, all too often, there is a breakdown of 'equivalence' between decision-makers and decision-takers, between decision-makers and stakeholders, and between the inputs and outputs of the decision-making process. As a result, we face the challenge of:

• *matching circles of stakeholders and decision-makers* – to create opportunities for all to have a say about global public goods that affect their lives;

• *systematizing the financing of global public goods* – to get incentives right and to secure adequate private and public resources for these goods;

[15] Rosenau, 'Governance in a New Global Order', op. cit.

[16] Moore, *A World without Walls*, op. cit., p. 218.

[17] See D. Held, *Democracy and the Global Order*, Cambridge, Polity Press, 1995.

[18] Kaul et al., 'How to Improve the Provision of Global Public Goods', op. cit., pp. 27–8.

• *spanning borders, sectors, and groups of actors* – to foster institutional interaction and create space for policy entrepreneurship and strategic issue management.[19]
Failures or inadequacies in global political processes often result from the mismatch between the decision-making circles created in international arenas and the range of spillovers associated with specific public goods or public bads. 'The challenge is to align the circles of those to be consulted (or to take part in the decision-making) with the spillover range of the good under negotiation.'[20]

Traditionally, the tension between the sphere of decision-makers and the sphere of decision-takers has been resolved by the idea of political community – the bounded, territorially delimited community in which decision-makers and decision-takers create processes and institutions to resolve the problem of accountability. During the period in which nation-states were being forged – and the territorially-bound conception of democracy was consolidated – the idea of a close mesh between geography, political power and democracy could be assumed. It seemed compelling that political power, sovereignty, democracy and citizenship were simply and appropriately bounded by a delimited territorial space. These links were by and large taken for granted and generally unexplicated. But they can be no longer. Globalization, global governance and global challenges raise issues concerning the proper scope of democracy and of a democracy's jurisdiction, given that the relation between decision-makers and decision-takers is not necessarily symmetrical or congruent with respect to territory.

The principle of inclusiveness and subsidiarity is often regarded in democratic theory as a helpful means to clarify the fundamental criterion for drawing proper boundaries around those who should be involved in particular decision-making domains, those who should be accountable to a particular group of people, and why.[21] At its simplest, it states that those significantly (i.e., nontrivially) affected by

---

[19] I. Kaul et al., 'Why Do Global Public Goods Matter Today?', in Kaul et al., *Providing Global Public Goods*, op. cit., pp. 5–6.

[20] Kaul et al., 'How to Improve the Provision of Global Public Goods', op. cit., p. 28.

[21] See D. Held, *Models of Democracy*, 2nd edn, Cambridge, Polity Press, 1996, part 3.

public decisions, issues or processes should, *ceteris paribus*, have an equal opportunity, directly or indirectly through elected delegates or representatives, to influence and shape them. Those affected by public decisions ought to have a say in their making.[22]

While this principle points in an important direction, it is only in association with the idea of a political community that it is compelling; for here decision-makers and decision-takers meet by convention to resolve matters of common fate. But the issue is: how is the notion of 'significantly affected' to be understood when the relation between decision-makers and decision-takers is more spatially complex – when, that is, decisions affect people outside a circumscribed democratic entity? To take some examples: a decision to permit the 'harvesting' of rainforests may contribute to ecological damage far beyond the borders which formally limit the responsibility of a given set of decision-makers. A decision to build a nuclear plant near the frontier of a neighbouring country is a decision likely to be taken without consulting those in the nearby country (or countries) despite the many risks for them. A decision by large US corporations such as IBM or Microsoft can have profound effects on the economic opportunities in countries such as India, but it will in all likelihood be taken without consultation with those in far-off lands.[23] In these situations, as Robert Keohane put it, 'the normative question arises . . .: should the acting entity be accountable to the set of people it affects? . . . Merely being affected cannot be sufficient to create a valid claim. If it were, virtually nothing could ever be done, since there would be so many requirements for consultation and even veto points.'[24]

This is a hard issue to resolve. The issue becomes a little easier to think through if the all-affected principle is connected directly to the idea of impact on people's needs or interests. If we think of the impact of powerful forces on peoples' lives, then impact can be divided into three categories: strong, moderate and weak. By strong

---

[22] See M. Saward, 'A Critique of Held', in B. Holden (ed.), *Global Democracy*, London, Routledge, 2002.

[23] Other examples include the decision to go to war. However, war raises a number of exceptional questions which I will not address in this article.

[24] R. O. Keohane, 'Global Governance and Democratic Accountability', in D. Held and M. Koenig-Archibugi (eds), *Taming Globalization*, Cambridge, Polity Press, 2003, p. 141.

I mean that vital needs or interests are affected (from health to housing) with fundamental consequences for people's life expectancy. By moderate I mean that needs are affected in such a way that people's ability to participate in their community (in economic, cultural and political activities) is in question. At stake here is the quality of life chances. By weak I mean an effect which impacts upon particular lifestyles or the range of available consumption choices (from clothes to music). These categories are not watertight and require further theoretical analysis,[25] but they provide some useful guidance:

• if people's urgent needs are unmet their lives will be in danger. In this context, people are at risk of serious harm;

• if people's secondary needs are unmet they will not be able to participate fully in their communities and their potential for involvement in public and private life will remain unfulfilled. Their choices will be restricted or depleted. In this context, people are at risk of harm to their life opportunities;

• if people's lifestyle needs are unmet their ability to develop their lives and express themselves through diverse media will be thwarted. In this context, unmet need can lead to frustration. (Frustration could be thought of as a weak term, but it can give rise to serious tension and conflict.)

In the light of these considerations, the principle of inclusiveness and subsidiarity needs restating. I take it to mean here that those whose life expectancy and life chances are significantly affected by social forces and processes ought to have a stake in the determination of the conditions and regulation of these, either directly or indirectly through political representatives. Democracy is best located when it is closest to and involves those whose life expectancy and life chances are determined by powerful entities, bringing the circles of stakeholders and decision-makers closer together. The argument for extending this consideration to decisions and processes which affect lifestyle needs is less compelling, since these are fundamentally questions of value and identity for communities to resolve for themselves. Whether McDonald's should be allowed access across China, or US media products given free range in Canada, are questions largely for

---

[25] Cf. L. Doyal and I. Gough, *A Theory of Human Need*, London, Macmillan, 1991; and Held, *Democracy and the Global Order*, op. cit., part 2.

those countries to resolve, although clearly serious cross-border issues concerning, for example, the clash of values and consumption choices can develop, posing questions about regional or global trade rules and regulations.

The principle of inclusiveness and subsidiarity points to the necessity of both the decentralization *and* centralization of political power. If decision-making is decentralized as much as possible, it maximizes the opportunity of each person to influence the social conditions that shape his or her life. But if the decisions at issue are translocal, transnational, or transregional, then political institutions need not only to be locally based but also to have a wider scope and framework of operation. In this context, the creation of diverse sites and levels of democratic forums may be unavoidable. It may be unavoidable, paradoxically, for the very same reasons as decentralization is desirable: it creates the possibility of including people who are significantly affected by a political issue in the public (in this case, transcommunity public) sphere. If diverse peoples beyond borders are effectively stakeholders in the operation of select regional and global forces, their de facto status as members of diverse communities would need to be matched by a de jure political status, if the mechanisms and institutions that govern these political spaces are to be brought under the rubric of the principle of inclusiveness and subsidiarity. Stakeholders in de facto communities and networks of local, national, regional and global processes will be politically empowered only if they achieve the necessary complementary de jure status.

Properly understood, the principle of inclusiveness and subsidiarity should be taken to entail that decision-making should be decentralized as much as possible, maximizing each person's opportunity to influence the social conditions that shape his or her life. Concomitantly, centralization is favoured if, and only if, it is the necessary basis for avoiding the exclusion of persons who are significantly affected by a political decision or outcome.[26] These considerations yield, as one analyst has written, 'the result that the authority to make decisions of some particular kind should rest with the democratic political process of a unit that (1) is as small as

---

[26] T. Pogge, 'Cosmopolitanism and Sovereignty', in C. Brown (ed.), *Political Restructuring in Europe: Ethical Perspectives*, London, Routledge, 1994, pp. 106–9.

possible but still (2) includes as equals all persons significantly
. . . affected by decisions of this kind'.[27]

Elsewhere, I have proposed three tests to help filter policy issues
to different levels of democratic governance: the tests of extensity,
intensity and comparative efficiency.[28] The test of extensity assesses
the range of people within and across borders whose life expectancy
and life chances are significantly affected by a collective problem and
policy question. The test of intensity examines the degree to which
the latter impinges on a group of people(s) and, therefore, the
degree to which regional or global initiatives are warranted. The
third test – the test of comparative efficiency – is concerned to
provide a means of examining whether any proposed regional or
global initiative is necessary insofar as the objectives it seeks to meet
cannot be realized satisfactorily by those working at 'lower' levels of
local or national decision-making. Accordingly, the principle of inclusiveness and subsidiarity may require diverse and multiple democratic public forums for its suitable enactment. It yields the possibility
of multilevel democratic governance. The ideal number of appropriate democratic jurisdictions cannot be assumed to be embraced
by just one level – as it is in the theory of the liberal democratic
nation-state.

STRENGTHENING GLOBAL GOVERNANCE

To restore symmetry and congruence between decision-makers and
decision-takers, and to entrench the principle of equivalence in a
manner that is consistent with inclusiveness and subsidiarity, requires
a strengthening of global governance and a resolve to address those
challenges previously discussed – institutional competition, overlapping jurisdictions, the excessive costs of inaction, the failures of
accountability, etc. In the first instance, this agenda can be thought
of as comprising three interrelated dimensions:
- promoting co-ordinated state action to tackle common problems;
- reinforcing those international institutions that can function
effectively;

---

[27] Ibid., p. 109.
[28] Held, *Democracy and the Global Order*, op. cit., ch. 10.

• and developing multilateral rules and procedures that lock in all powers, small and major, into an accountable multilateral framework.[29]

Such a strategy means promoting intergovernmentalism and interstate action to tackle problems like international criminal networks and the containment of new epidemics; and adopting the widest possible strategies for intergovernmental and interstate consultation and coalition building. This amounts to a policy of creating an enlightened multilateralism, a useful first step in establishing democratic accountability at the global level. But it can only be regarded as a first step – ambitious as it is in the current political climate.[30]

Systematizing the provision of global public goods requires not just building on existing forms of multilateral institutions, but also extending and developing them in order to address questions of transparency, accountability and democracy. A programme in this regard has been set out recently by the UNDP. It suggests the necessity of developing a number of new global institutional tools to foster both the provision and the public nature of decision-making. The following recommendations are made:

• promoting the principle of stakeholder–decision-maker equivalence;
• developing criteria for fair negotiations;
• strengthening the negotiating capacity of developing countries;
• developing rules for interactions between state and non-state actors;
• creating advisory scientific panels for all major global issues, following the example of the Intergovernmental Panel on Climate Change;
• creating negotiating arenas for new priority issues (such as the right of access to water for all people) together with appropriate grievance panels (such as a world water court);
• creating demand-driven review and response facilities to promote flexible implementation of policy regimes, such as a trade and development review council within the WTO.[31]

---

[29] See P. Hirst and G. Thompson, 'The Future of Globalization', *Cooperation and Conflict*, 37: 3 (2002), pp. 252–3.

[30] Ibid.

[31] Kaul et al., 'How to Improve the Provision of Global Public Goods', op. cit., p. 35.

The programme offers an imaginative leap forwards in the thinking about how to provide global public goods in a framework of public involvement.

Jean François Rischard has recently also stressed that the current international system is simply not effective, accountable or fast enough to solve many of the big global issues we face, issues concerning our planet, our humanity and our rulebook: see Figure 1. In this regard, he argues that the creation of major treaties is typically too slow a process, and often leads to legal agreements and instruments that are not enforced; big UN conferences are good and helpful at raising levels of awareness about a global issue but often fail to produce detailed solutions to those issues; G7/G8-type meetings can be very productive but are mostly reactive to problems that have occurred; and the world's leading IGOs, while they are sometimes quite effective, are rarely in a position to take a major initiative with regard to pressing global public problems.[32] Rischard stresses too that it is not enough simply to develop existing multilateral institutions, but that new innovative solutions are required if the core political problems we face are to have any hope of effective resolution within a legitimate framework of accountability. He is sceptical about our ability to create new institutions in sufficient time to resolve pressing global issues, and he is sceptical too about the ability of such institutions to act effectively in the short term. So against such notions, he proposes a series of global issue networks (GINs). He argues that what we require is a distinct global issue network for each urgent policy problem (see Figure 1). What would this look like?

Rischard argues that it is possible to conceive of the development of global issue networks in three stages:
• a constitutional phase, when the network is convened and set in motion;
• a norm-producing phase, beginning with a rigorous evaluation of options and alternatives; and
• an implementation phase, in which the network takes on a rating role, helping the norms exert their influence through reputation effects.[33]

---

[32] See J. F. Rischard, *High Noon*, New York, Basic Books, 2002, part 3.
[33] Ibid., p. 171.

Figure 1
Twenty Global Issues

Sharing our Planet: issues in volving the global commons

- Global warming
- Biodiversity and ecosystem losses
- Fisheries depletion
- Deforestation
- Water deficits
- Maritime safety and pollution

Sharing our Humanity: issues requiring a global commitment

- Massive step up in the fight against poverty
- Peacekeeping, conflict prevention, combating terrorism
- Education for all
- Global infectious diseases
- Digital divide
- Natural disaster prevention and mitigation

Sharing our Rulebook: issues needing a global regulatory approach

- Reinventing taxation for the twenty-first century
- Biotechnology rules
- Global financial architecture
- Illegal drugs
- Trade, investment and competition rules
- Intellectual property rights
- E-commerce rules
- International labour and migration rules

Source: Rischard, *High Noon*, op. cit., p. 66.

Such networks could be permanent or temporary and each would be charged with initiating policy recommendations for core pressing problems, such as global warming, biodiversity and ecosystem losses. Each network would be initiated by a leading international actor working purely as a facilitator – not a problem-solver in its own right. The GINs' membership would include representatives of governments concerned by and experienced with the issue at hand, as well as knowledgeable people from business and international NGOs. The GINs' brief would be to dissect a global problem and search for solutions. They would be asked to draw up detailed norms and standards which could, in principle, resolve the issue, and which could be used to put formal and informal pressure on the various players involved in the generation, and future solution, of the problem. The core phases in the development of global issue networks are set out in Figure 2.

GINs would seek to set out new standards of behaviour required by key agents to solve global problems, and would then act as a kind of rating agency to expose countries, businesses or other players that were not living up to the new standards. For example, they would regularly 'name and shame' governments that had not passed legislation conforming to the standards, or had not ratified or enforced a perfectly useful treaty, or had not altered domestic policy where it mattered.

The creation of a global issue network is clearly, in principle, a very flexible instrument to help bypass or circumvent organizations that have insufficient clarity about the issue involved, confusing mandates, or an inability to act decisively.[34] But there are problems with this mechanism if used alone. While the new networks are designed to put pressure on government organizations and agencies to perform better and more effectively, they contribute little to the question of norm and rule enforcement in the face of a reluctant actor – political, economic or social – that might refuse to come into line or that, by virtue of taking no action, could perpetuate and add to the core problem involved. Nor do they provide a solution to the problem of how one determines the range of legitimate voices or stakeholders that ought to be involved in a GIN, or how this matter can be effectively arbitrated. In this respect, it is helpful to think of GINs as a useful short-term mechanism in the creation and

---

[34] It is interesting to note that the EU is exploring similar policy instruments through its 'Open Method of Coordination'. In utilizing this method, member states agree to formulate national action plans in particular areas by drawing upon their distinctive and common experiences; subjecting proposals to test by a panel of expert officials drawn from a broad spectrum of member states; reviewing performance against relevant targets; and considering various incentives, and sanctions if necessary, to ensure policy success. See J. Cohen and C. F. Sabel, 'Sovereignty and Solidarity: EU and US', in J. Zeitlin and D. Trubek (eds), *Governing Work and Welfare in a New Economy: European and American Experiments*, Oxford, Oxford University Press, 2003.

Figure 2
Global Issues Networks (GINs)

Phase 1 – The constitutional phase

1 year
_____

Each GIN enlists members from:
• Governments
• International civil society organizations
• Businesses

Facilitators:
• One global multilateral as lead facilitator
• One co-facilitator from civil society
• One co-facilitator from the business world

Phase 2 – The norm-producing phase

1 year   2–3 years
_____

Methodology used by the GIN:
• Disciplines and substance, no posturing
• Deliberative polling through electronic town meetings (ETMs)
• Rough consensus

Substance of the GIN's work:
• What is the problem?
• How much time do we have?
• Where do we want to be twenty years from now?
• How do we want to get there?
• What are the options?
• What should the norms be? Detailed norm packages
                              Other recommendations

Phase 3 – The implementation phase

1 year   2–3 years   >10 years
_____

New tasks:
• Rating countries and players against norms
• Creating reputation effects through naming-and-shaming
• Observatory and knowledge-exchange roles
_____

Source: Rischard, *High Noon*, op. cit., pp. 173, 175, 177.

extension of an enlightened multilateralism, but an insufficient mechanism to reshape global governance alone.

The policy issues and suggestions discussed above lay out an agenda for thinking about the reform of global governance in the immediate future. But a democratic agenda for global governance reform also needs to think about how the current form of intergovernmentalism, with its existing problems of overlapping jurisdictions and fragmented structures, can be developed and improved in the longer run. Here, it is necessary to think more boldly about a cosmopolitan multilateralism. This is not a multilateralism that can, of course, be implemented in all respects in the immediate future. But setting it out helps set down paths and goals for democratic reform at the global level. With this in mind, the following section lays out an agenda for a robust cosmopolitan multilateralism.

COSMOPOLITAN MULTILATERALISM

Cosmopolitan multilateralism must take as its starting point a world of 'overlapping communities of fate'. Recognizing the complex processes of an interconnected world, it ought to view certain issues – such as housing, education and policing – as appropriate for spatially delimited political spheres (the city, region or state), while seeing others – such as the environment, world health and global economic regulation – as requiring new, more extensive institutions to address them. Deliberative and decision-making centres beyond national territories are appropriately situated when the principles of inclusiveness, subsidiarity and equivalence can only be properly upheld in a transnational context; when those whose life expectancy and life chances are significantly affected by a public matter constitute a transnational grouping; and when 'lower' levels of decision-making cannot manage satisfactorily transnational or international policy questions. Of course, the boundaries demarcating different levels of governance will always be contested, as they are, for instance, in many local, sub-national regional and national polities. Disputes about the appropriate jurisdiction for handling particular public issues will be complex and intensive; but better complex and intensive in a clear public framework than left simply to powerful geopolitical interests (dominant states) or market-based organizations to resolve them alone.

The possibility of a cosmopolitan polity must be linked to an expanding framework of states and agencies bound by the rule of law, democratic principles and human rights. How should this be understood from an institutional point of view? Initially, the possibility of a cosmopolitan polity could be enhanced if the UN system actually lived up to its charter. Among other things, this would mean pursuing measures to implement key elements of the rights conventions, and enforcing the prohibition of the discretionary right to use force.[35] However, while each move in this direction would be helpful, it would still represent, at best, a move towards a very incomplete form of accountability and justice in global politics. For the dynamics and logic of the current hierarchical interstate system (with the US in pole position) would still represent an immensely powerful force in global affairs; the massive disparities of power and asymmetries of resource in the global political economy would be left virtually unaddressed; ad hoc responses to pressing international and transnational issues would remain typical; and the accountability gaps between decision-makers and decision-takers would remain unbridged. As a result, the deeply embedded difficulties of the UN system would be unaddressed and unresolved – the susceptibility of the UN to the agendas of the most powerful states, the weaknesses of many of its enforcement operations (or lack of them altogether), the underfunding of its organizations, the continued dependency of its programmes on the financial support of a few major states, the inadequacies of the policing of many environmental regimes (regional and global) and so on.

Thus, a cosmopolitan polity would need to establish an overarching network of democratic public forums, covering cities, nation-states, regions and the wider transnational order. It would need to create an effective and accountable political, administrative and regulative capacity at global and regional levels to complement those at national and local levels. This would require:[36]
• the formation of an authoritative assembly of all states and agencies – a reformed General Assembly of the United Nations, or a complement to it. The focus of a global assembly would be the examination of those pressing problems which are at the heart of

---

[35] See R. Falk, *On Humane Governance*, Cambridge, Polity Press, 1995.

[36] The following points are adapted from D. Held, 'Cosmopolitanism: Globalization Tamed?', *Review of International Studies*, 29 (2003), pp. 465–80.

concerns about life expectancy and life chances – concerns, for instance, about health and disease, food supply and distribution, the debt burden of the developing world, global warming and the reduction of the risks of nuclear, chemical and biological warfare. Its task would be to lay down, in framework-setting law, the standards and institutions required to embed the rule of law, democratic principles, and the minimum conditions for human agency to flourish;[37]

• the creation, where feasible, of regional parliaments and governance structures (for example, in Latin America and Africa) and the enhancement of the role of such bodies where they already exist (the European Union) in order that their decisions may become recognized and accepted as legitimate independent sources of regional and international regulation;

• the opening-up of functional IGOs (such as the WTO, IMF and World Bank) to public examination and agenda-setting. Not only should such bodies be transparent in their activities, but they should be open to public scrutiny (on the basis perhaps of elected supervisory bodies, or functional deliberative forums, representative of the

---

[37] Agreement on the terms of reference of a global assembly would be difficult to say the least, although there is no shortage of plausible schemes and models. Ultimately, its terms of reference and operating rules would need to command widespread agreement and, hence, ought to be generated in a stakeholder process of consensus-building – a global constitutional convention – involving states, IGOs, international nongovernmental organizations (INGOs), citizen groups and social movements. A global process of consultation and deliberation, organized at diverse levels, represents the best hope of creating a legitimate framework for accountable and sustainable global governance. Three core issues would need to be addressed: Who is to be represented, governments or citizens? What is to be the principle of representation, one state, one vote, proportional representation, or a mixture of both? What are the proper scope and limits of action of a global assembly? These are demanding questions which admit of a number of sound theoretical answers. The case for each would have to be considered and weighed in the context of the diversity of interests which would be brought to a global constitutional convention, for example the inevitable differences that would emerge between the developed and developing countries on whether population size or economic strength, or a mixture of both, should count in the determination of the basis of representation. While the legitimacy and credibility of a new global assembly would depend on it being firmly grounded on the principle of consent and electoral inclusiveness, it is likely that any assembly in the foreseeable future would be constituted by compromises between theoretical ideas and practical constraints. Accordingly, rather than set out blueprints for the nature and form of a global assembly, it seems better to stress the importance of a legitimate process of consensus-building in and through which these issues might be deliberated upon and settled.

diverse interests in their constituencies), and accountable to regional and global assemblies;
• the establishment, where IGOs are currently weak and/or lacking in enforcement capability, of new mechanisms and organizations, e.g. in the areas of the environment and social affairs. The creation of new global governance structures with responsibility for addressing poverty, welfare and related issues is vital to offset the power and influence of market-oriented agencies such as the WTO and IMF;
• the enhancement of the transparency and accountability of the organizations of national and transnational civil society, addressing the potentially disturbing effects of those who are able to 'shout the loudest' and of the lack of clarity about the terms of engagement of nonstate actors with IGOs and other leading political bodies.[38] Experiments are necessary to find ways of improving the internal codes of conduct and modes of operation of nonstate actors, on the one hand, and of advancing their capacity to be represented in IGOs and other leading political bodies preoccupied with global policy processes, on the other. Moreover, to avoid citizens of developed countries being unfairly represented twice in global politics (once through their governments and once through their NGOs) special attention and support needs to be given to enhance the role of NGOs from developing countries;
• the use of general referendums cutting across nations and nation-states at regional or global levels in the case of contested priorities concerning the implementation of core cosmopolitan concerns. These could involve many different kinds of referendums including a cross-section of the public, and/or of targeted and significantly affected groups in a particular policy area, and/or of the policy-makers and legislators of national parliaments;
• the development of law-enforcement and coercive capability, including peace-keeping and peace-making, to help deal with serious regional and global security threats. It is necessary to meet the concern that, in the face of the pressing and violent challenges to fundamental human rights and priorities, 'covenants, without the sword, are but words' (Hobbes).

---

[38] See M. Edwards and S. Zadek, 'Governing the Provision of Global Public Goods: the Role and Legitimacy of Nonstate Actors', in Kaul et al., *Providing Global Public Goods*, op. cit.

In the long term, a cosmopolitan polity must involve the development of administrative capacity and independent political resources at regional and global levels. It would not call for the diminution *per se* of state power and capacity across the globe. Rather, it would seek to entrench and develop political institutions at regional and global levels as a necessary supplement to those at the level of the state.[39] This conception of politics is based on the recognition of the continuing significance of democratic nation-states, while arguing for layers of democratic governance to address broader and more global questions. The aim is to forge an accountable and responsive politics at local and national levels alongside the establishment of representative and deliberative assemblies in the wider global order; that is, a political order of transparent and democratic cities and nations as well as of regions and global networks.

MULTILEVEL CITIZENSHIP

Against this background, the basis of a new conception of citizenship can be disclosed – a citizenship based not on exclusive membership of a territorial community, but on general rules and principles which can be entrenched and drawn upon in diverse settings. This conception relies on the availability and clarity of the principles of democracy and human rights. These principles create a framework for all persons to enjoy, in principle, equal freedom and equal participative opportunities. The meaning of citizenship shifts from membership in a community which bestows, for those who qualify, particular rights and duties to an alternative principle of world order in which all persons have equivalent rights and duties in the cross-cutting spheres of decision-making which affect their vital needs and interests. It posits the idea of a global political order in which people can enjoy an equality of status with respect to the fundamental processes and institutions which govern their life expectancy and life chances. As a result, the opportunities of citizenship would be extended to cover all political communities in which people have a critical stake.[40] Citizenship would become multilevel and multidimensional, while anchored in common rules and principles.

[39] Cf. M. Doyle, 'A More Perfect Union?', *Review of International Studies*, 26 (2000), pp. 81–94.

[40] See D. Held, *Democracy and the Global Order*, op. cit., ch. 12.

Within this context, the elusive and puzzling meaning of global citizenship becomes a little clearer. Built on the fundamental rights and duties of all human beings, global citizenship underwrites the autonomy of each and every human being, and recognizes their capacity for self-governance at all levels of human affairs. Although this notion needs further clarification and unpacking, its leading features are already within our grasp. Today, if people are to be free and equal in the determination of the conditions which shape their lives, there must be an array of forums, from the city to global associations, in which they can hold decision-makers to account. If many contemporary forms of power are to become accountable and if many of the complex issues that affect us all – locally, nationally, regionally and globally – are to be democratically regulated, people will have to have access to, and membership in, diverse political communities. As Jürgen Habermas has written, 'only a democratic citizenship that does not close itself off in a particularistic fashion can pave the way for a *world citizenship*. . . . State citizenship and world citizenship form a continuum whose contours, at least, are already becoming visible'.[41] There is only a historically contingent connection between the principles underpinning citizenship and the national community; as this connection weakens in a world of overlapping communities of fate, the principles of citizenship must be rearticulated and re-entrenched. Moreover, in the light of this development, the connection between patriotism and nationalism becomes easier to call into question, and a case built to bind patriotism to the defence of core civic and political principles – not to the nation or country for their own sake.[42] Only national identities open to diverse solidarities, and shaped by respect for general rules and principles, can accommodate themselves successfully to the challenges of a global age.

The international community has already produced a body of common rules and standards which ground this possibility, and which can be elaborated and built upon in the future (see below). In addition, the changing practices of citizenship itself are pushing in this direction. For example, a typical resident of Glasgow can participate and vote in city elections, as well as in those of Scotland, the UK and Europe. And if this is not enough, he or she can participate in the rich web of relations of global civil society. These complex and

[41] J. Habermas, *Between Facts and Norms*, Cambridge, Polity Press, 1995, pp. 514–15.
[42] See D. Heater, *World Citizenship*, London, Continuum, 2002.

overlapping political relations anticipate a world increasingly defined by multiple forms of citizenship, anchored in clear and established general rules and principles.

COSMOPOLITANISM

I refer to a global polity with multilevel citizenship as a cosmopolitan order. Why? What does 'cosmopolitan' mean in this context?[43] In the first instance, cosmopolitanism refers to those basic values which set down standards or boundaries that no agent, whether a representative of a global body, state or civil association, should be able to violate. Focused on the claims of each person as an individual, these values espouse the idea that human beings are in a fundamental sense equal, and that they deserve equal political treatment; that is, treatment based upon the equal care and consideration of their agency, irrespective of the community in which they were born or brought up. After over 200 years of nationalism, and sustained nation-state formation, such values could be thought of as out of place. But such values are already enshrined in the law of war, human rights law and the statute of the International Criminal Court (ICC), among many other international rules and legal arrangements.

Second, cosmopolitanism can be taken to refer to those forms of political regulation and law-making that create powers, rights and constraints which go beyond the claims of nation-states and which have far-reaching consequences, in principle, for the nature and form of political power. These regulatory forms can be found in the domain between national and international law and regulation – the space between domestic law which regulates the relations between a state and its citizens, and traditional international law which applies primarily to states and interstate relations.[44] This space is already filled by a plethora of legal regulation, from the legal instruments of the EU, and the international human rights regime as a global framework for promoting rights, to the diverse agreements of the arms control system and environmental regimes. Cosmopolitanism is not

[43] See D. Held, 'Law of States, Law of Peoples', *Legal Theory*, 8: 1 (2002), pp. 1–44, from which I have adapted the following four paragraphs.

[44] P. Eleftheriadis, 'The European Constitution and Cosmopolitan Ideals', *Columbia Journal of European Law*, 7: 1 (2002), pp. 21–39.

made up of political ideals for another age, but embedded in rule systems and institutions which have already transformed state sovereignty in distinct ways.

Yet the precise sense in which these developments constitute a form of 'cosmopolitanism' remains to be clarified, especially given that the ideas of cosmopolitanism have a long and complex history. For my purposes here, cosmopolitanism can be taken as the moral and political outlook which builds upon the strengths of the post-1945 multilateral order, particularly its commitment to universal standards, human rights and democratic values, and which seeks to specify general principles upon which all could act. These are principles which can be universally shared, and can form the basis for the protection and nurturing of each person's equal interest in the determination of the institutions which govern their lives.

Cosmopolitan values can be expressed formally, in the interests of clarification, in terms of a set of principles.[45] Eight principles are paramount. They are the principles of: 1) equal worth and dignity; 2) active agency; 3) personal responsibility and accountability; 4) consent; 5) collective decision-making about public matters through voting procedures; 6) inclusiveness and subsidiarity; 7) avoidance of serious harm; and 8) sustainability. While eight principles may seem like a daunting number, they are interrelated and together form the basis of a compelling internationalist orientation.

The eight principles can best be thought of as falling into three clusters. The first cluster (principles 1–3) set down the fundamental organizational features of the cosmopolitan moral universe. Its crux is that each person is a subject of equal moral concern; that each person is capable of acting autonomously with respect to the range of choices before them; and that, in deciding how to act or which institutions to create, the claims of each person affected should be taken equally into account. Personal responsibility means, in this context, that actors and agents have to be aware of, and accountable for, the consequences of their actions, direct or indirect, intended or unintended, which may substantially restrict and delimit the choices of others. The second cluster (principles 4–6) form the basis of translating individually initiated activity, or privately determined activities more broadly, into collectively agreed or collectively sanctioned

---

[45] See Held, 'Law of States, Law of Peoples', op. cit., for an elaboration of the first seven principles.

frameworks of action or regulatory regimes. Public power can be conceived as legitimate to the degree to which principles 4, 5 and 6 are upheld. The final principles (7 and 8) lay down a framework for prioritizing urgent need and resource conservation. By distinguishing vital from non-vital needs, principle 7 creates an unambiguous starting point and guiding orientation for public decisions. While this 'prioritizing commitment' does not, of course, create a decision procedure to resolve all clashes of priority in politics, it clearly creates a moral framework for focusing public policy on those who are most vulnerable. By contrast, principle 8 seeks to set down a prudential orientation to help ensure that public policy is consistent with global ecological balances and that it does not destroy irreplaceable and non-substitutable resources.

These principles are not just western principles. Certain of their elements originated in the early modern period in the west, but their validity extends much further. For these principles are the foundation of a fair, humane and decent society, of whatever religion or cultural tradition. To paraphrase the legal theorist Bruce Ackerman, there is no nation without a woman who yearns for equal rights, no society without a man who denies the need for deference, and no developing country without a person who does not wish for the minimum means of subsistence so that they may go about their everyday lives.[46] The principles are building blocks for articulating and entrenching the equal liberty of all human beings, wherever they were born or brought up. They are the basis of underwriting the autonomy of others, not of obliterating it. Their concern is with the irreducible moral status of each and every person – the acknowledgement of which links directly to the possibility of self-determination and the capacity to make independent choices.[47]

The eight cosmopolitan principles can be thought of as the guiding ethical basis for a cosmopolitan polity. They lay down some of the universal or organizing principles which delimit the range of diversity and difference that ought to be found in public life. And

[46] B. Ackerman, 'Political Liberalism', *Journal of Political Philosophy*, 91 (1994), pp. 382–3.

[47] It is frequently alleged that democracy itself is a western imposition on many developing countries. Yet, as George Monbiot has pointed out, 'the majority of those who live in parliamentary democracies, flawed as some of them may be, live in the poor world' (*The Age of Consent*, London, Flamingo, 2003, p. 109).

they disclose the proper framework for the pursuit of argument, discussion and negotiation about particular spheres of value, spheres in which local, national and regional affiliations will inevitably be weighed. These are principles for an era in which political communities and states matter, but not only or exclusively. In a world where the trajectories of each and every country are tightly entwined, the partiality, one-sidedness and limitedness of 'reasons of state' need to be recognized. States are hugely important vehicles to aid the delivery of effective public regulation, equal liberty and social justice, but they should not be thought of as ontologically privileged. They can be judged by how far they deliver these public goods and how far they fail; for the history of states is, of course, marked not just by phases of corruption and bad leadership but also by the most brutal episodes. A system of democratic accountability relevant to our global age must take this as a starting point, and build a politically robust and ethically sound conception of the proper basis of political community, and of the relations among communities.

Index

argument
  and bargaining compared, 173–4,
    176
  and compliance, 181–5
  conceptual issues, 170–6
  definitions, 172–3
  and global governance, 186–9
  as learning mechanism, 164–5
  roles, 6
  and rule-setting, 176, 177–80
  see also bargaining; persuasion
argumentative entrapment, 176, 177
argumentative rationality, 170
  Habermasian, 171–2
argumentative self-entrapment, 184
arms control, 90
Asia, financial crises, 21–2, 36
Asia Pacific Economic Cooperation
  (APEC), 46
Association for the Taxation of
  financial Transactions for the
  Aid of Citizens (ATTAC), 156–7
Australia, 44, 202
  antitrust cooperation
    agreements, 57

Bank for International Settlements
  (BIS), 17, 92
  and civil society organizations, 102
banks (central) *see* central banks
bargaining
  and argument compared, 173–4,
    176
  compromises, 177
  definitions, 172–3
  in negotiations, 178
  and rule-setting, 169
  see also argument; negotiations
Basel Committee, 45
Battle of Seattle (1999), 104
Beck, U., 152
beef, export bans, 160
Beitz, Charles, 152

Benner, Thorsten, 6
Benvenisti, Eyal, 65
Berufungsgrundlagen, 174
Bhopal (India), 101, 119
BIS *see* Bank for International
  Settlements (BIS)
Black Friday, 139
black people's movement, 96, 101
Bolton, John, 216
BONGOs (business-organized
  nongovernmental
  organizations), 77
Brazil, 125
  civil society organizations, 96, 97
  corporate social responsibility
    schemes, 98
Brazil Network on Multilateral
  Financial Institutions, 94
Bretton Woods Agreement (1944),
  27, 87, 97, 142, 153
briefcase nongovernmental
  organizations (BRINGOs), 107
British Toy and Hobby Association,
  128
Brookings Institution, 99
Brussels (Belgium), 226, 230
BSE crisis, 160
bureaucratic despotism, 225–6
Bush, George W., 35
Business Council for Sustainable
  Development, 125
business-organized
  nongovernmental
  organizations (BONGOs), 77

Canada, 25, 46, 250
  antitrust cooperation
    agreements, 57
  civil society organizations, 94,
    105
  corporate social responsibility
    schemes, 98
  environmental policy, 37